The ACE BAKERY
COOKBOOK

The ACE BAKERY COOKBOOK

Recipes for and with Bread

ACE BAKERY

Linda Haynes

FOREWORD BY JAMES CHATTO

whitecap

Edited by Kathy Evans
Proofread by Lesley Cameron
Cover and interior design by Dinnick & Howells
Colour photographs by Christopher Freeland
Photography assistance by Tracy Cox
Food styling by Claire Stubbs
Black and white photographs and author photograph by Laura Arsie

Printed and bound in Canada

National Library of Canada Cataloguing in Publication Data

Haynes, Linda, 1951-
    The ACE Bakery cookbook : recipes for and with bread / Linda Haynes ;
James Chatto, foreword ; Christopher Freeland, photographer.

    Includes bibliographical references and index.
    ISBN 1-55285-507-4

    1. Cookery (Bread) 2. Bread. I. Title.
TX769.H39 2003   641.8'15   C2003-911232-2

The publisher acknowledges the support of the Canada Council for the Arts and the Cultural Services Branch of the Government of British Columbia for our publishing program. We acknowledge the financial support of the Government of Canada through the Book Publishing Industry Development Program for our publishing activities.

Note: Some of the recipes in this book call for the use of raw eggs. Pregnant women, the elderly, young children and anyone with a compromised immune system are advised against the consumption of raw eggs.

Contents

Dedication

To Martin, Devin, and Luke
for making every breakfast, lunch,
and dinner a joyous occasion.

To my mother for all her guidance
in the kitchen and elsewhere and
to my father for always being there
when I needed him.

Acknowledgments

Many thanks to

Seanna, Ted, John, Shauna, Lindsey, and Barb for eating all the experiments and giving such positive feedback;

My colleagues at ACE for all their encouragement, not to mention recipe testing;

Joe Laface, Marcus Mariathas, and Tom Vas for all their help in adapting ACE bread recipes for home use;

Robert McCullough for not taking no for an answer;

Kathy Evans for thoughtful and intelligent guidance through the editing process;

Jonathan Howells and Pam Lostracco of Dinnick and Howells, and Devin Connell for designing a book that looks as delicious as I hope you will find the recipes;

Christopher Freeland, brilliant photographer, and Claire Stubbs, food stylist extraordinaire, for translating written words into delicious, stunning photographs;

Laura Arsie for her wonderful photographs of a day in the life of ACE Bakery;

Robin Rivers and Roberta Batchelor of Whitecap for generously sharing their knowledge and expertise, while taking me down the road from manuscript to finished book;

Mechtilde Hoppenrath for pushing me to start the book and for being an exacting recipe tester;

Sandy Stermac for testing more recipes than I thought humanly possible;

Charles Oberdorf for taking a first look at the manuscript;

Noel Comess for the early mentoring;

Hyacinth Anderson for all the teamwork in my kitchen;

Anya Oberdorf for all her research as well as for being a pleasure to work with;

Allison Fryer of The Cookbook Store for her advice and insights;

Alison Maclean for enthusiastically answering all my emails;

and last, but definitely not least, the wonderful Rosalind Whelan for the benefit of all her years of experience, her wisdom, and her months of working on copy.

Foreword

More than ten years have passed (in less time than it takes to eat a sandwich) since the morning in March, 1993, when Linda Haynes and Martin Connell pulled their first loaves from the oven and introduced Toronto to ACE. Almost overnight, the little bakery on King Street West became a place of pilgrimage.

For a food press weary of recessionary closures, it was a story from headline heaven— a glamorous and successful couple, renowned philanthropists, bringing bread to the people. Everyone seemed to know the idea had begun as a private hobby but this was clearly no vanity project. Linda devoted extraordinary energies to the new business and she and Martin guaranteed the quality of each loaf with their signatures, right under that cleverly naïve, instantly recognizable woodcut of happy bakers. ACE bread was cool and it was righteous—a portion of the profits were diverted to Calmeadow, the charitable foundation the couple had created—but, above all, it was absolutely delicious. Under the dark, crunchy crust, the crumb had the fleeting, complex, fruity, nutty subtlety that is the hallmark of a properly timed, properly fermented sourdough. Food writers waxed poetic, dusting off memories of long-ago loaves in Europe, instant experts on the wayward lives of wild yeasts.

Ten years later, ACE has become a Toronto institution, a commercial success that has nevertheless stayed true to its first, artisanal inspiration. Linda still takes every single loaf personally so it's hardly surprising that this book is also a labor of love, a personal collection of her favorite recipes. Happiness is a warm bun, a fresh baguette, a slice of tangy ACE sourdough, but none of us lives by bread alone. Those loaves have stood at the heart of so many meals, from the most casual picnics to the grandest banquets: now we have the rest of the menu.

James Chatto

Introduction

When I moved away from home I left with my mother's recipes and a gift of new cookbooks from my father. I had been brought up in a household in which every dinner was a celebration—a time to catch up, debate, and enjoy one another's company. From an early age, my Belgian mother encouraged me to cook and experiment and, best of all, not clean up—what a way to learn.

The pleasure of cooking for friends and family had been a large part of my childhood, and it became a large part of my life as an adult. I cooked when I was alone and with friends, with and without a boyfriend, during the work week and on weekends, employed and unemployed, sad and happy. I cooked for Martin and we fell in love and married.

Sometime during the winter of 1985 my husband decided he wanted to bake bread. When we talk about it now, neither of us can remember why this urge came over him. We had a country house about an hour out of Toronto where we went every weekend and moved to for the summer months. The snow was particularly heavy that year and, in looking back, Martin thinks that learning to make bread seemed like a wonderful way to while away a few hours on a weekend morning. He decided to try to make a baguette, little realizing that it is one of the hardest breads to get right. So sprouted the initial seeds of ACE Bakery.

Martin bought *Bernard Clayton's Complete Book of Breads*, and every Saturday morning that winter, he and our 3-year-old daughter, Devin, shared the ritual of getting up early and mixing dough. Saturday night dinner with extended family and friends became the testing ground. We ate dozens of questionable baguettes but always complimented our two bakers on their results.

Then, as now, we enjoyed traveling in France. We loved to rent a car and meander from village to village, plotting where the good restaurants were and arriving in time for dinner. The bread was wonderful and, more times than not, the chef had bought it from the village boulangerie. The next morning, in my fractured French, I would explain to the boulanger that my husband was an amateur baker and ask if we could watch the baking process. The bakers were generally amused by us and would invite us into the back to watch the mixing, shaping, and baking. Many times they would take us aside to tell us the secrets of how their bread got its distinctive flavor.

Our interest in the mysteries of bread baking accelerated, and we found ourselves seeking out old wood-burning ovens in villages all across Europe. Traditionally, in many places, when the baker finished his bread baking, the villagers would arrive with roasts and vegetables and even cakes to be cooked in the oven as it slowly lost its heat.

Back at home in Toronto, our bread making became more refined and daring. Sometimes, two or three different doughs would appear at those Saturday dinners. Shapes became more experimental. Braiding, wheat sheaves, and grape clusters appeared on large boules (rounds)—but still the baguette remained elusive.

One day Martin announced that he was ready to build his own wood-burning oven. We had brought back plans from France and found a man who was up to the challenge. Within six months we were proud owners of a small bake house with an oven capable of baking 20 loaves at a time, the first of which appeared on our Thanksgiving table.

Meanwhile, the U.S. and Canada were becoming the center of creative bread baking. In Europe, small bakeries we had loved to visit were becoming few and far between. More large companies were shipping out factory-made frozen dough that was being baked off for mass consumption. But Acme Bakery was open in San Francisco and James McGuire of Passe Partout was baking in Montreal. Artisan bakers were springing up in L.A., New York, and numerous smaller cities, and all were committed to turning out natural, preservative-free bread.

Martin had a birthday coming up, and through a friend of a friend I arranged an introduction to Noel Comess, the chef-turned-baker extraordinaire who owns Tom Cat Bakery in New York. He agreed to let Martin come, watch, and learn.

When we returned to Toronto, it struck us that, although there were great ethnic bakeries in the city, no one was baking the kind of bread we had seen and tasted at Tom Cat and Eli's in New York and Acme and La Brea in California. We decided to start a bakery.

There were only three prerequisites. The bread had to taste great, we wanted to have fun, and we wanted a percentage of our profits to go to a Canadian aid agency we had founded, called Calmeadow.

In March 1993, ACE Bakery sold its first loaf of bread. Today we have more than 700 clients in hotels, restaurants, gourmet food stores, and airlines, and that elusive baguette has become our best seller.

I developed some of the recipes in this book for the café and fresh bread shop that has always been a part of ACE. Others were conceived for dinners with family and friends, and still others were inspired by our travels. All have been tested by critical home cooks and all are meant to be improvised on. I hope you enjoy them.

And by the way, our daughter, Devin, now cooks when she's alone and with friends, with and without a boyfriend, during the work week and weekends, in school and out of school, sad and happy. I expect that our son, Luke, will do the same.

"Cooking is like love. It should be entered into with abandon or not at all." —Harriet van Horne

Breads and Basics

"The smell of buttered toast simply talked to Toad, and with no uncertain voice; talked of warm kitchens, of breakfasts on bright frosty mornings, of cozy parlour firesides on winter evenings..."
— Kenneth Grahame, The Wind in the Willows

Baking 101

TEN RULES FOR HASSLE-FREE HOME BREAD BAKING

1 Measure all your ingredients first.

2 Whenever possible, use a kitchen scale to measure ingredients, as weight measurements will be more accurate than volume, such as cups or milliliters. Different flours, even different salts, will weigh the same although their volumes will be different. A ton of feathers does weigh the same as a ton of stone. For example, ½ ounce (14 g) of kosher salt will measure 3½ teaspoons (17.5 mL), while the equivalent weight in table salt will measure 2 teaspoons (10 mL). For the bread recipes in this first section, I have listed the dry ingredients by weight rather than volume. In the past, whenever I've relied on cups, tablespoons, or milliliters, the final product has not turned out as well as it should have. But because household scales are not precise enough to weigh small quantities, I have converted those to volume measurements.

3 Since you will be working in fits and starts, begin by making a schedule of when each step should take place before you even start the recipe. Leave it beside your bowl or pan.

4 For the bread recipes in this book I have used unbleached bread flour, traditional dry yeast, unsalted butter, and kosher salt.

5 You will need a standing mixer with a dough hook, a low-temperature thermometer (some meat thermometers will do), a spray bottle, an oven thermometer, and patience. All the bread recipes can be hand mixed except for the Focaccia and Scaciatta.

6 Always cover your dough after each procedure to prevent it from forming a dry crust that will inhibit rising.

7 Spraying hot water into the oven just before baking will ensure what bakers call a good spring (accelerated rise) and a crisp crust.

8 In humid weather you will need slightly less liquid, and in dry weather you will need slightly more.

9 Do not let your starter sit too long or it may over-ferment and your dough will not rise.

10 Your room temperature will affect how quickly your starter or dough will rise. These recipes were tested in a home kitchen where the temperature ranged from 70° to 74°F (21° to 24°C). Dough will rise faster in a warm kitchen.

"What many bakers don't realize is that good wheat can make bad bread. The magic of bread baking is in the manipulation and the fermentation. What has been lost is this method." —Lionel Poilâne

Pain au Lait

MAKES 3 LOAVES

Pain au Lait is a very typical French bread, made with similar ingredients to those for brioche—egg, butter, and sugar—although Pain au Lait is slightly heavier, denser, and not as rich. This recipe involves creating a *pâte fermentée*, a mixture of flour, water, and yeast that is used as a starter and gives the bread a more complex flavor. The recipe looks complicated and time-consuming, but it really isn't. The only complication is that you need two 15-minute periods, approximately four hours apart, then two more brief periods at roughly two-hour intervals. In other words, don't be intimidated by the length of the recipe—just take it in bite-sized pieces.

If your standing mixer bowl cannot hold at least 5 lb. (2 kg) of dough, hold back about ¼ to ⅓ of the flour mix. After finishing the final mixing, remove the dough, which will be sticky, to a countertop and knead the rest of the flour in by hand.

PÂTE FERMENTÉE (STARTER)
½ tsp. (2.5 mL) traditional dry yeast
⅓ cup (80 mL) lukewarm water, 75° to 95°F (24° to 35°C)
4¼ oz. (120 g) unbleached hard white flour

PAIN AU LAIT
⅔ cup (160 mL) lukewarm water, 75° to 95°F (24° to 35°C)
25 oz. (710 g) unbleached hard white flour
8½ oz. (240 g) semolina flour
3 oz. (90 g) sugar

¾ cup (180 mL) unsalted butter, at room temperature
1¼ cups (300 mL) homogenized milk, at room temperature
2 extra large eggs
4 tsp. (20 mL) traditional dry yeast
1 recipe Pâte Fermentée, fermented 4 to 6 hours
4 tsp. (20 mL) salt
canola oil to lightly coat mixing bowl and pans
1 egg white for glazing
cornmeal (for baking boules)

FOR THE PÂTE FERMENTÉE

Carefully measure all the ingredients. In a small bowl, dissolve the yeast in 1 Tbsp. (15 mL) of the water. The yeast should take on a creamy-looking consistency within a few minutes. (If it has not, discard it and buy new yeast.) Add the remaining warm water and stir. Place the flour in the standing mixer bowl with the dough hook attachment. Add the water and yeast mixture and mix on slow (#2 speed) for 2 minutes until the flour is incorporated and the mixture has the look of playdough or silly putty.

Transfer the *pâte fermentée* to a lightly oiled, medium-sized bowl. Cover with plastic wrap and leave to ferment at room temperature for 4 to 6 hours. It should look puffy and have a few air bubbles when it is done.

When the *pâte fermentée* is complete, it can be used immediately or refrigerated for a few hours. Bring to room temperature before continuing the recipe.

Pour ⅓ cup plus 3 Tbsp. (125 mL) of the water into the standing mixer bowl. Add the white flour and semolina flour, the sugar, butter, milk, and eggs. Hold back ¼ to ⅓ of the flour mixture if your bowl is not large enough. Attach the dough hook and mix on slow (#2 speed) for 3 minutes. Drape a kitchen towel or plastic wrap over the bowl and let the dough rest for 15 minutes. This process is called *autolyse*. It allows the dough to absorb water and the gluten to develop. Don't be concerned if the dough clings to the dough hook.

Pour the remaining ⅛ cup plus 1 tsp. (35 mL) of lukewarm water into a small bowl and stir in the yeast until dissolved. Add the *pâte fermentée* and the dissolved yeast to the dough and mix on slow (#2 speed) for 1 minute. Add the salt and mix for 2 minutes on slow (#2 speed) and then on fast (#4 speed) for 3 minutes. If you have not added all the flour, remove the dough from the bowl and knead it in now. Use the push-pull method, allowing your palms to push the dough away from you along the surface. Pull it back over itself and continue the action for about 4 minutes. The dough, when ready, should feel slightly sticky when pressed with your palm.

Pat the dough into a ball and place in a large, lightly oiled bowl. Turn it over so that it is completely coated in oil. Cover with a kitchen towel or plastic wrap and allow to rise at room temperature for about 1½ to 2 hours. The dough should almost double. Leave it up to an extra hour if necessary.

TO MAKE LOAVES

Lightly oil 3 pans approximately 3¾ x 7½ x 2½ inches (9½ x 19 x 6½ cm) in size—Teflon-coated if possible. Remove the dough from the bowl and place on a lightly floured surface. Cut the dough in 3 equal pieces, approximately 1½ lbs. (700 g) each. Shape each piece into a ball, cover with plastic wrap or a towel and let them rest for 15 minutes. Gently pat each piece of dough into a rectangle 8 inches (20 cm) long and of even thickness. Using your palms, roll one long side of the dough toward the other like a long jelly roll and pat into a shape that will fit your pan. Gently press the seams together. Put the dough into the pans, seam-side down. Again, drape with a kitchen towel or plastic wrap. Allow to rise at room temperature until approximately 1½ inches (4 cm) above the rim of the pan (about 2 to 3 hours). Press your finger into the dough. If it leaves a slight indentation, the bread is ready to be baked. If it springs back, cover it and check again in 15 minutes.

As the dough is proofing, preheat the oven to 375°F (190°C), or 325°F (165°C) for a convection oven. Check the temperature with an oven thermometer.

Uncover the loaves. Brush the top of each loaf with lightly whisked, room temperature egg white. Open the oven door and generously spray the sides of the oven with hot water. Alternatively, place 5 or 6 ice cubes on the oven floor. Close the door. Wait 10 to 20 seconds and place the pans on a rack a third from the bottom of the oven. Bake for 30 to 40 minutes. Breads put in a convection oven may bake slightly faster.

The bread should be a golden brown and produce a hollow sound when you tap the bottom crust. To do this, carefully tip the bread out of the pan. It should just slip out. Tap the bottom crust with your fingertips. If it is fully baked, it will sound hollow. If not, return the bread to the pan and bake a further 5 minutes. Repeat until the bread is done.

Remove the loaves immediately from the oven and cool, well spaced, on a wire rack. Resist the temptation to cut into them immediately. They will taste much better about an hour or two later.

If you prefer to make 3 boules (rounds), place your hands on either side of the cut pieces of dough after the first rising and gently rotate both your hands and the dough until the dough is rounded on top. Place seam-side down in a lightly oiled, shallow-lipped bowl that is slightly larger than the boule. Some rimmed soup bowls work perfectly. Gently drape with a kitchen towel or plastic wrap. Allow to rise at room temperature for about 2 hours.

Preheat a pizza stone or smooth bricks on a rack a third from the bottom of the oven at 375°F (190°C) or 325°F (165°C) for a convection oven. Lightly sprinkle cornmeal over the stones and gently place the boules seam-side down onto the cornmeal. Brush the tops with lightly whisked, room temperature egg white. Don't worry if some of the egg white drizzles down the sides. Generously spray the sides of the oven with hot water and close the door. If you prefer, place 5 or 6 ice cubes on the oven floor and bake for 25 to 35 minutes. Breads put in a convection oven may bake slightly faster. See above for testing doneness.

PAIN AU LAIT WITH RAISINS

Follow the recipe for Pain au Lait, then, after the salt is added, mix for 1 minute on slow (#2 speed) and then 3 minutes on fast (#4 speed). Add 9½ oz. (270 g) of moist sultana raisins that have been rinsed in water and then drained and left to sit for about 1 hour and mix for an additional 2 minutes on slow (#2 speed). Proceed as above for either loaves or boules.

"The oven supplied steam ... to ensure a fully expanded light loaf with a thinner, more crackling crust. The dough was very soft — moist — and the moisture gave bigger holes and better flavor. (Flavorful dough contains a lot of water, although contrary to baking lore, the kind of water has hardly any influence on the taste.)"

— Edward Behr, The Art of Eating, Winter 1998.

Focaccia and Scacciata

MAKES 2 LOAVES

This is a slightly simpler version of the focaccia we make at ACE. The use of a *biga* (Italian starter) will give your bread a deeper, richer flavor. I have given you two variations on the recipe—one will make focaccia over an inch (2.5 cm) high with a light interior; the other (what the Tuscans call *scacciata*), is a lower, denser focaccia. Extra oil and salt in the final dough and one less rise is the only difference in the method. With the exception of the 12-hour refrigeration of the *biga*, the focaccia will be out of the oven in less than 5 hours after you mix the final dough. You will have three 20-minute "work" periods interspersed with fermentation and proofing time. Since the scacciata has no final proof, it will be ready in about 4 hours. While all the other breads in this book can be made without a standing mixer, I have not had any luck making this recipe by hand. Feel free to experiment with other toppings—a few lightly sautéed but not browned cooking onions, olives, thyme, or black pepper.

BIGA (STARTER)
¼ tsp. (1.2 mL) traditional dry yeast
1 Tbsp. (15 mL) water at 75° to 95°F (24° to 35°C)
7 oz. (200 g) unbleached hard white flour
⅓ cup + 1½ Tbsp. (100 mL) water at 75°F (24°C)

FOR THE BIGA

In a small bowl, dissolve the yeast in the water. Within a few minutes, the yeast should have taken on a creamy-looking consistency. If it has not, the yeast should not be used. Combine the flour, water, and the yeast mixture in a standing mixer bowl and mix with the dough hook for 4 minutes on slow (#2 speed) to blend. Scrape down the bowl with a plastic spatula as needed. Increase to fast (#4 speed) and mix for an additional 4 minutes.

Place the mixture, which will be stiff, in a lightly oiled bowl large enough to let it double in size. Cover with plastic wrap and allow to ferment in a warm, draft-free area for 12 to 14 hours. The *biga* will have expanded by about 50% and have a few small holes in it. If need be, the *biga* can be held or retarded in the refrigerator for up to 24 hours. Bring to room temperature (72° to 75°F or 22° to 24°C) before continuing with your bread making.

FINAL DOUGH—FOCACCIA
13.2 oz. (375 g) unbleached hard white flour
1¼ cups (300 mL) water at 75°F (24°C)
1 Tbsp. (15 mL) olive oil
1½ tsp. (7.5 mL) traditional dry yeast
3 Tbsp. + 1 tsp. (50 mL) water at 75°F (24°C)
1 recipe Biga
2 tsp. (10 mL) kosher salt
olive oil for the baking pans, your hands, and the top of the dough

FINAL DOUGH—SCACCIATA
13.2 oz. (375 g) unbleached hard white flour
1¼ cups (300 mL) water at 75°F (24°C)
2 Tbsp. (30 mL) olive oil
2 tsp. (10 mL) traditional, dry yeast
3 Tbsp. + 1 tsp. (50 mL) water at 75°F (24°C)
1 recipe Biga
1 Tbsp. + 1½ tsp. (22.5 mL) kosher salt
olive oil for the baking pans, your hands, and the top of the dough

FOR BOTH FOCACCIA AND SCACCIATA

Put the flour, 1¼ cups (300 mL) water, and olive oil in a standing mixer and mix with a dough hook on slow (#2 speed) for 4 minutes. Drape a kitchen towel or plastic wrap over the bowl and allow the mixture to rest for 15 to 20 minutes. This process is called *autolyse*. It allows the gluten to develop and the dough to absorb water better.

Dissolve the yeast in 3 Tbsp. + 1 tsp. (50 mL) water. Add the *biga*, salt, and yeast to the mixture in the bowl and mix for 2 minutes on slow (#2 speed) followed by 6 minutes on fast (#4 speed). Your final dough should look shiny and be able to stretch about 6 inches (15 cm) without ripping.

FOR FOCACCIA

Transfer the dough to an oiled bowl large enough to let the dough expand. Cover lightly with a kitchen towel or plastic wrap, place in a draft-proof area, and allow to ferment for 2 hours or until the dough has more than doubled. Generously oil 2 pans roughly 8½ x 6½ x 2 inches (21.2 x 16.2 x 5 cm) or 1 roughly 10 x 8 x 2 inches (25 x 20 x 5 cm) in size. Non-stick or enamelware works well too, but must still be oiled. Oil your hands, then turn the dough onto a surface and either cut the dough in half and place into the 2 pans or keep in one piece for the larger pan. Spread out the dough to an even thickness. Cover the pans with plastic wrap or a kitchen towel and let the dough rest for 15 minutes. Sprinkle more oil over the dough and dimple it with the tips of your fingers. Loosely cover the pans with a kitchen towel or plastic wrap and allow to proof (rise) at room temperature for 1 to 3 hours or until the dough is almost double in size.

Preheat the oven to 425°F (220°C) or 375°F (190°C) for a convection oven.

FOR SCACCIATA

Generously oil 2 pans roughly 8½ x 6½ x 2 inches (21.2 x 16.2 x 5 cm) or 1 roughly 10 x 8 x 2 inches (25 x 20 x 5 cm) in size. Non-stick or enamelware can be used, but must also be oiled. Oil your hands, turn the dough onto a surface, and either cut it in half (for two pans) or keep in one piece for the larger pan. Place into the pan or pans. Sprinkle more oil on the dough and dimple it with your fingertips, spreading it out to an even thickness. Cover the pans loosely with plastic wrap or a kitchen towel and allow the dough to proof (rise) for about 2 to 3 hours at room temperature. The dough should almost double in size.

Preheat the oven to 425°F (220°C) or 375°F (190°C) for a convection oven. If using a pizza stone or bricks, preheat them as well.

TOPPINGS FOR FOCACCIA AND SCACCIATA
3 Tbsp. (45 mL) grated Parmigiano Reggiano cheese and ½ tsp. (2.5 mL) coarse sea salt

or 1 tsp. (5 mL) coarse sea salt and 1 heaping tsp. (5 mL), or to taste, fresh rosemary removed from the stalk and coarsely chopped, or ½ heaping tsp. (2.5 mL), or to taste, dried rosemary soaked in olive oil for 1 hour and patted dry.

Brush the focaccia and/or the scacciata with more oil if the top looks dry. Sprinkle the dough with either the rosemary and salt or the Parmigiano and salt. Place the pans on a rack a third from the bottom of the oven and bake for about 30 minutes. Remove the bread from the pans and tap the bottom crust with your fingertips. The bread should sound hollow. If it does not, bake for another 5 minutes. Immediately remove the bread from the pans and put them on a rack to cool.

ORGANIC HARD 20 KG 02 55 A 24 06 03 CERTIFIED BY OCPP

ORGANIC HARD 20 KG 02 48 A 24 06 03 CERTIFIED BY OCPP

ORGANIC HARD 20 KG 02 44 A 24 06 03 CERTIFIED BY OCPP

ORGANIC HARD 20 KG 02 54 A 24 06 03 CERTIFIED BY OCP

ORGANIC HARD 20 KG 02 47 A 24 06 03 CERTIFIED BY OCP

Organic flour for our
Organic White Oval.

ORGANIC HARD 20 KG 02 42 A 24 06 03 CERTIFIED BY OCP

Calabrese

Calabrese originated in the province of Calabria in southern Italy. Because of its even crumb, it is a natural for bruschetta and sandwiches and can also be used for French toast, stratas, as well as savory or sweet bread puddings. Your total "real" work-time will be about 1¼ hours spread over a 16-hour period. For 11 to 12 of those hours, your Old White Dough (starter) is developing in the refrigerator. You will have three periods, of about 15 minutes each, of mixing and kneading interspersed with 1 *autolyse* (resting time) and 2 long fermentation times. There is no need to be close at hand during the proofing, but you will want to check the progress of the dough from time to time.

At ACE, we add rye and corn flour to give our Calabrese a more complex taste than the original. We like to think the bakers of Calabria would appreciate our twist on their traditional recipe.

OLD WHITE DOUGH (STARTER)
½ tsp. (2.5 mL) traditional dry yeast
½ cup (120 mL) water at 75° to 95°F (24° to 35°C)
6½ oz. (185 g) unbleached hard white flour
½ tsp. (2.5 mL) kosher salt

Dissolve the yeast in the water. The yeast will take on a creamy-looking consistency within 5 to 10 minutes. If it has not, it should not be used. Combine the flour, salt, and yeast in a standing mixer with a dough hook and mix on slow (#2 speed) for 4 minutes and then on fast (#4 speed) for 2 minutes. Remove the dough from the food processor and place it in a well-oiled bowl. It will be quite stiff. Cover the bowl with plastic wrap and place in the refrigerator for 11 to 12 hours. Remove from the refrigerator, bring to room temperature, and continue with the recipe. You will have 10½ oz. (300 g) of Old White Dough.

FINAL DOUGH
1½ oz. (40 g) rye flour
1½ oz. (40 g) corn flour

21 oz. (600 g) unbleached white bread flour
1 Tbsp. + 1½ tsp. (22.5 g) malt powder
2 cups (475 mL) water at 68° to 75°F (20° to 24°C)

Combine all of the above ingredients in the standing mixer and mix with the dough hook on slow (#2 speed) for 5 minutes. Remove the bowl and cover with plastic wrap or a kitchen towel. Allow the dough to *autolyse* (relax) for 15 minutes.

FINAL MIXING
1 tsp. (5 mL) traditional dry yeast
2 Tbsp. (30 mL) water at 75° to 95°F (24° to 35°C)
1 recipe Old White Dough

1 recipe Final Dough
2 tsp. (10 mL) kosher salt
canola oil or butter (if making a loaf) for greasing pan
¼ to ½ cup (60 to 120 mL) cornmeal

"Honest bread is very good — it's the butter that makes the temptation."
—Douglas Jerrold, 1803–1857

Dissolve the yeast in the water. Combine the Old White Dough, the Final Dough, the salt, and the yeast in the standing mixer. Mix with the dough hook on slow (#2 speed) for 3 minutes and then on fast (#4 speed) for 4 minutes. If your standing mixer has trouble mixing this amount of dough, mix on slow (#2 speed) for 3 minutes, remove the dough to a floured surface and knead by hand. Using your palms, push the dough along the surface away from you. Pull it back over itself and continue the action for about 5 minutes. This is called the "push-pull" method of kneading.

Place the dough back into the well-oiled bowl making sure the dough is completely coated with oil. Cover loosely with plastic wrap or a kitchen towel, and allow it to ferment for 2 hours at room temperature.

After 2 hours, turn the dough onto a floured surface and cut the dough into one piece, approximately 1½ lb. (650 g) and two 10½-oz (300-g) pieces. Pat the pieces into rectangles, then fold the two ends into the middle. Repeat twice. Place seam-side down on a floured surface. Loosely cover with plastic wrap or a kitchen towel and allow to rest 8 to 10 minutes. Shape the 1½-lb. (650-g) piece of dough into a boule (see page 21) or a loaf (see page 20). Shape the two 10½-oz. (300-g) pieces into baguettes. For the baguettes, gently flatten the dough into a rough circle about 8 inches (20 cm) in diameter. Fold the furthest third of the circle to the middle and then bring the third closest to you to the middle. Press down on the seam with the heel of your hand. Take the cylinder of dough and roll it back and forth under your palms and fingers. The cylinder will lengthen. Stop once you have it 12 to 14 inches (30 to 36 cm) in length. Make sure all the seams are pinched closed. Place the boule and baguettes (seam-side down) on the back of a cookie sheet that has either been dusted with cornmeal or well oiled. (This will make it much easier to transfer the dough onto the hot pizza stone or bricks.) If you have decided to make a loaf-shaped bread, oil or butter a 3¾- x 7½- x 2½-inch (9½- x 19- x 6½-cm) pan, Teflon-coated, if possible, and place the dough seam-side down in the pan. Brush whichever shapes you make gently with oil and sprinkle with cornmeal. Cover the dough loosely with plastic wrap and allow it to proof from 35 minutes up to 2 hours, until it has grown approximately 50%. The baguettes will proof more quickly than the larger loaves. You may be able to bake them off first.

Place a pizza stone or smooth, clean bricks on a rack a third from the bottom of your oven and preheat to 400°F (200°C) or 375°F (190°C) for a convection oven. Allow the stone 20 to 25 minutes to heat up. For the boule, use a very sharp knife to cut a halo ¼ inch (.6 cm) deep a third from the top of the loaf. Dust the pizza stone with cornmeal to prevent sticking, and transfer the loaves to the oven. Before closing the oven door, spritz the roof and sides of your oven with warm water. If you prefer, place 5 or 6 ice cubes on the floor of the oven. This will create steam, which will help crisp the crust.

Bake the baguettes for approximately 25 minutes, the boule for 30 to 35 minutes, and the pan loaf for 35 to 40 minutes or until the crust becomes crisp and turns a medium brown. Breads put in a convection oven may bake slightly faster. Carefully remove the bread from the oven. To test if the bread is fully baked, tap your fingertips on the bottom of the loaf. If it is, it will sound hollow. If not, return the bread to the oven and bake in 5-minute increments until done. Place the bread on a rack to cool. You will not be able to appreciate the true taste or texture of the bread if it has not rested for at least 1½ to 2 hours.

Whole Wheat Bran

MAKES 3 LOAVES

Most whole wheat recipes call for oil in the mix. This home version of ACE's whole wheat bran doesn't, and is denser and more flavorful than the supermarket variety. So, if you like light, fluffy bread, this isn't for you. On the other hand, if you enjoy rustic European-style bread, you may want to give this a try. Coincidentally, it is the most foolproof of the yeasted bread recipes in this book. The Old White Dough has a slow fermentation in the refrigerator for 11 hours. Don't be concerned if you leave it an extra hour. The next stage will take about 40 minutes of your time, autolyse included. A 2-hour fermentation follows, another 10 minutes of work on your part, a final proof of about 1 hour and it's ready to bake. All in all, you will have spent a little over an hour of your time to produce these delicious loaves of bread.

OLD WHITE DOUGH (STARTER)
½ tsp. (2.5 mL) traditional dry yeast
½ cup (120 mL) water at 75° to 95°F (24° to 35°C)
6½ oz. (185 g) unbleached hard white flour
½ tsp. (2.5 mL) kosher salt

Dissolve the yeast in the water. The yeast will take on a creamy-looking consistency within 5 to 10 minutes. If it does not, discard it and start again with new yeast. Combine the flour, salt, and dissolved yeast in a standing mixer with a dough hook and mix on slow (#2 speed) for 4 minutes and then on fast (#4 speed) for 2 minutes. Remove the dough from the mixer and place it in a well-oiled bowl. Cover the bowl with plastic wrap and place in the refrigerator for 11 to 12 hours. Remove from the refrigerator, bring to room temperature, and continue with the recipe. You will have 10 ½ oz. (300 g) of Old White Dough.

FINAL DOUGH
21 oz. (600 g) whole wheat flour
13 oz. (365 g) unbleached hard white flour

4¼ oz. (120 g) bran
1½ Tbsp. (22.5 mL) molasses
3⅓ cups (800 mL) water at 75° to 95°F (24° to 35°C)

Combine all of the above ingredients in a standing mixer and mix with the dough hook on slow (#2 speed) for 3 minutes. Remove the bowl and cover with plastic wrap or a kitchen towel. Allow the dough to *autolyse* (relax) for 15 minutes.

FINAL MIXING
1½ tsp. (7.5 mL) traditional dry yeast
3 Tbsp. (45 mL) water at 75° to 95°F (24° to 35°C)
1 recipe Old White Dough

1 recipe Final Dough
1 Tbsp. (15 mL) kosher salt
butter for greasing pans
1 egg white, lightly whisked, for glazing

Dissolve the yeast in the water. The yeast will take on a creamy-looking consistency within 5 to 10 minutes. If it does not, discard it and start again with new yeast. Combine the Old White Dough, the Final Dough, salt and the dissolved yeast in the standing mixer bowl. Mix with the dough hook on slow (#2 speed) for 4 minutes and then on fast (#4 speed) for 7 minutes. If your mixer has trouble mixing this amount of dough, mix on slow (#2 speed) for 4 minutes. Remove the dough to a floured surface and knead by hand. Use the push-pull method, allowing your palms to push the dough along the surface away from you. Pull it back over itself and continue the action for about 8 minutes.

Place the dough back into the well-oiled bowl making sure the dough is completely coated in oil. Cover loosely with plastic wrap or a kitchen towel, and allow it to ferment for 2 hours at room temperature.

After 2 hours, turn the dough onto a floured surface and cut the dough into 3 even-sized pieces of approximately 1½ lb. (700 g) each. Shape the pieces into rectangles and fold the two ends into the middle. Repeat this twice. Place seam-side down on a floured surface. Loosely cover with plastic wrap and allow to rest for 8 to 10 minutes.

Lightly butter 3 pans approximately 3¾ x 7½ x 2½ inches (9½ x 19 x 6½ cm) in size, Teflon-coated if possible. Gently pat each piece of dough into a rectangle of even height. Using the palms of your hands, roll one long side of the dough toward the other like a long jelly roll and pat into a shape that will fit your pan. Gently press the seams together. Put the dough into the 3 pans, seam-side down. Again, gently drape with a kitchen towel or plastic wrap. Allow to rise at room temperature until approximately 1½ inches (3.8 cm) above the rim of the pan (about 1 hour). Press a finger into the dough. If the indentation remains, place the pans in the oven. If the dough springs back, proof for another 15 minutes and check again.

Preheat the oven to 400°F (200°C) or 375°F (190°C) for a convection oven. Place the rack a third from the bottom of the oven. Check the temperature with an oven thermometer. Spray the inside sides of the oven with hot water or place 5 or 6 ice cubes on the oven floor, and then close the door. Immediately uncover the loaves, brush with lightly whisked, room temperature egg white, and place in the preheated oven. Bake for 35 to 40 minutes. Loaves put in a convection oven may bake slightly faster.

The bread should be a golden brown and produce a hollow sound when you tap the bottom crust. To do this, carefully tip the bread out of the pan. It should just slip out. Tap the bottom crust with your fingertips. If it is fully baked, it will sound hollow. If not, return the bread to the pan and bake a further 5 minutes. Repeat until the bread is done.

Remove the loaves immediately from the oven and cool, well spaced, on a wire rack. Resist the temptation to cut into them immediately. They will taste much better about 2 hours later.

If you prefer to make boules, see page 21 (Pain au Lait) for instructions. Follow the baking instructions above.

Irish Soda Bread Three Ways

EACH RECIPE MAKES ONE LOAF

Irish Soda Bread was originally made with only four ingredients—flour, baking soda, salt, and buttermilk. In this version, I've added a little butter and an egg. Traditionalists would be rolling in their graves. It's a loaf best suited to great lashings of butter and jam or honey. Variations on the theme include raisins or herbs. Either addition provides a welcome change to an old favorite. The Herbed Soda Bread marries well with a chunk of old cheddar or as an accompaniment to lamb or beef stew, whereas the Lemon-Raisin version can substitute for dessert. Tradition has it that the deep cuts in Irish Soda Bread allow the fairies to fly out.

BASIC RECIPE

1 cup (240 mL) whole wheat flour

1 cup (240 mL) unbleached all-purpose flour

1 cup (240 mL) quick-cooking (not instant) oats

1 tsp. (5 mL) kosher salt

2 tsp. (10 mL) baking powder

1 tsp. (5 mL) baking soda

3 Tbsp. (45 mL) unsalted butter, melted and brought to room temperature

1 egg

1 cup (240 mL) buttermilk, at room temperature (see Cook's Tips)

Preheat the oven to 350°F (175°C).

Combine the 2 flours, oats, salt, baking powder, and baking soda.

Lightly mix the melted butter and the egg into the room temperature buttermilk. Make a well in the center of the dry ingredients and pour the liquid in the middle. Mix together with your hands until the ingredients just hold together.

Gently knead the dough—still in the bowl—with your knuckles for 2 minutes, then transfer to a lightly floured surface and roll with two hands into a flat disk, 2 to 2½ inches (5 to 6.2 cm) high. Place on a baking sheet and cut a cross at least 1 inch (2.5 cm) deep into the top.

Bake for 40 minutes or until a skewer inserted into the middle comes out dry. Cool on a rack and wait at least 2 hours before eating. Cut in slices or break the bread into 4 wedges along the cross.

HERBED IRISH SODA BREAD

Follow the Basic Recipe, and add 2 Tbsp. (30 mL) total of minced fresh thyme, rosemary, basil, oregano, marjoram, and savory—any or all—to the dry ingredients.

LEMON-RAISIN IRISH SODA BREAD

Follow the Basic Recipe, with the following changes:

Reduce the salt to ¾ tsp. (4 mL).

Add 3 Tbsp. + 1 tsp. (50 mL) sugar to the dry ingredients.

Add ⅔ cup (160 mL) sultana raisins* and ¼ tsp. (1.2 mL) grated lemon peel before kneading.

Sprinkle the top with ½ tsp. (2.5 mL) sugar before baking.

* Toss the raisins in 1 Tbsp. (15 mL) lemon juice. Leave for half an hour, pat dry, and discard any lemon juice not absorbed.

COOK'S TIPS

1. As a substitute for the buttermilk, mix 1 Tbsp. (15 mL) lemon juice or white vinegar with 1 cup (240 mL) less 1 Tbsp. (15 mL) homogenized milk, and let stand for 5 minutes before incorporating into the recipe. Another alternative for buttermilk can be found in Cook's Tip (see page 36).

2. Although I never recommend storing bread in a plastic bag, I make an exception for Soda Bread, as a crisp crust is not integral to the enjoyment of eating the loaf. You will get an extra day out of it.

Although you can bake Irish Soda Bread successfully in an oven, a traditionalist would insist that the real stuff can only be made in a bastible — much like a Dutch oven — in a peat fire.

Almond, Apricot, and Honey Scones

MAKES 8 TO 10 SCONES

Lightly toasted almonds, small pieces of dried apricot, and honey create a delicate, sophisticated scone that needs only a touch of butter as a complement.

1 Tbsp. (15 mL) baking powder
2 tsp. (10 mL) baking soda
1 large pinch kosher salt
2¾ cups (655 mL) unbleached all-purpose flour
1 Tbsp. (15 mL) sugar
¾ cup (180 mL) buttermilk
1 egg
⅓ cup (80 mL) delicately flavored liquid honey, such as wildflower

5 Tbsp. (75 mL) very cold unsalted butter cut into ¼-inch (.6-cm) pieces
½ cup (120 mL) ¼-inch (.6-cm) chopped dried apricots
½ cup (120 mL) lightly chopped slivered almonds (not sliced), toasted in a dry frying pan until golden brown

TOPPING
1 egg
1 Tbsp. (15 mL) water
1 Tbsp. (15 mL) sugar

Preheat the oven to 400°F (200°C).

Toss the baking powder, baking soda, salt, flour, and sugar in a large bowl until well mixed. In another bowl, whisk together the buttermilk and the egg. Add the honey and whisk again. Don't worry if the liquid thickens slightly.

Add the butter to the flour mixture and rub between your fingers until it looks grainy. It will feel very dry, and there should be no big chunks of butter left. Make a well in the flour mixture and add the egg mixture. Toss with a fork until just blended. Add the chopped fruit and nuts. Mix just until incorporated. Turn onto a floured working surface.

Lightly sprinkle the dough with flour so it doesn't stick, and pat the dough down to 1 inch (2.5 cm) thick. Use a 2½- to 3-inch (6.2- to 7.5-cm) metal circle or glass, and cut out as many circles as possible. Flour the cutter as you go along to prevent sticking. Gather the extra dough and gently knead it together, flatten, and cut out more scones. Repeat until all of the dough is gone. Work the dough as little as possible.

Place the scones on an ungreased cookie sheet.

For the topping, make a wash by whisking together the egg and 1 Tbsp. (15 mL) water. Brush each scone with the wash and then sprinkle with sugar. Bake on the middle rack for 15 minutes, then place on a baking rack to cool.

COOK'S TIP

1. When cutting dried fruit, spray your knife with cooking spray and the fruit won't stick.

2. See Cook's Tip page 31 and 36 for substitutes for buttermilk.

Apricots derive their name from the Latin word preacocium, meaning precocious. The Romans called them that because they ripened so early in the year.

Pain au Lait p.19

Baked Tortilla Shards p. 42

Motley Croutons
p. 44

Strawberry Orange Classico p. 65

Apple-Rhubarb Muffins p. 34

Focaccia p.22

Blueberry Cornmeal Muffins

MAKES 8 REGULAR OR 6 LARGE MUFFINS

From kitchen to table in 45 minutes, these muffins are wonderful with unsalted butter or liquid honey. They freeze well, so make a double batch for a treat on workday mornings.

canola oil for greasing tin
½ cup + 2 Tbsp. (150 mL) unbleached all-purpose flour
½ cup (120 mL) sugar, preferably fine
½ tsp. (2.5 mL) baking soda
1½ tsp. (7.5 mL) baking powder
1½ tsp. (7.5 mL) kosher salt
1½ tsp. (7.5 mL) ground cinnamon

1 cup (240 mL) cornmeal (not corn flour)
2 extra large eggs or 3 large eggs
¾ cup (180 mL) sour cream
½ tsp. (2.5 mL) vanilla extract
½ cup (120 mL) canola or vegetable oil
½ tsp. (2.5 mL) lemon zest
6 oz. (170 g) fresh blueberries or 7 oz. (200 g) frozen blueberries (do not defrost)

Preheat the oven to 350°F (175°C). Grease the muffin tin with canola oil.

Mix together the flour, sugar, baking soda, baking powder, salt, cinnamon, and cornmeal in a bowl large enough to hold all the ingredients. Lightly whisk the eggs, sour cream, and vanilla together in a smaller bowl. Gently stir into the dry ingredients, then pour the oil into the mixture while mixing continuously. When the oil is completely incorporated, fold in the lemon zest and the blueberries.

Fill the greased muffin tins to the top and bake for 15 to 20 minutes. Insert a cake tester to ensure that the muffins are fully cooked; it should come out clean.

COOK'S TIP

Break the frozen blueberries apart and add frozen to the dough. Defrosted frozen blueberries will bleed into the dough giving the finished muffins a blueish tinge.

Apple-Rhubarb Muffins

Moist and full of flavor, these muffins have an almost cake-like quality. Serve them warm with unsalted butter or a dollop of yogurt drizzled with honey.

canola oil for greasing tin
½ cup (120 mL) unsalted butter
½ cup + 2 Tbsp. (150 mL) unbleached all-purpose flour
½ cup (120 mL) sugar, preferably fine
½ tsp. (2.5 mL) baking soda
1 heaping tsp. (6 mL) baking powder
1½ tsp. (7.5 mL) kosher salt
1½ tsp. (7.5 mL) ground cinnamon

1⅓ cups (320 mL) bran
2 extra large eggs or 3 large eggs
¾ cup + 1 Tbsp. (200 mL) sour cream
½ tsp. (2.5 mL) vanilla extract
5 oz. (150 g) frozen unsweetened rhubarb, defrosted and cut into ¼-inch (.6-cm) pieces, or fresh rhubarb
1½ Granny Smith or Spy apples, peeled, cored, and diced in ¼-inch (.6-cm) pieces

Preheat the oven to 350°F (175°C). Grease the muffin tin with the canola oil.

Melt the butter and bring to room temperature.

Mix together the flour, sugar, baking soda, baking powder, salt, cinnamon, and bran in a mixing bowl large enough to hold all the ingredients. Lightly whisk the eggs, sour cream, and vanilla in a smaller bowl. Gently stir into the dry ingredients. In three additions, add the butter to the mixture while mixing continuously. When the butter is blended into the dough, fold in the rhubarb and apple.

Fill the greased muffin tins to the top and bake for 15 to 20 minutes. Insert a cake tester to ensure that the muffins are fully cooked; it should come out clean.

Date and Walnut Loaf

An 80-year-old friend of my mother gave her this recipe in 1948. It was always a treat when Mom made it for our family. She serves each piece slathered with unsalted butter, accompanied by a cup of black tea or, better still, a glass of good, dry sherry.

1 cup (240 mL) roughly chopped dried dates
¾ cup (180 mL) roughly chopped walnuts
½ tsp. (2.5 mL) baking soda
½ tsp. (2.5 mL) kosher salt
¾ cup + ⅛ cup (210 mL) boiling water

3 Tbsp. (45 mL) unsalted butter
1 cup (240 mL) sugar
1½ cups (360 mL) cake flour
1 tsp. (5 mL) vanilla extract
2 eggs
1 tsp. (5 mL) dark rum or Cognac, optional

Preheat the oven to 350°F (175°C). Lightly grease a loaf pan, approximately 8½ x 4½ x 2 inches (21.2 x 12.5 x 5 cm), with butter.

Mix the dates, walnuts, baking soda, and salt in a medium-sized bowl. Then stir in the boiling water and the butter. Let stand for 20 minutes.

Sift the sugar and the flour together into a smaller bowl. Lightly whisk the vanilla, eggs, and rum or Cognac (if using) in a large mixing bowl. Stir the flour and sugar into the egg mixture in 3 additions. Fold in the date and nut mixture, making sure the ingredients are well combined. The final mixture will be thick.

Pour the batter into the greased loaf pan and bake for about 1 hour. Check with a cake tester or skewer after about 50 minutes. Don't worry if little pieces of the dates and some moisture stick to the tester. It's better to take it out a little earlier than to risk overcooking the loaf.

Take out of the oven and let stand for 10 minutes before removing from the pan.

Dates are very sweet — the Ancient Romans used them in place of sugar — but they also have many other nutritional benefits. In fact, they are so nutritious that, in combination with milk, they made up the staple diet of desert travelers, who subsisted for long periods of time on little else.

Jalapeño Cornbread

Ten minutes prep time and 15 minutes in the oven—it doesn't get much easier than this. The buttermilk gives the cornbread a rich, deep flavor, and the jalapeño contributes a nice bite. Enjoy this bread for brunch with scrambled eggs and back bacon (or "Canadian bacon" in the U.S.), and with any pork or chicken dish.

1 cup (240 mL) cake flour
1¼ cups (300 mL) cornmeal
4 tsp. (20 mL) baking powder
1 tsp. (5 mL) kosher salt
1 egg
1¾ cups (420 mL) buttermilk
¼ tsp. (1.2 mL) hot chili powder

6 Tbsp. (90 mL) unsalted butter, melted and brought to room temperature
1½ cups (360 mL) corn kernels from approximately 2 cobs (or frozen and defrosted)
1 tsp. or more (5 mL+) minced, seeded, green jalapeño pepper
1 Tbsp. (15 mL) vegetable oil

Preheat the oven to 425°F (220°C). Warm an 8- to 10-inch (20- to 25-cm) iron skillet in the oven while mixing the batter.

In a medium-sized bowl, sift together the flour, cornmeal, baking powder, and salt. In a small bowl, lightly whisk together the egg and the buttermilk. Pour the buttermilk mixture into the flour mixture and stir with a wooden spoon until blended. Sprinkle the chili powder into the butter and then mix into the batter. Stir in the corn and jalapeño.

Carefully remove the hot skillet from the oven and place on the stove over high heat. Pour the vegetable oil into the skillet. When it is heated and easily coats the bottom of the skillet, add the batter and smooth the top. Turn the heat down to medium and cook for about 1 minute; this will give the cornbread a nice crust. If you prefer a softer crust, take the skillet off the heat immediately. In either case, place it back into the oven for about 15 minutes. Test with a cake tester or skewer. The cornbread should rest in the skillet for 5 minutes before you turn it out.

Cut in pie-shaped wedges and serve warm, with Hot Pepper Honey Butter (see page 89).

COOK'S TIP
You can substitute 1¼ cups (300 mL) homogenized milk mixed with ½ cup (120 mL) yogurt or sour cream for the buttermilk. Another alternative for buttermilk can be found in Cook's Tip (see page 31).

Just as the first European settlers of North America had to adapt in order to survive, so did their recipes. Cornbread is a traditional bread from those times. Its combination of cornmeal and wheat or rye flours brings together their old-world ingredients and baking techniques with the great grain from their new country.

Cornmeal Drop Biscuits

MAKES 6 BISCUITS

This is one of the easiest recipes for biscuits I know. Serve them right out of the oven—they stale quickly and are best eaten warm—with a good dollop of honey or jam, or split them open and pile with scrambled eggs. They are a great accompaniment to roasted pork, chicken, or turkey if you add the sage.

1¼ cups plus 3 Tbsp. (345 mL) unbleached all-purpose flour
⅓ cup (80 mL) cornmeal plus 2 tsp. (10 mL) for sprinkling on top
2 tsp. (10 mL) baking powder
1 tsp. (5 mL) baking soda
½ tsp. (2.5 mL) kosher salt

1 Tbsp. (15 mL) finely minced fresh sage (optional)
4 Tbsp. (60 mL) cold, unsalted butter, cut in ½-inch (1.2-cm) cubes
2 Tbsp. (30 mL) cold vegetable shortening, cut in ½-inch (1.2-cm) cubes
¾ cup (180 mL) buttermilk plus 1 Tbsp. (15 mL) for brushing tops

Preheat the oven to 400°F (200°C).

In a medium-sized bowl, stir together the flour, cornmeal, baking powder, baking soda, and salt. Add the cold butter and shortening. Using both hands, rub the butter and flour mixture together. Move quickly so as not to soften the butter too much. The mixture should be crumbly, with small pieces of butter and shortening visible.

Using a fork, stir in the buttermilk until the mixture holds together. Mix in the sage if using. Drop 6 free-form pieces of dough onto a greased or parchment-lined baking pan. Brush with the remaining buttermilk and sprinkle with cornmeal. Bake for about 16 minutes.

Serve warm.

COOK'S TIP
Buttermilk substitutions can be found in Cook's Tip (see page 31 and page 36).

There are two types of cornmeal—steel ground (common), and stone or water ground (less so). Stone grinding preserves some of the germ and husk of the grain. As a result, stone ground meal is more nutritious, but also more apt to spoil, so it should be stored in the refrigerator.

Apple and Dried Cranberry Stuffing

This full-flavored, delicious stuffing was created by Michele Heywood, a great cook and the Customer Service Manager at ACE Bakery. She developed the recipe as a use for our Sage Bread, which we make every Thanksgiving and Christmas. It's also a wonderful stuffing for chicken, pheasant, or partridge.

1 large loaf sage bread or 1 large loaf, about 1.1 lb. (500 g) white bread and 3 to 4 Tbsp. (45 to 60 mL) finely chopped fresh sage

½ cup (120 mL) unsalted butter

4 cups (950 mL) sliced leeks, white and pale green parts only

4 medium-sized tart green apples, peeled, cored, and diced

4 celery stalks, coarsely chopped

½ cup (120 mL) dried cranberries

½ cup (120 mL) minced fresh parsley

1 cup (240 mL) turkey or chicken stock

salt and freshly ground black pepper to taste

1 lb. (455 g) sweet Italian sausage, casings removed, meat crumbled and sautéed over medium-high heat for about 10 minutes, or until cooked (optional)

Cut the bread into ½-inch (1.2-cm) cubes, trimming the crust if you wish. Put the cubes on cookie sheets and bake in a 275°F (135°C) oven until crisp but not browned, about 15 to 20 minutes.

Heat the butter in a large skillet over medium-high heat. Add the leeks, apples, and celery, and sauté until the leeks soften, about 8 minutes. Remove the pan from the heat, mix in the dried cranberries, and cool to room temperature. The recipe, up to this point, can be made one day ahead and refrigerated.

In a large bowl, mix the bread cubes, the cooled fruit and vegetable mixture, parsley, stock, salt and pepper to taste, and toss gently. Add the sausage, if using.

Stuff the turkey just before roasting.

The practice of stuffing meats dates back at least to Ancient Rome, when Trimalchio's famous feast included a roast pig stuffed with sausages and black puddings.

Mom's Rustic Sage Stuffing

This is the easiest stuffing you will ever make. It's a second-generation family recipe, and in our house any attempt to make a more "sophisticated" stuffing is always voted down. It works equally well with Cornish hens or chicken.

1½ large loaves about 1.7 lb. (750 g) white or country bread, crusts removed
2 bunches fresh sage, washed and finely chopped
⅔ to ¾ lb. (285 to 340 g) unsalted butter, melted
salt and freshly ground black pepper to taste

Ideally, the bread should be a day old—slightly stale but not dried out. I sometimes tear it up the day before I need it, put it in a bowl and cover it with a towel.

Rip the bread into ½-inch (1.2-cm) pieces and put in a bowl. The stuffing will have a nicer consistency if the pieces are smaller. Add three-quarters of the sage, ½ cup (120 mL) of the butter, 1 tsp. (5 mL) salt, and ¼ tsp. (1.2 mL) pepper. Toss.

Taste and add more sage, butter, salt, and pepper. The sage flavor should be pronounced. All the bread should be moist, and the mixture should be slightly salty.

COOK'S TIPS

1. Stuff the turkey just before roasting. If you have too much stuffing for the turkey, wrap the excess in foil and bake it with the turkey for the last hour. When serving, mix the stuffing baked in foil with the stuffing that you've removed from the bird. The delicious juices of the bird will permeate it all.

2. If just the thought of the amount of butter in this recipe sends your cholesterol level soaring, use roughly ½ lb. (225 g) butter and ¾ cup (180 mL) chicken stock.

"Why should a man die in whose garden sage grows?"
— Medieval Latin proverb

Melba Toast (Spa and Decadent)

SPA MELBA TOAST

MAKES UP TO 30 TOASTS

Traditional Melba toast is made only with white bread, but feel free to try any type you want. My favorites are pain au lait, white, or brown.

10 or more slices of any type of bread you want, crusts removed

Preheat the oven to 350°F (175°C).

Roll out the bread slices with a rolling pin until they are about ⅛ inch (.3 cm) thick. Cut into triangles, fingers, squares, or circles.

Put the pieces of bread on a baking sheet and bake in the oven for 10 minutes or more, turning over once, until they become dark golden brown on both sides.

Store in an airtight container for up to 3 weeks.

COOK'S TIP

Any bread containing egg or butter will be easier to roll out. Other breads will tend to spring back, but if you persevere, you will end up with a great Melba toast no matter what type of bread you are using.

DECADENT MELBA TOAST

Sweet variations on a Spartan theme. Great crumbled over ice cream or with a 4 o'clock cup of tea.

10 or more slices Pain au Lait (see page 19), challah, brioche, or white bread, crusts removed
3 Tbsp. (45 mL) unsalted butter, or more, if needed

2 Tbsp. (30 mL) finely granulated sugar mixed with 1 scant Tbsp. (15 mL) ground cinnamon *or* 2½ Tbsp. (37.5 mL) finely granulated sugar, or more if needed

Preheat the oven to 350°F (175°C).

Roll out the bread slices with a rolling pin until they are about ⅛ inch (.3 cm) thick. Lightly spread both sides of each slice of bread with butter.

Mix together the sugar and cinnamon, if using that option.

Cut the bread into triangles, fingers, squares, or circles.

Cover a baking sheet with foil. Place the bread on the foil and bake in the oven for about 5 minutes. Turn the bread over and lightly sprinkle the sugar or the cinnamon-sugar mixture on the bread after you have turned it.

Bake until golden brown. Cool and store in an airtight container for up to 1 week.

Baked Tortilla Shards

You may have to make these two or three times to find the right balance of oil, salt, and pepper for you. When I first made them, I found them too bland. The second time they were too salty. By the third time they were just right.

8 tsp. (40 mL) olive oil
8 large corn or wheat tortillas
coarse sea salt and freshly ground pepper to taste

Pour a scant ½ tsp. (2.5 mL) of oil into the center of each tortilla and spread with a pastry brush. Do this on both sides of each tortilla.

Sprinkle 1 side of the tortilla with salt and pepper.

Cut into triangles and bake at 375°F (190°C) for about 10 minutes. If you prefer a darker chip with a more toasted taste, increase the baking temperature to 400°F (200°C), but keep an eye on the chips, as they darken very quickly.

The chips will keep in an airtight container for up to 1 week.

Different regions of Mexico are known for their different tortillas. Oaxaca is said to have the thinnest ones, Guadalajara's are thicker, and the blue color of the corn grown in the mountains of Central Mexico is preserved in the tortillas made there.

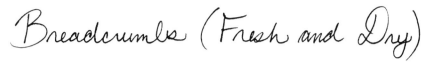
Breadcrumbs (Fresh and Dry)

FRESH BREADCRUMBS

MAKES 4¾ CUPS (1.1 L)

Fresh breadcrumbs are lighter, more absorbent, and generally larger than dried. Don't try substituting the two in recipes. Obviously, white bread is the most versatile for crumbs, but whole wheat, rye, sourdough, country, and grain breadcrumbs can also be used in some recipes. Pain au lait, brioche, and challah crumbs are good for desserts. Make fresh breadcrumbs from bread that is fresh or no more than one day old. It can't be bone dry.

> 1 loaf of bread, crust removed

Tear the bread into approximately ½-inch (1.2-cm) pieces. Place in a food processor fitted with the sharp mixing blade and process until the bread is shredded into pieces about ⅛ inch (.3 cm) or smaller. Don't overprocess; you may end up with a ball of gummy bread. For finer crumbs, spread crumbs on a baking sheet and let them air dry a bit, then force them through a sieve.

Place in a plastic bag and freeze for up to 6 months. Use as needed.

DRY BREADCRUMBS

MAKES 2 CUPS (475 ML)

> 1 stale loaf of bread

If you want, cut the crusts off the bread. If the bread is very, very dry, break it in pieces, place the pieces in a food processor with the sharp mixing blade, and process until the crumbs are the consistency of grainy sand.

If the bread is not completely dry, tear it into ½-inch (1.2-cm) pieces and toast these in a 325°F (165°C) oven until a test piece crumbles between your fingers; timing will depend on the freshness of the bread. Turn the heat down if the bread is getting too dark. Process as above. Place in a plastic bag and freeze for up to 6 months. Use as needed.

Motley Croutons

This is a great way to use up leftover bread. Cube your odd pieces of bread and toss them in the freezer in a tightly sealed plastic bag until you have accumulated a few cups. Purists may prefer to use just one kind of bread, but I like my croutons mixed, so I use white, country, Calabrese, focaccia, whole wheat—any bread. All croutons will keep for a week in a plastic bag stored in a cool, dark place—but not in the refrigerator.

EXTRA VIRGIN CROUTONS

These croutons can be made either in the oven or on the stovetop.

4 cups (950 mL) ½- to 1-inch (1.2- to 2.5-cm) crustless bread cubes, defrosted if previously frozen
¼ to ½ cup (60 to 120 mL) extra virgin olive oil

Oven Method: Preheat the oven to 375°F (190°C). Toss the bread cubes and half the oil in a large bowl. Add more oil if all the bread is not coated.

Place the bread cubes on a baking sheet in a single layer and bake for approximately 10 to 15 minutes depending on their size and how dark you want the croutons to be. Stir occasionally to prevent burning.

Stovetop Method: Pour 1½ Tbsp. (22.5 mL) of the oil into a frying pan and warm over medium heat. Add half the bread cubes. Sauté, stirring often, until the croutons are golden brown. Add more oil if necessary. Repeat with the rest of the bread cubes. Cool before using.

SPA CROUTONS

Most croutons are secret little bomblets of butter or oil, but if you bake them carefully, you can spare the fat and no one will be the wiser.

4 cups (950 mL) ½- to 1-inch (1.2- to 2.5-cm) crustless bread cubes, defrosted if previously frozen

Preheat the oven to 375°F (190°C).

Place the bread cubes on a baking sheet in one layer and bake for approximately 10 to 15 minutes, depending on their size and how dark you want the croutons to be. Stir once or twice to prevent them from burning. Cool before using.

GARLIC PARMIGIANO CROUTONS

If you have time, marinate 2 cloves of bruised garlic in the oil for up to 1 hour. Discard the garlic before tossing the oil with the croutons and cheese. Do not add minced garlic if you have used this method.

4 cups (950 mL) ½- to 1-inch (1.2- to 2.5-cm) crustless bread cubes, defrosted if previously frozen
¼ to ½ cup (60 to 120 mL) olive oil
½ to ¾ cup (120 to 180 mL) grated Parmigiano Reggiano
2 large cloves garlic, very finely minced

Preheat the oven to 375°F (190°C).

Toss the bread cubes with ¼ cup (60 mL) of oil and ¼ cup (60 mL) of the cheese, and all the garlic. Add more oil and cheese, if necessary, until all the bread is coated. Remember, the cheese needs enough oil to cling to the bread. Put the bread cubes on a baking sheet in one layer and bake for approximately 10 to 15 minutes, stirring occasionally, until the cheese has melted and the croutons are golden brown. Don't let the garlic burn. Cool before using.

HERBED CROUTONS

Try a combination of breads for these. Mixed herbed croutons add a crunchy lift to a salad of hearty greens, while white-based breads will let the herbs shine through. You could marinate 2 cloves of bruised garlic in the oil for up to 1 hour. Discard the garlic before using the oil.

4 cups (950 mL) of ½- to 1-inch (1.2- to 2.5-cm) crustless bread cubes, defrosted if previously frozen
½ cup (120 mL) olive oil

up to ¼ cup (60 mL) finely minced fresh parsley
up to ¼ cup (60 mL) combination of finely minced fresh chives, sage, and basil

Preheat the oven to 375°F (190°C).

Place the oil in a small bowl and add ⅛ cup (30 mL) of parsley, and ⅛ cup (30 mL) of mixed herbs. Toss half of this oil into the bread cubes and mix until coated. Add the rest of the oil and herbs in increments until the bread cubes are coated to your liking. Place the bread cubes on a baking sheet in a single layer. Bake for 10 to 15 minutes, stirring occasionally. Remove from the oven when the croutons are golden. Be careful not to let the herbs burn. Cool before using.

More Than Toast and O.J.

"It was one of those mornings when a man could face the day only after warming himself with a mug of thick coffee beaded with steam and a good thick crust of bread, and a bowl of bean soup."

—Richard Gehman

ACE Granola with Yogurt and Fresh Fruit

Toasted Grain Bread with Chèvre and Honey

Classic French Toast with Choice of Toppings

Cinnamon Banana French Toast with Chocolate Drizzle

Ham and Gruyère French Toast with Sautéed Apples

Camembert and Green Onion Strata

Chicken, Onion, and Mushroom Strata

Smoked Salmon, Spinach, and Chèvre Strata

Canadian Bacon and Egg Sandwich with Gruyère, Tomato Chutney, and Chives

Egg in the Hole

Spinach Gratin with Baked Eggs and Parmigiano

Coddled Eggs with Mushrooms and Tomato

Le mélange doux de ma mère

Souffléd Cheddar and Chive Gratin

Strawberry Orange Classico

Ginger and Honey Tea

ACE Granola with Yogurt and Fresh Fruit

MAKES 20 CUPS (4.8 L)

This granola was so popular at our café that we couldn't keep it in stock. We had to start bagging it so customers could take it home. It looks beautiful if you layer the granola, yogurt, and fruit in glass bowls or wide-mouthed glasses.

2 cups (475 mL) buckwheat (cooked quinoa or amaranth can be substituted)
5 cups (1.2 L) rolled oats
2 cups (475 mL) oat bran
1 cup (240 mL) shredded or flaked unsweetened coconut
½ cup (120 mL) unsalted sunflower seeds
1 cup (240 mL) unsalted peanuts, measured then chopped
1 cup (240 mL) whole unsalted almonds, measured then chopped
1 cup (240 mL) honey

½ cup (120 mL) vegetable oil
1 Tbsp. (15 mL) ground cinnamon
2 Tbsp. (30 mL) vanilla extract
1½ cups (360 mL) chopped dried apricots
1½ cups (360 mL) chopped dried prunes
1 cup (240 mL) dried banana, broken up if necessary
1½ cups (360 mL) chopped dried papaya
1½ cups (360 mL) sultana raisins

ACCOMPANIMENTS
yogurt
your choice of fresh berries

Preheat the oven to 325°F (165°C).

In a large bowl, combine all ingredients except the dried fruit and raisins.

Divide the mixture into thirds and spread each on a separate baking sheet. Place all the baking sheets in the oven and bake for 15 to 20 minutes, or until lightly golden, turning once. Remove from the oven and allow to cool for approximately 2 hours.

When the mixture has cooled, return to the bowl and toss with the dried fruit and the raisins.

In serving dishes, layer the granola with yogurt and fresh fruit. Store the remaining granola in an airtight container for up to 1 month. If making this much granola seems excessive, you can halve the recipe.

COOK'S TIP

If your supermarket doesn't stock buckwheat—most don't—look for it in a health food or bulk food store. Quinoa and amaranth are readily available in most grocery and health food stores.

In 1877, Dr. John Harvey Kellogg invented a new breakfast food made of oats, wheat, and cornmeal baked into biscuits, and then ground. He originally called it granula, but that name had already been claimed for a similar breakfast cereal, so Kellogg was forced to rename his creation granola.

Toasted Grain Bread with Chèvre and Honey

SERVES 4

Bea Villani, a terrific chef who worked for ACE as our Café Manager and then moved on to run our Sales department, created this for "Feast of the Fields," an organic food festival held each fall at different conservation areas in Ontario. If you can't find an organic granary loaf, try this with a multigrain or a dense whole wheat.

¼ cup (60 mL) sunflower seeds
4 slices organic granary bread
4 to 6 oz. (113 to 170 g) soft chèvre
1 to 2 Tbsp. (15 to 30 mL) homogenized milk (if needed)
1 Tbsp. (15 mL) liquid honey

Preheat the oven to 400°F (200°C).

Spoon the sunflower seeds onto a baking pan. Place in the oven for approximately 5 to 7 minutes, stirring often, until they are a dark golden color. Watch carefully, as the seeds burn easily. Keep the oven on, at the same temperature.

Toast the bread and let cool. Spread each slice generously with the chèvre. If the cheese isn't creamy enough, mix it with 1 to 2 Tbsp. (15 to 30 mL) of the homogenized milk. Bake in the oven until slightly softened, about 3 to 5 minutes. Drizzle with the honey and sprinkle with the toasted sunflower seeds. Serve warm or at room temperature.

"I am the one who eats his breakfast gazing at morning glories." — Basho

Classic French Toast with Choice of Toppings

SERVES 4 GENEROUSLY

Pure and simple breakfast or brunch food. Each topping adds its own distinctive taste to this classic, and can be made days before. Feel free to use slightly stale bread here, as the dip in the cream and eggs will revive it.

5 eggs
2½ cups (600 mL) whipping cream
2 tsp. (10 mL) ground nutmeg
4 tsp. (20 mL) ground cinnamon
1 tsp. (5 mL) finely grated lemon zest (optional)
2 Tbsp. (30 mL) unsalted butter
8 ¾-inch (1.9-cm) slices Pain au Lait (see page 19), brioche, challah, white, or fruit bread

TOPPINGS

maple syrup and toasted pecans *or*
Raspberry Honey Butter (see page 88) *or*
Honey Citrus Yogurt (see below) *or*
fresh strawberries and whipped cream *or*
sautéed pears and toasted almond slivers

Preheat the oven to 400°F (200°C). In a bowl, whisk the eggs, cream, spices, and zest, if using. Melt the butter in a frying pan over medium heat. Dip both sides of each slice of bread into the egg mixture, and lightly fry each side until golden. Transfer to a baking sheet and bake for 5 minutes.

Lay on plates, and serve with any of the toppings mentioned above.

HONEY CITRUS YOGURT
½ cup (120 mL) yogurt
1 tsp. (5 mL) orange zest
1 tsp. (5 mL) lemon zest
2 tsp. (10 mL) wildflower honey or any other delicate-tasting honey

Mix the yogurt, zest, and honey together. Taste and add more honey or citrus zest if you want a more pronounced taste.

COOK'S TIP

French toast can be fried up to 2 hours before serving. To reheat, place the room temperature slices on a baking pan and bake in a preheated 400°F (200°C) oven for approximately 5 minutes.

Just as residents of Hamburg have another name for hamburgers, the French have another name for French Toast. They call it pain perdu (lost bread) because they see it as a way of reviving bread that has gone stale.

Cinnamon Banana French Toast with Chocolate Drizzle

SERVES 2 (WITH ENOUGH MELTED CHOCOLATE LEFT OVER TO MAKE A GREAT MUG OF COCOA)

This French toast recipe is a glammed-up version of my son's favorite breakfast. Luke still likes it his way—made without orange zest, topped with mashed banana, and drizzled with maple syrup. The best part is that either version can be assembled and almost finished up to 2 hours before eating. It looks very pretty served with a mango, orange and pineapple fruit salad topped with pomegranate seeds and mint.

3 eggs
1½ cups (360 mL) whipping cream
1½ tsp. (7.5 mL) ground cinnamon
½ tsp. (2.5 mL) ground nutmeg
½ tsp. (2.5 mL) orange zest

2 1½-inch (3.8-cm) thick slices white bread
1 to 2 ripe bananas, mashed
butter for pan—about 2 Tbsp. (30 mL)
1½ oz. (42 g) semi-sweet chocolate, melted (see below)
2 Tbsp. (30 mL) icing sugar

Preheat the oven to 400°F (200°C).

Whisk together the eggs, cream, spices, and zest in a bowl.

In the bottom part of the 2 slices of bread, cut a horizontal pocket large enough and deep enough to stuff with at least half a mashed banana. Stuff both pieces of bread.

Over medium heat, melt the butter in a frying pan until it sizzles.

Generously dip both sides of each bread slice in the egg and cream mixture. Fry, flipping once, until both sides are golden brown. Remove from the pan and place on a baking sheet. You can stop the recipe at this point, up to 2 hours ahead.

Place the French toast in the hot oven for approximately 10 minutes.

Remove the French toast from the oven. Cut each piece on the diagonal and drizzle the melted semisweet chocolate over. Dust with icing sugar.

TO MELT CHOCOLATE

Microwave Version: Coarsely chop the chocolate, place in a bowl, and microwave on high for 20 seconds. Remove from microwave and stir. Continue cooking it in 20-second intervals, stirring in between, until only a few soft lumps remain. Move the chocolate to a counter and stir until the lumps melt. Don't overcook or the chocolate will congeal.

Stovetop Version: Coarsely chop the chocolate and place in the top of a double boiler or in a metal bowl over a saucepan. Bring water to a boil in the saucepan. Place the metal bowl on top of the saucepan, taking care that the hot water doesn't touch the bottom of the bowl. Stir occasionally until the chocolate is melted.

Although the name _cinnamon_ can legally be applied to the bark of a tree called _cassia_, true cinnamon is the bark of a _Cinnamomum zeylanicum_ tree found in Sri Lanka, Myanmar, and parts of India.

Ham and Gruyère French Toast with Sautéed Apples

SERVES 4

Not everyone likes sweet French toast, so this recipe is for them. I love the fact that it can be prepared ahead, leaving you time to read the paper, go for a walk, or entertain your guests.

5 eggs
2½ cups (600 mL) whipping cream
2 Tbsp. (30 mL) butter

8 slices sourdough or white country bread
2 tsp. (10 mL) Dijon mustard
4 to 6 oz. (113 to 170 g) sliced Gruyère cheese
4 to 8 slices Black Forest ham

Preheat the oven to 400°F (200°C).

Whisk the eggs and cream in a bowl.

Melt the butter in a frying pan over medium heat.

Dip both sides of each slice of bread in the egg and cream mixture and lightly fry until golden. Turn and fry the other side. Remove from heat.

Spread 4 slices of the slightly cooled French toast with the mustard, followed by a layer of cheese, then ham, and ending with another layer of cheese. Top with the remaining slices of bread. The assembled sandwiches can be held at room temperature for up to 2 hours.

Place the sandwiches in the oven until the cheese melts, about 5 to 8 minutes. Remove from the oven, cut diagonally, and serve, preferably accompanied by Sautéed Apples (see below).

SAUTÉED APPLES

2 Tbsp. (30 mL) unsalted butter
2 Golden Delicious or Spy apples, peeled, cored, halved, and cut into 10 pieces each
1 Tbsp. (15 mL) Calvados (optional)
large pinch of ground cinnamon (optional)

Melt the butter in a frying pan over medium heat. Add the apple slices and sauté, stirring often, until tender. Off the heat, add the Calvados, if using. Return to the heat and gently toss the apples until the alcohol evaporates. Sprinkle with cinnamon.

This can be prepared ahead and heated in the oven with the French Toast.

Never be afraid to buy more Gruyère than you think you need, as it keeps remarkably well when tightly wrapped and refrigerated. It tastes wonderful on its own or with apples and pears, makes a great fondue, and works beautifully in sandwiches.

12 noon: Ron weighs ingredients for today's batches.

Camembert and Green Onion Strata

SERVES 8 GENEROUSLY

This strata works with brie or a gentle blue cheese, but my favorite cheese for it is Camembert. It makes a soothing brunch or lunch dish with a salad of tomato, Vidalia onion, and baby spinach. It's also a good accompaniment to simply roasted pork or chicken.

6 eggs
3½ cups (840 mL) homogenized milk
1⅔ cups (400 mL) whipping cream
1½ tsp. (7.5 mL) minced garlic
1 tsp. (5 mL) kosher salt
¼ tsp. (1.2 mL) freshly ground white pepper
¾ tsp. (4 mL) chopped fresh thyme

1 Tbsp. (15 mL) unsalted butter, plus enough to coat the casserole dish
1½ cups (360 mL) ¼-inch (.6-cm) pieces of green onion, green and white parts
5 thin slices ham, julienned into ¼- x 2-inch (.6- x 5-cm) strips (optional)
20 to 25 slices country or olive bread, crusts removed
9 oz. (255 g) cold Camembert, cut in ¼-inch (.6-cm) cubes or ⅛-inch (.3-cm) slices

Lightly whisk the eggs in a bowl large enough to also hold the milk and whipping cream. Pour the milk and cream into a saucepan and bring to a simmer. Add the minced garlic. Slowly pour the warm milk into the eggs, whisking continuously. Add the salt, pepper, and thyme.

Sauté the onions in the 1 Tbsp. (15 mL) of butter until just softened. Remove from the heat and reserve. Butter an 8- x 11-inch (20- x 28-cm) casserole dish. Cover the bottom with a layer of slightly overlapping bread slices. Sprinkle the onions and ham, if using, over the bread and top with another layer of bread. Lay the Camembert pieces on next. Cut the remaining bread into 1-inch (2.5-cm) pieces and cover the cheese with them.

Stir the egg mixture so that the garlic rises from the bottom, and pour it evenly over the strata. Cover with plastic wrap and press down so that all the bread soaks up the liquid. Leave for at least half an hour.

Preheat the oven to 375°F (190°C).

Bake for 50 minutes to 1 hour. The top should be golden. If it starts to get too dark, cover with foil. Remove from the oven and let sit 10 minutes before serving.

Although Camembert is sold all year, it is at its best in September and October. Cows produce the best milk in the summer, when they are eating fresh grass. As Camembert takes about two months to make, July and August milk will be in the early fall cheese.

Chicken, Onion, and Mushroom Strata

SERVES 6 TO 8

A great strata for an autumn brunch or a casual supper. Using leftover chicken will cut down the preparation time considerably. Serve with a salad made of Belgian endive, frisée, and oak leaf lettuce in a citrus vinaigrette or with Green Beans with a Soffrito and Toasted Breadcrumbs (see page 177).

3 Tbsp. (45 mL) canola oil
2½ cups (600 mL) cooking onion, sliced ⅛ inch
  (.3 cm) thick
3 cups (720 mL) coarsely chopped button mushrooms
pinch of kosher salt
1½ cups (360 mL) sliced shiitake mushrooms
2 tsp. (10 mL) minced garlic
2 tsp. (10 mL) minced fresh sage
1 tsp. (5 mL) fresh thyme leaves

2 cups (475 mL) homogenized milk
1 cup (240 mL) 18% cream
1 cup (240 mL) chicken stock
5 large eggs, slightly beaten
salt and freshly ground white pepper to taste
about 20 slices of white bread, crusts removed
12 oz. (340 g) cooked chicken, cut into bite-sized pieces
  (see below)
¼ to ½ cup (60 to 120 mL) grated Parmigiano Reggiano

Heat 2 Tbsp. (30 mL) of the oil in a frying pan and add the onions. Cook for about 15 minutes over medium heat, stirring often until soft and slightly caramelized. Reserve.

Heat the remaining oil in the same frying pan and toss in the button mushrooms, stirring them until coated. Add the pinch of salt to draw out the water from the button mushrooms, and continue cooking. When the water from the button mushrooms is almost evaporated, add the sliced shiitakes. Sauté until almost done, about 5 to 8 minutes, adding more oil if necessary. Then add the garlic, sage, and thyme and sauté for another 2 to 3 minutes. Be careful not to burn the garlic.

Combine the milk, cream, and chicken stock in a saucepan and heat to a simmer, and very gradually whisk the hot liquid into the beaten eggs. Add salt and pepper. Be generous.

In a greased 10-cup (2.4-L) baking dish, place a layer of bread slices, then a layer of the chicken. Add another layer of bread, then the mushrooms and onions. Finish with a layer of bread cut in cubes. Pour the milk mixture over the strata. Cover with plastic wrap and press down so that all the bread soaks up the liquid. Leave for at least half an hour.

Preheat the oven to 375°F (190°C).

Sprinkle with the Parmigiano, then bake for 50 minutes to 1 hour. If the top starts to get to dark, cover with foil. The strata should rest for 10 minutes before serving.

CHICKEN
Any leftover chicken will do for this dish, or use the recipe for poaching chicken from Persian Chicken Salad (see page 116), leaving out the ginger. You could also marinate breasts in lemon, garlic, olive oil, and pepper and pan-fry or grill them.

Smoked Salmon, Spinach, and Chèvre Strata

SERVES 6 TO 8

This is great cold-weather food. If you want a less hearty version, use white bread instead of dark rye, but the rye bread really complements the salmon. Try pairing this with an arugula salad, or steamed asparagus for a delicious brunch or informal supper.

1 bunch or 1 bag spinach, washed, drained, and stems removed

1 to 2 tsp. (5 to 10 mL) unsalted butter, for buttering the dish

15 to 20 slices dark rye or dense whole wheat bread, crusts on

½ lb. (225 g) smoked salmon, sliced and cut into 1-inch (2.5-cm) strips

½ to 1 Tbsp. (7.5 to 15 mL) chopped fresh dill

3½ oz. (100 g) creamy chèvre

2 cups (475 mL) homogenized milk

1¼ cups (300 mL) 18% cream

5 large eggs

½ tsp. (2.5 mL) salt

¼ to ½ tsp. (1.2 to 2.5 mL) freshly ground white pepper

Blanch the spinach in boiling water. Drain on paper towels.

Butter an 8- to 9-cup (2- to 2.3-L) baking dish. Place a layer of bread slices on the bottom of the dish. Cover with all of the salmon. Sprinkle the dill over the salmon. Spread all the chèvre on enough bread slices to cover the salmon, and add to the baking dish, cheese side up. Layer the spinach evenly over the bread slices that have been spread with the cheese. Cut the remaining bread into 1-inch (2.5-cm) cubes and toss over the spinach, covering it completely.

Note: The strata can be prepared to this point up to 12 hours before serving. Keep in the refrigerator, tightly covered.

Mix the milk, cream, eggs, and salt and pepper together and gently pour over the strata. Cover with plastic wrap and press down so that all the bread soaks up the liquid. Leave for at least half an hour.

Preheat the oven to 350°F (175° C).

Cook for 50 minutes to 1 hour. Remove from the oven and let the strata sit for 10 minutes before cutting into pieces. Serve with Mustard-Yogurt Sauce (see page 163).

At one time in Medieval England, salmon became so inexpensive that apprentices had to request that their free meals would include it no more than three times a week.

1:05 pm : Olives and thyme ready
to be mixed into the dough.

Canadian Bacon and Egg Sandwich with Gruyère, Tomato Chutney, and Chives

SERVES 2

This delicious breakfast sandwich takes just minutes to prepare. I like it open-faced, followed by a bowl of whatever fruit is in season. You could also make it with grilled prosciutto, poached eggs, and fontina cheese for a change of pace. A non-stick pan works well here.

canola oil for cooking the bacon and eggs
6 slices Canadian bacon, thinly sliced
2 large eggs
2 to 4 slices country or white bread

2 Tbsp. (30 mL) Tomato Chutney (see page 152)
  or 4 slices tomato
salt and freshly ground white pepper to taste
2 to 4 Tbsp. (30 to 60 mL) grated Gruyère
1 tsp. (5 mL) minced fresh chives

Sauté the bacon in a small amount of oil, turning once. The bacon should be cooked through. Drain on paper towels.

Heat a thin layer of oil in a pan large enough to hold both eggs. When the oil is smoking, remove from heat and let sit until the smoke dissipates, about 45 seconds. Add the eggs; the residual heat of the pan should cook them. If it doesn't, put the pan back on the heat for a few seconds at a time. This will prevent them from darkening around the edges. The yolks should be soft but cooked by the time you are ready to assemble the sandwich. They will be getting another minute under the broiler, so cook them accordingly.

Toast the bread and spread a thin layer of chutney or the sliced tomatoes on two slices. Layer on the bacon and the cooked egg. Sprinkle each egg with salt and pepper and 1 to 2 Tbsp. (15 to 30 mL) of Gruyère. Finish under a hot broiler for about 1 minute or until the cheese is melted but not brown.

Remove from oven and sprinkle with chives. Top with another slice of toast if you like.

COOK'S TIP

To cook and hold poached eggs for a short time before using, bring water to a boil in a frying pan. Add a few drops of white vinegar and a pinch of salt. Break an egg into a cup. Swirl the water in circles with a spoon and slide the egg into the center of the swirl. Simmer until just cooked. Remove from the water with a slotted spoon and place into a bowl of cool water. Continue until all the eggs are cooked. The eggs will hold for at least 2 hours. To reheat, plunge them into simmering water for 30 to 45 seconds.

"We plan, we toil, we suffer — in hope of what? ... Simply to wake up just in time to smell the coffee and the bacon and eggs. And again I cry, how rarely it happens! But when it does happen — then what a moment, what a morning, what a delight!" —J. B. Priestley

Egg in the Hole

SERVES 2

For my parents' crowd, this was a standard late-night snack after an evening of cocktails and dancing. I tend to eat it the morning after, accompanied by a good café latte. If you have a child who doesn't like eggs, I guarantee he or she will love to help you make and eat this retro classic. The non-traditionalist may like to garnish the eggs with ketchup or Tomato Chutney (see page 152).

2 slices white bread
1 to 2 Tbsp. (15 to 30 mL) unsalted butter
2 large eggs
salt and freshly ground white pepper

With a glass or cookie cutter, cut out a circle, 2 inches (5 cm) in diameter, in the middle of each slice of bread.

In a frying pan large enough to hold the two slices of bread, melt enough butter over medium heat to nicely coat the bottom. Put the bread in the pan and break an egg into each hole. Sprinkle with salt and pepper.

When the egg white is almost cooked through but the yolk is still very runny, check the underside of the bread to make sure it is golden. Add more butter if necessary. Gently flip the toast and egg over and cook briefly until the underside is golden but the yolk is still runny. Eat immediately. Serve with ketchup or Tomato Chutney if you wish.

"Eggs in an hour, bread of a day, wine of a year, a friend of thirty years." —Italian proverb

Spinach Gratin with Baked Eggs and Parmigiano

SERVES 4 TO 8, DEPENDING ON APPETITES

This easy dish always gets compliments. You can also make it in individual portions, using 1 or 2 eggs per person. Serve with plenty of thickly cut buttered toast. Back bacon—Canadian bacon to Americans—would be good on the side too.

4 bunches spinach—approximately 2¼ lb. (1 kg)—
  cleaned, drained, and stems removed
2 Tbsp. (30 mL) unsalted butter
¼ cup (60 mL) finely minced cooking onion
2 Tbsp. (30 mL) finely minced garlic
7 Tbsp. (105 mL) all-purpose flour
3 cups (720 mL) warm homogenized milk

½ tsp. (2.5 mL) freshly grated nutmeg
1 tsp. (5 mL) kosher salt
large pinch of white pepper
8 large eggs
½ cup (120 mL) fresh breadcrumbs (see page 43)
1 Tbsp. (15 mL) unsalted butter, melted
½ cup (120 mL) finely grated Parmigiano Reggiano

Preheat the oven to 375°F (190°C).

In manageable batches, plunge the spinach into boiling water. Allow the water to come to a boil again. Cook for 1 minute and drain on paper towels. Roughly chop.

Melt the butter in a frying pan large enough to hold all the ingredients except the eggs. Add the onions and sauté over medium heat for 2 minutes. Stir in the garlic, then mix in the spinach and cook for 1 minute. Sprinkle with the flour and, stirring, gently cook for 1 minute more. Pour in the warm milk and bring to a simmer. Cook, stirring, until the mixture thickens, about 5 minutes. Add the nutmeg, salt, and pepper. The recipe can be prepared to this point up to 1 day ahead.

Spoon the spinach mixture into an 8- to 10-cup (2- to 2.4-L) buttered baking dish (or 4 to 8 individual baking dishes). Make 8 indentations in the spinach and break an egg into each well. Sprinkle each egg with a pinch of salt. Bake for 15 to 18 minutes or until the egg white is set but still soft.

Mix together the breadcrumbs, melted butter, and the Parmigiano Reggiano. Remove the baking dish from the oven. Turn on the broiler. Sprinkle the crumb mixture over the eggs and place under the broiler for 30 seconds, until lightly golden.

Many recipes that feature spinach, including this one, combine nutmeg with the spinach. One explanation, other than the fact that the flavors combine nicely, is that spinach was often part of sweet dishes in medieval cooking.

Coddled Eggs with Mushrooms and Tomato

SERVES 6

This is what you want someone to bring to you when you're in bed—sick or otherwise. Feel free to add or subtract ingredients with the eggs. Sautéed onions, small pieces of cooked bacon, or grilled, chopped peppers with a little ham would be good too. I make these eggs in glass ramekins for two reasons: I can see how they are cooking, and the layers look lovely at the table. My friend Gillian Diamond introduced me to coddled eggs, and for that I am eternally grateful.

1 Tbsp. (15 mL) unsalted butter
10 mushrooms of your choice, cleaned and sliced
large pinch kosher salt for cooking mushrooms
1 Tbsp. (15 mL) finely minced celery leaves

12 cherry tomatoes, quartered
6 extra large eggs
3 Tbsp. (45 mL) heavy cream *and/or*
4 Tbsp. (60 mL) grated Gruyère
salt and freshly ground white pepper

Preheat the oven to 350°F (175°C).

Melt the butter in a sauté pan and add the mushrooms. Sauté for 2 to 3 minutes, then add a large pinch of salt. Continue cooking until the mushrooms are almost cooked and the pan is dry. Add the celery leaves and sauté for another 30 seconds or so. Reserve.

Drop 2 quartered tomatoes into each of 6 half-cup (120-mL) ramekins. Divide the mushrooms on top of the tomatoes. Gently crack the eggs over the mushrooms. To each dish, add either 1½ tsp. (7.5 mL) of cream or 2 tsp. (10 mL) of cheese—or both, if you're feeling greedy. Sprinkle with salt and pepper. Cover with foil or, if you have them, individual lids.

Cook in the oven for about 18 minutes or until all the egg white is set but the yolk is still runny. The eggs with cream may take a minute or so longer to cook. Serve immediately, with batons of toast.

"A simple enough pleasure, to have a breakfast alone with one's husband, but how seldom married people in the midst of life achieve it."
— Anne Morrow Lindbergh

Le mélange doux de ma mère

SERVES 1

My mother swears by this recipe for upset stomachs or general malaise. Her mother served it to her as a child, and she in turn fed it to my brother and me when we were children. When it's gray outside and you're feeling blue, try making yourself a bowl and crawl back into bed where you can savor it. Add a dusting of cinnamon and nutmeg if you want.

2 slices white bread
1 to 2 tsp. (5 to 10 mL) unsalted butter
1 to 2 Tbsp. (15 to 30 mL) sugar, brown or white
1 cup (240 mL) or more hot homogenized milk

Butter both slices of bread. Cut or tear into 2-inch (5-cm) cubes.

Place in a shallow bowl. Sprinkle with sugar and pour the hot milk over the bread.

Eat while still very warm.

"All sorrows are less with bread."
— Miguel de Cervantes

1:25 pm:
ACE bags line the counter in our Fresh Bread Store.

Souffléd Cheddar and Chive Gratin

SERVES 8

This is a family recipe that I have been making for years. It can be assembled in about 20 minutes and makes a sophisticated brunch or lunch when served with a simple mesclun salad. I've also served it as a side dish with an herb-stuffed roasted chicken. In my house, we fight over the delicious crust. It's the best part.

1 to 1½ tsp. (5 to 7.5 mL) unsalted butter for greasing dish
10 ½-inch (1.2-cm) slices white or country bread, crusts removed
1 lb. (455 g) old white cheddar, grated
⅓ cup (80 mL) grated Parmigiano Reggiano
6 large eggs
3½ cups (840 mL) homogenized milk

1½ tsp. (7.5 mL) dry mustard
1½ Tbsp. (22.5 mL) finely chopped fresh chives
½ tsp. (2.5 mL) salt
¼ tsp. (1.2 mL) freshly ground white pepper

GARNISH
1 cup (240 mL) sour cream and some minced chives (optional)

Preheat the oven to 375°F (190°C) and butter a 12-cup (3-L) baking dish or soufflé dish.

Cut the bread into ¼-inch (.6-cm) cubes and place in a bowl large enough to hold all the ingredients. Toss the cheeses with the bread.

Put 2 whole eggs and 4 egg yolks in a bowl. Reserve the 4 leftover egg whites in another bowl.

Whisking, add the milk, mustard, chives, salt, and pepper to the whole eggs and egg yolks. Pour over the bread and cheese mixture and mix gently. Let stand at least half an hour. Whisk the reserved egg whites with a pinch of salt until they hold stiff peaks. Stir a third of the whites thoroughly into the bread mixture, and then gently fold in the rest.

Pour the mixed ingredients into the baking dish. If using a shallow baking dish, cook for 45 minutes. A higher soufflé dish will need to bake for about 1 hour and 15 minutes. The top should become a dark golden brown. Cover during baking if it starts to burn. Serve immediately. If you want, garnish each serving with sour cream and chives. The soufflé may sink in the middle, but that won't affect the taste.

The literal translation of soufflé is "puffed up," which is exactly how a successful soufflé will look. In most cases, don't let temptation make you open the oven door to check your soufflé; the fluctuation in temperature is sure to deflate it. But because we have added bread cubes to this soufflé, the structure is strong and you can afford to take a peek without danger to the recipe

Cinnamon Banana French Toast with
Chocolate Drizzle p. 51

Smoked Salmon, Spinach,
and Chèvre Strata

p. 56

Jalapeño Cornbread p. 36

Focaccia p. 22

Coddled Eggs with Mushrooms and Tomato p. 61

Strawberry Orange Classico

SERVES 2

This welcome change to plain orange juice should perk up any morning. It's especially pleasing when fresh strawberries are at their best, but I have made it with frozen ones when I needed a mid-winter lift.

2 cups (475 mL) orange juice
6 medium strawberries, cleaned and chopped, or the equivalent in frozen strawberries

¾ cup (180 mL) ice
3 oz. (90 mL) vodka (optional)
2 whole strawberries for garnish

Pour the orange juice into a blender and add the berries and ice. Blend until smooth. Add the vodka, if desired, and blend again. Pour into 2 glasses and place a partially cut strawberry on each rim.

Ginger and Honey Tea

MAKES ONE LARGE MUG

I give this comforting tea to my family to soothe a sore throat and help ease the symptoms of laryngitis. It seems to have many curative properties. Rosalind Whelan, Administrative Coordinator at ACE, was given ginger tea by her mother to cure an upset tummy when she was a child.

5 thin slices of peeled ginger
1½ cups (360 mL) boiling water
1 tsp. (5 mL) honey, or to taste

Steep the ginger in the hot water for 4 to 5 minutes. Press the ginger gently with a spoon to release more ginger flavor. Remove the ginger and add honey to taste. Drink while very warm.

Ginger is one of the oldest and most useful folk medicines. It warms the body and can induce sweating to fight off infections, help fevers run their course, and boost the immune system. It even eases nausea and has natural antibiotic properties.

Nibbles, Spreads, and Other Openers

House-Brand Olives

Basil and Black Pepper Bruschetta

Devin's Spring Green Crostini

Grilled Shrimp and Avocado Butter Crostini

Pan con Tomate

Grilled Radicchio and Fontina Bruschetta

Homemade Swedish Gravlax with Mustard-Dill Sauce

Basil-Garlic Dip

Zataar

Red Pepper and White Bean Hummus

Edamame Hummus

Smoked Trout Pâté

Marinated Chèvre

Spa Yogurt Cheese

Oven-Roasted Tomatoes

Mayonnaise—Four Types

Flavored Butters—Four Tastes

Roasted Apple Cranberry Compote

" 'A loaf of bread,' the Walrus said 'is what we chiefly need.' "
—Lewis Carroll, Alice Through the Looking Glass

House-Brand Olives

MAKES 4½ LBS. (2 KG)

This may seem like a lot of olives, but they keep for quite a while and taste delicious. Friends will ask where you get them; you will smile and change the subject. Buy the largest, best-tasting olives possible, as they will make the most dramatic and mouth-watering presentation, or alternatively use four or five different shapes and sizes of olives for an eclectic look and taste.

2¼ lbs. (1 kg) large, unpitted green olives (Green Super Mammoth, if possible)

2¼ lbs. (1 kg) large, unpitted black olives (Kalamata Colossal, if possible)

½ jalapeño pepper, seeded

1 bunch rosemary, cleaned and chopped, reserving 3 to 5 sprigs for garnish

2 large sprigs thyme, cleaned and chopped

3 to 4 bay leaves

2 garlic cloves, 1 minced, the other thinly sliced

juice of ½ lemon

zest of ⅓ orange, reserving 1 to 2 tsp. (5 to 10 mL) for garnish

⅔ cup (160 mL) olive oil

Mix all ingredients together in a large container. Cover and marinate, tossing occasionally, in a cool place for at least 36 hours. Serve portions in a shallow bowl decorated with the additional rosemary sprigs and orange zest. The olives will keep in the refrigerator for a month. Bring to room temperature before serving.

"The whole Mediterranean, the sculpture, the palms, the gold beads, the bearded heroes, the wine, the ideas, the ships, the moonlight, the winged gorgons, the bronze men, the philosophers — all of it seems to rise in the sour, pungent smell of these black olives between the teeth. A taste older than meat, older than wine. A taste as old as cold water." — Lawrence Durrell

Basil and Black Pepper Bruschetta

SERVES 2

Bruschetta is traditionally made with thick, coarse bread—grilled, rubbed with garlic, drizzled with oil, and topped with salt or pepper. Toronto's Trattoria Giancarlo's version is the *ne plus ultra*. This is my interpretation of their popular antipasto.

2 1- to 1¼-inch (2.5- to 3-cm) thick slices Calabrese (see page 26) or other dense white or country bread
1 to 2 cloves of garlic, sliced lengthwise

4 large basil leaves
up to ¼ cup (60 mL) extra virgin olive oil
fresh, coarsely ground black pepper
kosher salt, to taste

Grill, broil, or toast both sides of the 2 slices of bread.

Rub the cut side of the garlic clove 2 or 3 times over the top side of the bread. Next, rub the basil leaves over the bread and then discard them.

Place the bread on a serving dish and drizzle the oil over both pieces of bread. Be very generous. Coarsely grind the pepper very liberally over the top. Sprinkle with salt and serve immediately.

There are several varieties of basil, some green-leafed and some purple. Each has a distinct flavor, some very perfumed, others citrusy, and some even reminiscent of cloves.

Devin's Spring Green Crostini

Crostini is thinly sliced white bread, traditionally toasted or fried in oil. My daughter, Devin, came up with the idea for this one. It has all the tastes of spring and is fairly straightforward to make. I like the crunch of the toast with the smooth spread. You can use frozen peas if you're not inclined to spend time shelling the pods, or if peas are out of season.

1 generous Tbsp. (15 mL) olive oil
2 leeks, white and pale green parts, sliced in ¼-inch
  (.6-cm) rounds, soaked in water until clean, and drained
½ cup (120 mL) water
salt and freshly ground white pepper to taste
¾ cup (180 mL) fresh green peas or small frozen green peas

1 Tbsp. (15 mL) olive oil
¼ cup (60 mL) finely grated Parmigiano Reggiano
4 mint leaves, chopped
½ baguette
2 to 3 Tbsp. (30 to 45 mL) extra virgin olive oil
pea shoots for garnish

Heat the 1 generous Tbsp. (15 mL) of olive oil in a pan over medium heat. When the oil is hot but not smoking, add the leeks and sauté for 2 minutes. Add ¼ cup (60 mL) of the water and turn the heat down slightly until just at a simmer. Add ⅛ tsp (.5 mL) of both salt and pepper. Add the other ¼ cup (60 mL) of water if the pan becomes dry and the leeks are not yet soft. Cook until the water is evaporated. Reserve in a bowl.

Cook the green peas in water and a bit of salt. If the peas are very starchy, add ½ tsp. (2.5 mL) sugar. When they are cooked, drain and shock them under cold water. Drain again and add to the leeks. If using frozen peas, follow the package directions.

Put the leek and pea mixture in a food processor. Add the 1 Tbsp. (15 mL) of olive oil and pulse for about 45 seconds. The mixture should still be a little chunky.

Add the Parmigiano and mint, and blend for another 20 seconds. If you want a smoother mixture, pulse it for another 10 to 20 seconds.

The leek and pea mixture will keep in the refrigerator for up to a week, and it freezes well. Bring to room temperature before serving.

FOR THE CROSTINI

Slice as many pieces of bread as you need, about ¼ inch (.6 cm) thick. Grill, toast, or broil on both sides. Brush one side of each piece of bread with olive oil and mound with the leek and pea mixture. Decorate with fresh baby peas shoots if desired.

COOK'S TIP

Mint picked in the spring and early summer has a very strong flavor, so you might want to add it sparingly. Later in the season, the mint becomes milder, and you will need the full amount called for in the recipe. Also, different species of mint will have varying degrees of intensity and different tastes.

Grilled Shrimp and Avocado Butter Crostini

MAKES 12 PIECES

The crispness of the bread, the creaminess of the avocado, and the crunch of the shrimp make a mouthwatering combination. If you can't find the chipotle and ancho peppers, substitute chili or cayenne pepper to taste. You can prepare all the components ahead of time and serve cool, but I prefer the taste of these crostini when the bread and shrimp are still warm. Romesco Sauce (see page 168) instead of the avocado butter also tastes great.

AVOCADO BUTTER

1 avocado, peeled, pit removed
juice of 1 lime
1 Tbsp. (15 mL) finely minced onion
⅛ tsp. (.5 mL) kosher salt
⅛ tsp. (.5 mL) freshly ground white pepper
⅛ tsp. (.5 mL) chipotle pepper, or to taste
⅛ tsp. (.5 mL) ancho pepper, or to taste
2 tsp. (10 mL) shredded fresh basil

SHRIMP

½ cup (120 mL) vegetable or canola oil
2 Tbsp. (30 mL) lemon juice
1 Tbsp. (15 mL) minced garlic
12 large shrimp, head off, shell on and deveined
⅛ tsp. (.5 mL) freshly ground white pepper

CROSTINI

12 slices baguette cut ¼ inch (.6 cm) thick
1 Tbsp. (15 mL) extra virgin olive oil
1½ tsp. (7.5 mL) finely minced jalapeño pepper for garnish (optional)

FOR THE AVOCADO BUTTER

I like the avocado butter very smooth. If you prefer it chunky, mash accordingly. Place three-quarters of the lime juice and all the other ingredients, except the basil, in a blender or food processor. Blend and taste. Add the basil and more lime juice and spices if you like. Put in a bowl and press plastic wrap to the surface of the avocado butter to prevent it from turning brown. Refrigerate if not using within the hour. Bring to room temperature before assembly.

FOR THE SHRIMP

Pour the oil into a dish large enough to hold all the shrimp in one layer. Mix the lemon juice and the garlic into the oil. Toss the shrimps in the oil until they are well coated. Marinate at room temperature for half to three-quarters of an hour, turning occasionally.

Heat a grill, cast iron skillet, or grill pan until very hot. Cook the shrimp on both sides until they are bright pink and cooked through, approximately 90 seconds per side. Check to see if they are cooked to your liking by cutting a small piece from the thick part of one shrimp. Remove from the heat and cool just to the point at which you can peel them.

FOR THE CROSTINI

Toast or grill the bread and then brush with a little olive oil. Spread the avocado butter thickly over each slice and top with a warm shrimp. Garnish with some jalapeño pepper if you want a bit more bite.

Avocados are the most protein-rich of all fruits, and have the highest oil content.

Pan con Tomate

This Spanish tapas, when translated, means "bread with tomato." It tastes best, of course, made with juicy summer tomatoes, but it can be made with winter ones, as you will be using only the juice of the tomato, not the flesh. Kids love to make this. They get to use their hands and, if you'll let them, make a mess. It's a great start to a meal if you're barbecuing. Just throw the bread on the grill and let your guests do the rest.

4 thick slices Calabrese bread (see page 26) or
  10 to 12 white or Calabrese baguette pieces
1 large clove garlic, sliced in half, lengthwise

1 to 2 medium tomatoes, cut horizontally
up to 2 Tbsp. (30 mL) extra virgin olive oil
kosher salt to taste

Grill, toast, or broil the bread on both sides. Rub the cut garlic across the top side of each piece of bread until all parts of the toast have been covered.

Press the tomato firmly onto the bread and rub back and forth until the bread is pink in color. Drizzle with olive oil and sprinkle with salt. It's best served warm.

Save the tomato halves, cut into cubes, and toss in a salad.

"A day without bread lasts long." — Spanish proverb

Grilled Radicchio and Fontina Bruschetta

SERVES 4 TO 8

Grilled radicchio taste wonderful. They become slightly caramelized when cooked, giving the peppery taste a sweet undertone. Fontina cheese brings all the flavors together. No need to use your best quality balsamic vinegar here. A medium-priced bottle will do. If you prefer a less peppery taste, try making this with Belgian endive.

2 large long radicchio heads (Treviso), sliced lengthwise
1½ Tbsp. (22.5 mL) olive oil
1 Tbsp. (15 mL) balsamic vinegar
pinch of both salt and pepper

4 slices of Calabrese bread (see page 26) sliced ½ inch (1.2 cm) thick, or 8 to 12 slices Calabrese baguette
1 garlic clove, cut in half lengthwise
3 to 4 oz. (85 to 113 g) fontina cheese, thinly sliced
1 Tbsp. (15 mL) minced Italian parsley (optional)

Brush the radicchio with olive oil. Grill over high heat, 2 to 3 minutes on each side, or until the radicchio has softened slightly and is charred. Place in a shallow bowl and toss with the vinegar, salt, and pepper.

Preheat the oven to broil. Grill or toast the bread on both sides and rub one side gently with the cut side of the garlic clove. Brush with a little olive oil.

Chop the radicchio into ½-inch (1.2-cm) slices and mound on the bread. Top with slices of fontina. Don't worry about completely covering the radicchio. The bruschetta looks better with some of the vegetables peeking through.

Broil until the cheese melts. If using the Calabrese bread, not the baguette, cut the slices in smaller pieces. Sprinkle with a little parsley and serve.

Homemade Swedish Gravlax with Mustard-Dill Sauce

SERVES 8 TO 10

Swedes have been making gravlax for hundreds of years. Instead of smoking the salmon, they marinate it with dill—the most popular of Swedish herbs. The traditional way of serving gravlax in Sweden is with a mustard-dill sauce and rye bread. They also serve it as a first course with two or three new potatoes that have been steamed in butter and dill. The addition of vodka to the marinade breaks with tradition.

3 to 3½ pounds (1.4 to 1.6 kg) fresh salmon, center cut, cleaned and scaled
1 large bunch dill, washed and patted dry
⅓ cup (80 mL) coarse salt

¼ cup (60 mL) sugar
1 Tbsp. + 2 tsp. (25 mL) white peppercorns (or black), slightly crushed
2 Tbsp. (30 mL) vodka
1 recipe Mustard-Dill Sauce (facing page)

Cut the salmon in half lengthwise, and remove the backbone and small bones. Try to get your fishmonger to do this for you. Place half the fish, skin-side down, in a deep baking dish or casserole 4 to 6 inches (10 to 15 cm) high.

Lay the bunch of dill evenly on the fish.

Combine the salt, sugar, and crushed peppercorns in a bowl. Sprinkle this mixture evenly over the dill. Drizzle the vodka over the salt and sugar mixture. Top with the other half of the fish, skin-side up.

Cover the top of the fish lightly with foil and place a dish or platter slightly larger than the salmon on top of it. Pile the dish or platter with weights to allow the marinade to permeate the fish. Cans of food work well. Refrigerate 48 to 72 hours.

Take the fish out of the dish every 8 to 12 hours, turn it over, and drizzle it with the liquid that accumulates around it. Make sure to separate the halves and baste the salmon inside. Replace the covering dish or platter and the weights each time.

You will notice that the fish becomes more compressed with each turning. Before serving, throw away the dill and seasoning, and pat the fish with paper towels to dry, making sure to remove all the peppercorns. Try one slice. If too salty, rinse the fish lightly under cool water and pat dry before slicing.

Traditionally, Swedish cooks making this dish would bury the fish, either in barrels filled with weights or in the ground. Short-term burial resulted in fish that was immediately edible even though it was raw, and long-term burial kept the fish preserved during winter. In Swedish gravlax means buried fish.

Place the separate halves skin-side down on a carving board and slice the salmon thinly (but slightly thicker than smoked salmon slices) on a diagonal, leaving the skin behind.

Arrange 2 to 3 pieces of the gravlax on a plate, spoon some Mustard-Dill sauce on the side and accompany with buttered rye bread. You could also make open-faced sandwiches or hors d'oeuvres. In that case, top the salmon with a dollop of sauce and a tiny dill sprig.

MUSTARD-DILL SAUCE

MAKES ABOUT ¾ CUP (180 ML)

1 Tbsp. (15 mL) grainy mustard
3 Tbsp. (45 mL) Dijon mustard
1 tsp. (5 mL) powdered mustard

2 Tbsp. (30 mL) sugar
2 Tbsp. (30 mL) white vinegar
⅓ cup (80 mL) canola or safflower oil
2 to 3 Tbsp. (30 to 45 mL) fresh chopped dill

Mix the three mustards, sugar, and vinegar in a small bowl. Slowly whisk in the oil. The sauce will thicken. Stir in the chopped dill.

Canada is among the top five mustard seed producers in the world, and is the world's largest exporter of it. About 78 percent of Canada's mustard crop is grown for export, with about 31 percent sold to the United States, and up to 20 percent to Bangladesh.

Basil-Garlic Dip

MAKES ¾ CUP (180 ML)

The basil and garlic in this recipe need an assertive Tuscan extra virgin olive oil to round out the flavors. You can make it with a gentler oil, too, but it will just not be as gutsy. Because this dip is thick it can also be used as a spread for the ACE Grilled Cheese Sandwich (see page 128).

½ cup (120 mL) roughly chopped fresh basil
¼ cup (60 mL) roughly chopped fresh parsley, curly or Italian
½ cup (120 mL) Tuscan extra virgin olive oil

1 or 2 small-to-medium garlic cloves, peeled and chopped
white, sourdough, country bread, or focaccia, thickly sliced
a variety of fresh vegetables including: radishes, carrots, baby zucchini, and baby squash

Place the basil, parsley, and olive oil in a blender. A food processor will not emulsify the mixture, and the oil will separate from the basil and parsley. Add 1 chopped garlic clove. Pulse until fairly smooth. Taste and add more garlic if you like. Pulse again.

Serve in a small bowl with fresh or grilled bread and/or vegetables.

This dip mellows as it stands. It can be made ahead of time and will keep for 2 weeks if refrigerated. Bring to room temperature before serving.

When first introduced to Europeans, basil provoked great suspicion as well as approval. There was a common belief, enforced by old herbals (books about herbs), that basil bred scorpions.

76 THE ACE BAKERY COOKBOOK

2 pm: Sabeypan double
checks that the olives are
pit free for tomorrow's bake.

3:15 pm:
Ron adds raisins to the raisin walnut dough.

3:35 pm: Empty mixing bowls
await a cleaning; then the next
group of ingredients.

Zataar

MAKES ALMOST 2 CUPS (475 ML)

Zataar, a.k.a. duqqa (doo-khah), is a Middle Eastern mixture of ground seeds and nuts with a variety of uses. Try dipping pieces of baguette or country bread into good olive oil and then into zataar as an hors d'oeuvre with drinks, or use it as a coating for firm, white fish, or to sprinkle over a salad.

1 cup (240 mL) chopped hazelnuts
¾ cup (180 mL) white sesame seeds
½ cup (120 mL) poppy seeds

10 white peppercorns
¼ cup (60 mL) cumin seeds
½ cup (120 mL) coriander seeds

Preheat the oven to 400°F (200°C).

Mix all the ingredients on a baking sheet and roast for about 5 minutes or until the seeds look golden. Remove from the oven and let cool.

Spoon the mixture into a resealable plastic bag. Close the bag and, using a rolling pin, roughly crush the seeds and nuts, taking care not to reduce them to paste. This should take about 1 to 2 minutes. Alternatively, use a mortar and pestle.

Zataar will last 1 month if stored in a tightly sealed container.

Red Pepper and White Bean Hummus

MAKES 3 TO 4 CUPS (720 TO 950 ML)

Vaughan Chittock, a talented chef who worked at ACE, came up with this hummus recipe for a charity event. Extra canned or bottled peppers make a delicious sandwich when paired with fontina cheese and Basil-Garlic Dip (see page 76).

2 19-oz. (532-mL) cans cannellini or white kidney beans, rinsed and drained *or* 1⅓ cups (320 mL) dried white beans (see below for cooking instructions and extra ingredients)

4 medium red peppers or 5-oz. (150 mL) canned or bottled Spanish red peppers

¼ cup (60 mL) tahini

4 cloves garlic, peeled

1½ tsp. (7.5 mL) cumin

¼ tsp. (1.2 mL) cayenne

¼ tsp. (1.2 mL) kosher salt, or to taste

juice of 1 lemon, or to taste

up to ¼ cup (60 mL) vegetable oil, if necessary, to thin the hummus

IF USING DRIED BEANS

1 large carrot, chopped in large chunks

¾ of a medium-sized cooking onion, thinly sliced

1 stalk celery, chopped in large chunks

1 large clove garlic, crushed

6 grinds white pepper

1 tsp. (5 mL) kosher salt

Soak the dried beans in very warm water for about 1½ hours or until they look wrinkly. Drain and place in a medium-sized saucepan. Add the carrot, onion, celery, garlic, and pepper. Cover the beans with water by 3 inches (7.5 cm) and bring to a simmer. Cook for 45 minutes, checking periodically that the water has not evaporated. Add the salt and simmer for another 30 to 45 minutes, or until the beans are cooked. Drain and reserve.

FOR THE HUMMUS

Preheat the oven to broil.

Place the peppers on a baking tray and broil each side until the skin starts to blister. Remove from the oven and cool. Peel the skin off the peppers and remove seeds. If using canned or bottled peppers, they should be rinsed and patted dry.

In a food processor, place all the ingredients except the oil and half the lemon juice, and purée. Pulse until smooth, scraping down the sides occasionally. Dribble in oil, if necessary, until the hummus is spreadable, but not too thin. Add more lemon juice to taste. Serve with slices of baguette.

COOK'S TIP

If using canned beans, be sure to rinse and drain them well; otherwise, the hummus will be gummy.

Sesame seeds must soak for 26 hours before the bran and kernel can be separated with the crushing blow of a hammer. Then they need to soak again, in water so salty that it would "float an egg". The kernels float to the top, where they are gathered and then grilled before being ground into the oily paste, or tahini, called for in this recipe.

Edamame Hummus

Edamame are green soybeans, popular in Japan. Frozen edamame are sold in health food and gourmet stores as well as in Japanese grocery stores. You can buy them in their pods or not. All they need is a quick boil and they're ready to go. Italians make a similar purée to this one, with fava beans. If you have ever peeled, boiled, and peeled again a batch of fava beans, you'll know why I prefer this alternative. Serve this hummus warm with thinly sliced, toasted or grilled baguette. This purée is also wonderful as a warm bed for grilled scallops or salmon.

2½ cups (600 mL) cooked shelled edamame
  (see Cook's Tip)
½ cup (120 mL) or more extra virgin olive oil, and extra
  for drizzling

2 Tbsp. (30 mL) lemon juice
¼ to ½ tsp. (1.2 to 2.5 mL) kosher salt
⅛ tsp. (.5 mL) freshly ground white pepper
1 tsp. (5 mL) fresh minced chives (optional)
a pinch of chunky sea salt (optional)

Put the edamame in a food processor or blender and process for 10 seconds. Scrape down the sides and drizzle in ½ cup (120 mL) olive oil and the lemon juice. Pulse until fairly smooth, scraping down the sides when necessary.

Add salt and pepper. The beans tend to soak up a lot of oil, so add more if necessary. Fold in the chives, if using, and taste. Add more lemon juice, salt or pepper if needed.

Spoon into a bowl and drizzle with more oil and the chunky sea salt if desired. Serve with thinly sliced, toasted bread slices.

The hummus freezes well.

COOK'S TIP

Frozen edamame are sold two ways. One package of shelled beans yields 2½ cups (600 mL) of beans. If you buy unshelled beans, one package yields 1 cup (240 mL) after removing the beans from their shells.

In Japan, edamame are a popular snack food, much like chips, popcorn, or peanuts. The difference is in their nutritional value. A helping of edamame contains a significant amount of protein. The Japanese word eda-mame means "branch beans" because that is how they are sold — in pods still on their branches.

Smoked Trout Pâté

MAKES 1½ GENEROUS CUPS (360 ML)

This recipe makes a great open-face sandwich or delicious finger food when cut in small pieces. If it seems like too much trouble to assemble, put small bowls of the pâté and mayonnaise on a platter and surround with pieces of bread. Serve with rosé, sangria, or beer.

8 oz. (225 g) smoked trout, skinned and flaked
5 Tbsp. (75 mL) unsalted butter, room temperature
1½ Tbsp. (22.5 mL) lemon juice
salt and freshly ground white pepper to taste

¼ cup (60 mL) Lemon Mayonnaise (see page 87)
½ tsp. (2.5 mL) Dijon mustard
2 small branches fresh dill
6 slices granary, multigrain, rye, or dense whole wheat bread

Put the smoked trout and softened butter in a food processor and pulse until smooth. Add the lemon juice, salt, and pepper and pulse again until combined. Taste and add more seasonings if necessary.

Mix the Lemon Mayonnaise and the mustard together and transfer to a squeeze bottle. Pull the dill branches apart into small sprigs. Spread the pâté smoothly over the bread, lightly drizzle with the mayonnaise mixture, and garnish with the dill.

Refrigerate the remaining pâté and mayonnaise for future use. The pâté will keep for 1 week and the mayonnaise for 3 days. Bring to room temperature before using again.

The original meaning of the French word pâté referred to a pie or pastry filled with vegetables, fish, or meat. Over time the term came to be used as a name for the filling independent of its pastry shell.

Marinated Chèvre

MAKES 12 OZ. (350 G) CHEESE AND 3¾ CUPS (900 ML) MARINADE

I love this recipe because it has so many uses. Mash the cheese and some of the marinade, if necessary, and spread it over Calabrese, olive, or country bread and warm in the oven, or put the cheese pieces with some of the marinade in a shallow bowl and serve with thinly sliced pieces of bread. Another option is to use the marinade as part of a vinaigrette and top salad servings with a cheese disk. It is also wonderful in a sandwich made with whole wheat bread and garnished with crunchy lettuce or sliced cucumber. The cheese will keep in the refrigerator for about one week, but my experience is that it disappears much more quickly.

1 Tbsp. (15 mL) butter
⅓ cup (80 mL) finely chopped shallots
¾ lb. (340 g) creamy chèvre
3½ oz. (100 g) Roma tomatoes, submerged in boiling water, peeled and seeded (1 to 2 tomatoes)
3 Tbsp. + 1 tsp. (50 mL) balsamic vinegar

3 Tbsp. + 1 tsp. (50 mL) soy sauce
2 tsp. (10 mL) Worcestershire sauce
1¼ cups (300 mL) olive oil (average grade)
1 cup (240 mL) extra virgin olive oil
1 handful parsley, roughly chopped
½ tsp. (2.5 mL) fresh thyme leaves
salt and freshly ground white pepper

Melt the butter in a sauté pan over medium heat and add the shallots. Sauté until soft and golden, being careful not to let them burn.

Chop the peeled and seeded tomatoes into ¼-inch (.6-cm) pieces and place in a bowl.

Form the cheese into disks about ¾ to 1 inch (1.9 to 2.5 cm) thick and 1½ to 2 inches (3.8 to 5 cm) in diameter. If you want to make round balls or other shapes, mold the cheese with your hands. Lay the cheese in a flat dish. Spread the shallots over the cheese.

Add the remaining ingredients to the tomatoes and mix, and then pour over the cheese. Let stand, covered, for 24 hours in the refrigerator. Serve with sliced baguette.

Chèvre (goat cheese) is very different from cow cheese because it contains different amino acids, and because goats have a more interesting diet than cows. For example, goats often eat wild thyme — one of the reasons why chèvre is often paired with thyme in recipes.

Spa Yogurt Cheese

MAKES 1½ CUPS (360 ML)

Yogurt cheese is very easy to make, is low in fat, and keeps for up to two weeks in the refrigerator. It has a slightly tangy taste and the consistency of soft cream cheese. Best of all, it can be dressed up and used in a variety of ways. You can use low-fat yogurt, but the taste is flatter, and when you consider that most commercial yogurt has only 4% butterfat, what's the point? The basic recipe can be used in Honey Citrus Yogurt Spread (see page 50), which is wonderful on any grain bread, and in Mustard-Yogurt Sauce (see page 163), which is great as a dip for raw vegetables such as cauliflower, broccoli, celery, jicama (a root vegetable sometimes called "the Mexican potato"), and carrots.

BASIC RECIPE

2 cups (475 mL) 4% plain yogurt

Spoon the yogurt into a very fine mesh sieve or an ordinary sieve lined with cheesecloth. Rest the sieve on a bowl and refrigerate for at least 24 to 36 hours. Check occasionally and throw out the liquid that accumulates in the bowl. When the yogurt is as thick as soft cream cheese, remove it from the sieve and place in a covered bowl.

HERBED AND SPICED YOGURT CHEESE BALLS

3 Tbsp. (45 mL) minced chives
3 Tbsp. (45 mL) ground sumac
3 Tbsp. (45 mL) coarsely ground black pepper
3 Tbsp. (45 mL) each sweet and hot paprika

Roll small amounts of the cheese into 1- to 1 ½-inch (2.5- to 3.8-cm) balls. This is a messy job, and the balls will not be perfectly spherical. If the balls seem very wet, place them, uncovered, in the refrigerator overnight. Choosing from the list above, place each herb and spice that you like on a separate plate. Gently roll each ball in one of the seasonings until it is completely coated. Present the multi-colored balls on a serving dish with thin slices of toasted baguette.

HERBED YOGURT SPREAD

1 to 1½ Tbsp. (15 to 22.5 mL) chopped fresh thyme mixed with minced chives or garlic chives

Follow the basic recipe, and mix the herbs into the yogurt cheese. Mound on baguette, country, or whole wheat bread. This is also great as a spread for a vegetarian sandwich.

Sumac: This sour spice is made of ground, dried berries of the shrub _Rhus coriaria_. Sumac can be found in Middle Eastern grocery stores and some gourmet shops.

Oven-Roasted Tomatoes

MAKES 2 CUPS (475 ML)

These tomatoes are so easy to prepare and can be used in lots of ways. They make a quick bruschetta when used to top grilled bread that's been rubbed with garlic and drizzled with olive oil, and they are an integral part of the Asiago Cheese with Oven-Roasted Tomatoes and Caramelized Onions on Focaccia (see page 130). You could also serve them with grilled salmon or halibut or tossed with pasta.

1½ lb. (680 g) fresh plum tomatoes
⅔ cup (160 mL) medium-quality balsamic vinegar
¼ cup (60 mL) soy sauce
2 Tbsp. (30 mL) vegetable oil

Wash and halve the tomatoes lengthwise and place in a bowl. Combine the remaining ingredients, and pour over the tomatoes. Marinate at least 2 hours or overnight, in the refrigerator. Drain and reserve the marinade to use again. It will keep, refrigerated, for 10 days.

Preheat the oven to 300°F (150°C).

Place the tomatoes, cut-side up, on a baking pan covered with foil. Bake until slightly shriveled but not completely dried out, about 1 to 1½ hours—longer if they came out of the refrigerator.

Oven-roasted tomatoes can be stored in a covered container in the refrigerator for at least 1 week.

North American balsamic vinegar is but a thin imitation of its namesake, Aceto Balsamico Tradizionale. The real stuff, made only by artisans in Modena, Italy, is quite thick, hard to come by, and very expensive.

Mayonnaise — Four Types

MAKES 1 GENEROUS CUP (240 ML)

This is my Mom's recipe and one of the first things I learned to make. I always wanted to pour the oil in very quickly, which meant the sauce never emulsified, so my mother would pour the oil as I whisked. It was our first team effort. Even though it's not classic, Mom always started with that touch of Dijon. I like to use a delicate-tasting oil as I don't want an overpowering taste in the mayonnaise. For a more assertive flavor, use olive oil, as they do in the south of France and Italy.

BASIC MAYONNAISE

1 tsp. (5 mL) Dijon mustard

1 egg yolk

1 cup (240 mL) corn or canola oil

up to 1½ Tbsp. (22.5 mL) lemon juice

¼ heaping tsp. (1.2 mL) kosher salt

⅛ tsp. (.5 mL) freshly ground white pepper

Put the mustard in a bowl and whisk in the egg yolk. Dribble the oil very slowly into the egg, whisking continuously. If the whisking makes your arm tired, take a break. The mixture will not separate.

When all the oil is incorporated, start adding the lemon juice half a teaspoon (2.5 mL) at a time. Continue to whisk. Taste after each addition. Add salt and pepper and taste again.

If this method seems too daunting, put the mustard and egg yolk in a food processor and pulse to blend. With the processor on, slowly pour in the oil. When the mixture has emulsified, add the lemon juice, salt, and pepper.

Cover and keep in the refrigerator until ready to use.

ROASTED GARLIC MAYONNAISE

Follow the basic recipe, but substitute olive oil for half of the corn or canola oil. After incorporating all the oil, thoroughly mix in 2 to 4 cloves of mashed roasted garlic. Garlic mayo is great as a condiment for french fries or as a dip for raw or steamed vegetables. To roast the garlic, heat the oven to 400°F (200°C). Cut the tip off the garlic bulb, drizzle with a little oil and wrap lightly in foil. Roast for about 1 hour, depending on the size of the bulb. Roast garlic will keep in the refrigerator for up to 1 week.

LEMON MAYONNAISE

Follow the basic recipe, but use the whole egg instead of just the yolk, and up to 3 Tbsp. (45 mL) of lemon juice. This will result in a much thinner mayonnaise. Toss with romaine lettuce and Spa Croutons (see page 44).

TOMATO CHIVE MAYONNAISE

Add 1 tsp. (5 mL) tomato paste and 1 Tbsp. (15 mL) finely minced fresh chives to the finished basic recipe. Taste and add more tomato paste as desired. You can also use cooked puréed tomato, but start with 2 Tbsp. (30 mL) and add more as desired. Use in a roasted chicken sandwich or as an accompaniment to poached salmon or smoked trout.

COOK'S TIP

All the ingredients must be at room temperature or the mayonnaise will not emulsify. If your mom isn't there to help you, wrap the bottom of the bowl in a damp towel to prevent it from slipping as you whisk in the oil.

Saving a separated sauce: In emulsion sauces there is always the risk of separation, but this can be fixed. Simply mix some of the separated sauce with a bit of water and emulsifier (egg yolk, mustard) until it blends. Then dribble in the rest of the separated sauce slowly, beating constantly.

Flavored Butters — Four Tastes

EACH RECIPE MAKES ½ LB. (225 G)

You'll want to try the first two butters on grain bread or Classic French Toast (see page 50). Hot Pepper Honey Butter is terrific on cornbread or savory muffins. A cold disk of Lemon Herb Butter plopped on a just-off-the-grill steak, fish, or chicken breast will make a good meal better. All these butters can be frozen for up to 6 months.

ORANGE HONEY BUTTER

½ cup (120 mL) orange juice, preferably freshly squeezed
½ lb (225 g) unsalted butter, at room temperature
1 Tbsp. (15 mL) finely grated orange rind
1½ tsp. (7.5 mL) honey, preferably wildflower

Pour the orange juice into a small saucepan and boil down to ¼ cup (60 mL). Cool.

Put the softened butter in a bowl and add the orange juice. Slowly mix the juice into the butter. This will take a while. Add the orange rind and the honey. Mix again and taste. Add more rind if desired. If you plan to serve the butter cold, as opposed to room temperature, remember that the orange flavor will be dulled, so you may want to add more rind.

Serve at room temperature or form the butter into a log shape on foil, roll up and refrigerate or put in the freezer until hard. To serve, slice into disks.

RASPBERRY HONEY BUTTER

1 scant cup (240 mL) frozen unsweetened raspberries or 1½ cups (360 mL) fresh raspberries
½ lb. (225 g) unsalted butter at room temperature
1 Tbsp. (15 mL) honey, preferably wildflower or lavender

Defrost the raspberries. Purée in a food processor and strain through a fine-meshed sieve.

Place the butter in a small bowl. Mix 4 Tbsp. (60 mL) of the raspberry purée and the honey into the butter. Make sure the flavored butter is completely mixed and is a consistent color. Spoon the butter in a line along a piece of foil. Use the foil to roll the butter into a log. Refrigerate until hard. Slice in ¼- to ½-inch (.6- to 1.2-cm) disks just before serving. Place 1 disk on each piece of Classic French Toast (see page 50).

HOT PEPPER HONEY BUTTER

This butter is delicious spread over warm cornbread, especially when served with spareribs or grilled pork tenderloin. You could continue the southern accent by adding collard greens and rice and peas.

up to ½ a jalapeño pepper, finely minced
½ to 1 Tbsp. (7.5 to 15 mL) liquid honey, preferably wildflower
½ lb. (225 g) unsalted butter, at room temperature

With a fork, mix the pepper and honey into the butter, starting with ¼ of the minced jalapeño pepper and ½ Tbsp. (7.5 mL) of the honey. Keep adding both until you get a nice kick that is mellowed out by the honey. Spoon into a bowl or place the butter in a line along a piece of foil. Use the foil to roll the butter into a log. Refrigerate until hard. Slice in ¼- to ½-inch (.6- to 1.2-cm) disks just before serving.

LEMON HERB BUTTER

Lemon juice just doesn't want to mix into butter. It likes to bead and run along the surface. By using an ordinary dinner fork and persevering, you'll get a lovely infused butter. A simple grilled steak or any white fish will benefit greatly from a cold round of it placed on top just before serving.

½ lb. (225 g) unsalted butter, at room temperature
up to 2 tsp. (10 mL) lemon juice
½ tsp. (2.5 mL) Dijon mustard

1 small clove garlic, finely minced
1 Tbsp. (15 mL) minced, mixed fresh herbs such as parsley, chives, marjoram, or chervil

Place the butter in a small bowl. Use a fork to mix the lemon juice, mustard, and garlic into the softened butter. Gently mix in the herbs. Spoon the butter in a line along a piece of foil. Use the foil to roll the butter into a log. Refrigerate until hard. Slice in ¼- to ½-inch (.6- to 1.2-cm) disks just before serving.

4:15 p.m.:
86 lb. (39 kg) of country dough finishes mixing.

Roasted Apple Cranberry Compote

MAKES 1 9-INCH (23-CM) "CAKE"

Serve this thick compote as part of a cheese course. It is especially good with old cheddar, manchego, or any assertive hard cheese. You can also spread it on toast as a low-calorie jam, or serve it as a condiment for a roasted pork sandwich.

12 Granny Smith or Spy apples, peeled, cored, halved, and thinly sliced
⅛ cup (30 mL) sugar (slightly less with Spy apples)

2 Tbsp. (30 mL) minced fresh marjoram
½ cup (120 mL) dried cranberries
2 tsp. (10 mL) liquid honey

Preheat the oven to 200°F (95°C). Coat a round 9- x 5-inch (23- x 12.5-cm) high ovenproof dish with a light film of vegetable or canola oil. You can also use loaf pans or terrine dishes.

Arrange a layer of overlapping apple slices in the bottom of the dish. Sprinkle with a pinch of sugar, a pinch of marjoram, and a few cranberries. Add another layer of apples. Add another sprinkling of sugar, marjoram, and cranberries and honey. Continue layering the apples, adding sugar, marjoram, and cranberries between every layer. Drizzle every second layer with honey as well. End with an apple layer. They will be higher than the rim of the dish.

Gently press down on the apples. Cover tightly with foil and bake for about 10 hours. You can leave it unattended overnight.

Remove from the oven and let cool. When the dish has cooled enough to handle, gently drain the liquid off without dislodging the apples. Reserve the liquid—it's wonderful drizzled over ice cream. Put the foil back over the apples, place a light weight over the foil, and refrigerate for at least 6 hours.

Turn out on a serving dish. Refrigerated, the compote will keep well for about a week.

Cranberries grow in bogs and marshes and other wetlands, but not in water, as many people believe. This common misconception stems from the fact that cranberry farms are usually photographed at harvest time when the bogs are flooded to make berry collecting easier.

Soup, Soupe, Zuppa

Cauliflower Soup with Spinach and Indian Spices

Three-Onion Soup with Gruyère Croutons

Leek and Yukon Gold Potato Soup with Chive Oil Drizzle

Kate's Corn Chowder

Mushroom Consommé with Enoki Mushroom and Green Onion Garnish

Potage de la campagne

Roasted Squash and Sweet Potato Soup with Apple-Shallot Garnish

Zuppa alla Pavese

Tomato, Red Pepper, and Roasted Garlic Soup with Ham and Cheese Croutons

Poitou-Style Fresh Pea Soup

Pumpkin-Lemongrass Soup

Avocado and Cucumber Soup

Mariner's Medley

White Gazpacho

"Soup does its loyal best, no matter what undignified conditions are imposed upon it. But soup knows the difference. Soup is sensitive. You don't catch steak changing around when you're poor and sick do you?"
— Judith Martin, a.k.a. Miss Manners

Cauliflower Soup with Spinach and Indian Spices

MAKES 12 CUPS (2.8 L)

If you think Indian means spicy you'll be surprised at the fragrant, subtle flavorings of this soup. I love the saffron color the turmeric gives to it, and the spinach leaves turn a glossy green. Try serving it with Baked Tortilla Shards (see page 42), grilled country bread drizzled with good olive oil, or Jalapeño Cornbread (see page 36). Follow it with the Roasted Salmon Salad in Cumin-Scented Yogurt Dressing (see page 114), and you've got a casual summer supper.

3 Tbsp. (45 mL) vegetable or canola oil
6 green cardamom seeds
2 tsp. (10 mL) ground coriander (the flavor will be fresher if you grind your own)
1 tsp. (5 mL) ground turmeric
pinch of cayenne
½ cup (120 mL) finely chopped cooking onion
2 medium cloves garlic, minced

1 head cauliflower, washed, drained, and coarsely chopped
2 medium-sized Yukon gold potatoes, cut in ¼-inch (.6-cm) dice, approximately 2 cups (475 mL)
1 Tbsp. (15 mL) Dijon mustard
6 to 8 cups (1.5 to 2 L) light chicken stock
2 tsp. (10 mL) kosher salt
freshly ground white pepper
1 very large handful baby spinach, washed
yogurt to garnish

Heat the oil in a pot large enough to accommodate all the ingredients. Add the cardamom seeds and sauté about 1 minute until they give up their oils. Skim the seeds out of the oil and discard them. Lower the heat to medium low and add the coriander, turmeric, and cayenne. Sauté for about 20 seconds until you can smell the spices.

Add the onion and garlic. Sauté about 5 minutes, or until the onion is wilted. Lower the heat if the onion starts to brown. Add the cauliflower, potatoes, and mustard. Toss until the spices coat the vegetables and cook for 2 to 3 minutes until the vegetables are slightly roasted.

Pour in 6 cups (1.5 L) of the stock and simmer, covered, for 20 to 30 minutes or until the vegetables are soft.

If you have time, cool the mixture. Purée it in a food processor or blender. Add salt and pepper to taste. If the purée is too thick, add an extra 1 to 2 cups (240 to 475 mL) of stock.

Reheat and taste for seasonings. Stir in the spinach just before serving. The spinach will turn bright green and have a slight crunch. Pour into bowls and garnish with a dollop of yogurt.

This soup can be made ahead to the point just before you add the spinach. It will keep in the refrigerator for 5 days or in the freezer for 2 months. The spinach, once added to the soup, will keep its color for 2 days, but it will lose its crispness.

COOK'S TIP

Try to buy your spices for this soup at an Indian or Asian grocery. You'll be able to buy smaller amounts and they will be fresher. It's well worth buying them, too; they will last up to 6 months. Green and white cardamon seed come from the same plant, a member of the ginger family. Cardamom seed is naturally green, but is more often found in its bleached white form.

Three-Onion Soup with Gruyère Croutons

MAKES 10 CUPS (2.4 L)

A kitchen without onions would be a sorry place indeed. A member of the lily family, these bulbs are used in cooking in every culture in the world. This much lighter version of *soupe à l'oignon* would be wonderful followed by Roasted Salmon with Asparagus, Zucchini, Corn, Grilled Onions, and Tomatoes (see page 173). Make sure your frying pan is large enough to hold all the onions in a very thin layer. You want them to cook and slightly caramelize, not stew on top of each other.

6 strips of bacon
1 Tbsp. (15 mL) canola oil
1 large clove garlic, minced
1 Tbsp. (15 mL) unsalted butter
2 leeks, white only, cleaned and sliced in ¼-inch (.6-cm) rings, to make about 1 cup (240 mL)
1 cup (240 mL) sliced shallots (3 to 8 depending on size)
2 heaping cups (475 mL) cooking onions, peeled and sliced (about 4)

1 bay leaf
1 large sprig thyme
1 large pinch sugar
8 cups (2 L) good-quality chicken stock
salt and freshly ground white pepper
2 Tbsp. (30 mL) unsalted butter
2 to 3 large slices Calabrese or white bread, crusts removed and cut into ½-inch (1.2-cm) cubes (for croutons)
⅓ cup (80 mL) coarsely shredded Gruyère

Cut 3 strips of bacon in ¼-inch (.6-cm) dice. Fry the bacon over medium–low heat, starting with a cold pan, for about 5 minutes. Add the canola oil and heat for 10 to 20 seconds and then add the garlic. Fry for 30 seconds, then add the butter and the three types of onions.

Raise the heat to medium and cook for 5 minutes. Add the bay leaf, thyme, and sugar and continue cooking for another 10 to 15 minutes, until the onions are dark golden but not burned. Remove the onions and deglaze the pan with ⅓ cup (80 mL) of the stock. Reduce the liquid until you end up with about 2 to 3 Tbsp. (30 to 45 mL) of syrupy stock.

Heat the remaining stock and add the onion mixture and deglazed stock. Sprinkle in the salt and pepper and simmer for 15 minutes. Remove 1½ cups (360 mL) of the soup and purée it in a blender or food processor. Add back to the pot.

Cook the remaining 3 pieces of bacon. Drain and crumble into chunks. Meanwhile, make the croutons.

Melt 2 Tbsp. (30 mL) of butter in the frying pan in which the bacon and onions were cooked. Add the croutons and cook, tossing, until dark golden and crisp. Toss in the cheese until it melts and remove immediately from the heat.

Ladle the soup into heated bowls. Top with a few croutons and some crumbled bacon. The croutons may have clumped together but can be easily pulled apart. Pile the extra ones into a bowl and bring them to the table for your greedier diners.

COOK'S TIP
Leeks, notoriously dirty, can be difficult to clean. Slice them in rings, place the rings in a large bowl, and fill it with cold water. Let them soak for 5 minutes. The clean leeks will rise to the top and the dirt will be left at the bottom of the bowl.

Leek and Yukon Gold Potato Soup with Chive Oil Drizzle

MAKES 12 CUPS (2.8 L)

This beautiful pale green soup is wonderful in winter or summer. Adding some of the green of the leeks, the garlic, and the nutmeg gives it extra depth. There is no milk or cream in this recipe, but it still has a rich taste.

6 cups (1.5 L) sliced leeks, about 3 leeks (use the white and 2 inches (5 cm) of green from each leek)
2 Tbsp. (30 mL) olive oil
½ cup (120 mL) peeled and chopped shallots (about 4)
3 medium-sized Yukon Gold potatoes, peeled and cubed

3 medium-sized cloves garlic, halved
8 cups (2 L) chicken stock
salt and freshly ground white pepper to taste
large pinch of nutmeg
3 Tbsp. (45 mL) minced chives
¼ to ⅓ cup (60 to 80 mL) light-tasting olive oil

Put the sliced leeks in a bowl of cold water for 10 minutes to drain them of sand. Pat dry before using.

Heat the 2 Tbsp. (30 mL) of oil in a saucepan large enough to hold all the ingredients. Add the shallots and leeks and sauté over medium heat for about 5 minutes, until they just start to wilt.

Add the potatoes, garlic, and stock. Cover and bring to a simmer. Cook until the potatoes are soft. Season with salt, pepper, and nutmeg. Let cool, then purée in batches in a food processor or blender.

Put the chives and ¼ cup (60 mL) olive oil in a blender. (A food processor will not emulsify the mixture.) Purée. Add more oil as needed. The mixture should be thick but pourable. Heat the soup, pour into individual bowls and drizzle with the chive oil.

In the twelfth century, Arab traders introduced nutmeg from the Molucca Islands in Indonesia to Europe, where it quickly became a popular and coveted spice. By the seventeenth century, the islands were invaded by the Dutch, who went so far as to kill island inhabitants and chop down trees in order to limit nutmeg production.

House-Brand Olives p. 68

Oven-Roasted Tomatoes p. 85

Flavored Butters p. 88

Whole Wheat Bran p. 28

Zuppa alla Pavese p. 101

Avocado and Cucumber Soup p.105

Mariner's Medley
p. 106

Kate's Corn Chowder
p. 97

Kate's Corn Chowder

MAKES 10 CUPS (2.4 L)

Kate Cocks is a wonderful cook and caterer from Nova Scotia. This soup is lighter than most chowders and is perfect served as a light lunch or an appetizer before grilled lamb or chicken. She made it without the bacon for a family function that included some vegetarians. I've added the sautéed shrimp or scallops if you wish to turn it into a one-dish meal. Any light bread such as ciabatta or baguette is a good accompaniment.

5 slices bacon, cut into ¼-inch (.6 -cm) pieces (optional)
2 Tbsp. (30 mL) unsalted butter
2 cups (475 mL) chopped yellow onion
2 Tbsp. (30 mL) all-purpose flour
4 cups (950 mL) chicken or vegetable broth
2 large white potatoes, peeled and cut into ½-inch (1.2-cm) dice, or use red potatoes, scrubbed but unpeeled

1 cup (240 mL) light cream
¾ tsp. (4 mL) freshly ground white pepper
kosher salt to taste
4 cups (950 mL) corn kernels, fresh or frozen
1 large red pepper, cut into ¼-inch (.6-cm) dice
3 scallions or green onions, cut into ¼-inch (.6-cm) dice
1 Tbsp. (15 mL) chopped fresh coriander, for garnish
sautéed shrimp or scallops, for garnish (optional)

Wilt the bacon (if using) in a large stockpot over low heat until the fat is rendered, about 5 minutes. Add the butter to the pot and melt. Then add the onion and sweat over low heat for about 10 minutes until softened but not browned. Spoon in the flour and cook, stirring, for another 2 to 3 minutes.

Pour in the broth with the potatoes. Continue cooking over medium-low heat until the potatoes are just tender, 10 to 15 minutes.

Next add the cream, pepper, and salt and cook for about 3 minutes.

Toss in the corn, red pepper, and green onions and adjust the seasonings if necessary. Cook an additional 5 minutes. Serve immediately, garnished with coriander and sautéed shrimp or scallops (if using). If you make the soup with the bacon, you may find it rich enough without the shellfish. On the other hand, sometimes too much of a good thing is wonderful.

Chowders are always hearty soups, but there are many different kinds. The name likely comes from the French _chaudière_, the pot this soup would have been cooked in.

Mushroom Consommé with Enoki Mushroom and Green Onion Garnish

MAKES 15 CUPS (3.5 L)

This soup was inspired by a vegetable stew cooked by Gordon Hammersley of Hammersley's Bistro in Boston. The consommé is totally fat free, but its flavorful, satisfying taste belies that. Serve it with plenty of warm baguette or with Spa Melba Toast (see page 40). Both the consommé and the chopped mushrooms freeze well, so don't be concerned about the quantity of this recipe. The word *consommé* is the past participle of the French *consommer*, to consume, accomplish, or finish. In reference to this clear soup, it is taken to mean a finished soup rather than simply a broth to be used as an ingredient, or to have other things added to it.

2 large portobello mushrooms, stems included
2 lbs. (900 g) white button mushrooms
2 Tbsp. (30 mL) chopped garlic
1 large Spanish onion, chopped
3½ cups (840 mL) dry white wine
12 cups (2.8 L) water
1 cup (240 mL) dried porcini mushrooms

¾ to 1 cup (180 to 240 mL) light-colored soy sauce or tamari (wheat-free soy sauce)
¼ tsp. (1.2 mL) kosher salt
2 tsp. (10 mL) fresh thyme leaves

GARNISH

1 3½-oz. (100-g) package enoki mushrooms, washed and trimmed
3 green onions, green part only, finely sliced in rings

Scrape the gills out of the portobello mushrooms. Finely chop the portobello and the white mushrooms.

Over high heat, heat a stockpot large enough to hold all the ingredients. It is imperative that the pot be very hot before you add the mushrooms. This allows you to cook the mushrooms without oil. Add the mushrooms, garlic, and onion and cook, stirring, for about 5 minutes, until the mushrooms release their water. Don't be concerned if some of the mushroom mixture sticks to the bottom of the pot when you first start cooking it.

Add the wine, water, porcini mushrooms, ¾ cup (180 mL) soy sauce, salt, and thyme and bring to a boil. Remove from the heat, cover, and let sit for 45 minutes. Return to stove and simmer, still covered, for another 45 minutes.

Pour the consommé through a fine strainer twice. Taste and add up to a ¼ cup (60 mL) more soy sauce if the soup needs more seasoning. Reserve 3 cups (720 mL) of the chopped mushroom mixture. Spoon 2 Tbsp. (30 mL) of the mushrooms into individual heated bowls. Ladle 1½ cups (360 mL) of the consommé into each bowl and garnish with a few enoki mushrooms and some green onion rings.

"I believe I once considerably scandalized her by declaring that a clear soup is a more important factor in life than a clear conscience." —Saki

Potage de la campagne

MAKES 6 TO 7 CUPS (1.5 TO 1.7 L)

When I asked the owner of the restaurant Astrance in Paris what gave the marvelous soup we had just eaten its earthy flavor, he told me "darkly toasted bread." With a bit more prodding, he also mentioned bacon and chicken stock. This is my version of their bread soup.

4 slices of bacon, chopped
3 Tbsp. (45 mL) finely chopped cooking onion
4 slices sourdough or country bread, sliced ¾ inch
   (1.9 cm) thick
6 cups (1.5 L) chicken stock

2 Tbsp. (30 mL) Dijon mustard
1 bay leaf
1 cup (240 mL) homogenized milk
salt to taste
pinch of white pepper
parsley for garnish

Pan-fry the bacon over medium-low heat for about 5 minutes, until some of the fat is rendered but the bacon is still soft. Add the onion and continue cooking on low heat for about 8 minutes until the onions are soft and barely golden. Drain the bacon and onion on paper towel and pat off any extra grease.

Toast the bread until it is dark golden brown but not burned. Cut into 1-inch (2.5-cm) cubes.

In a large saucepan or stockpot, heat the stock and add the bacon and onion mixture, bread, mustard, and bay leaf. Simmer, covered, for 15 minutes. Remove the bay leaf and pour in the milk. Purée in batches in a food processor. Add salt and pepper to taste.

Heat and serve in large cups with a parsley sprig as garnish.

For a more unusual presentation, froth 1 cup (240 mL) of the soup in a blender or mixer and gently spoon a bit of it on top of each cup.

Roasted Squash and Sweet Potato Soup with Apple-Shallot Garnish

MAKES 16 CUPS (4 L)

This makes a large quantity of really scrumptious soup. You could halve the recipe, but because it freezes so well, I wouldn't bother. If you don't have time to make the garnish, don't worry; this soup tastes great on its own. Serve with warm Calabrese (see page 26) or country bread spread with unsalted butter.

1 large butternut squash, peeled and chopped, about 7 cups (1.7 L)
4 large sweet potatoes, peeled and chopped, about 8 cups (2 L)
1½ large Spanish onions, peeled and chopped, about 4 cups (950 mL)
3 Tbsp. (45 mL) wildflower honey
1 tsp. (5 mL) ground cinnamon
½ tsp. (2.5 mL) ground nutmeg
½ heaping tsp. (2.5 mL) toasted cumin

1 heaping Tbsp. (15 mL) minced fresh ginger
2 Tbsp. (30 mL) unsalted butter, cut in small cubes
8 cups (2 L) chicken or vegetable stock
salt and freshly ground white pepper

GARNISH
1 to 2 Tbsp. (15 to 30 mL) unsalted butter
1½ Golden Delicious apples, peeled and cut in ¼-inch (.6-cm) cubes
1½ Tbsp. (22.5 mL) vegetable oil or butter
4 large shallots, finely sliced

Preheat the oven to 375°F (190°C).

In 2 large roasting pans, toss together all the ingredients except the stock and salt and pepper. Mix well. Moisten with 1 cup (240 mL) of the stock. Cover tightly with foil and cook for 1 hour or until all the vegetables are soft.

Purée in a food processor, in batches, with the remaining stock. Season with salt and pepper. If you want a very smooth consistency, strain the soup through a sieve.

For the garnish, sauté the apples in the butter until soft and golden. Sauté the shallots in the oil or butter until crisp but not burned.

Pour the soup into warm bowls and garnish with the apples and shallots.

When Columbus arrived in Haiti in 1492, he and his crew also discovered the sweet potato, or _batata_, as the Haitians called it. Europeans didn't learn about the regular potato until 1537, when it was confused with the _batata_ and called the same thing — a misnomer that still causes confusion.

Zuppa alla Pavese

My version of this quick-to-make soup, named after the city of Pavia in Lombardy, depends on good chicken broth. Some cooks use beef or vegetable broth—also delicious. This simple recipe looks beautiful and tastes light but nourishing. My Croatian friend Sandy has made this with cumin seed or fresh coriander in place of the parsley.

9 cups (2.1 L) strong chicken broth
6 ½-inch (1.2-cm) slices country, Calabrese, or white bread
6 eggs
up to 6 Tbsp. (90 mL) grated Parmigiano Reggiano cheese
6 tsp. (30 mL) minced fresh Italian parsley

Bring the broth to a simmer. Cut each slice of bread to fit the bottom of your bowls. Toast the bread.

Poach the eggs. The eggs can be poached ahead of time and held until ready to serve. (See the Cook's Tip on page 58.)

Place the slices of toast in the bottom of 6 heated bowls. Carefully slide 1 poached egg onto each piece of toast. Gently ladle up to 1½ cups (360 mL) of broth into each bowl. Sprinkle 1 Tbsp. (15 mL) of cheese and 1 tsp. (5 mL) of parsley over each bowl.

COOK'S TIP

Improve store-bought chicken stock by adding some raw or roasted chicken wings, carrot, onion, celery, and a bay leaf. Simmer, covered, for 1 hour. Strain and refrigerate for a few hours. The fat will rise to the top and can be easily scraped off. Using the roasted chicken wings will result in a darker, stronger broth.

The word _zuppa_ doesn't describe just any soup, but one made with bread. In Italian, _zuppa_ comes from _soppa_, the name for bread that has absorbed—sopped up—a lot of liquid. Broths are _brodi_, and all soups made without bread are _minestre_, of which the grandest is _minestrone_.

Tomato, Red Pepper, and Roasted Garlic Soup with Ham and Cheese Croutons

MAKES 15 CUPS (3.5 L)

We serve this hearty soup all fall at the ACE Café. Substitute canned tomatoes for the Romas in the winter. Garlic Parmigiano Croutons (see page 45) can also be used as a garnish.

1 head of garlic
½ cup (120 mL) olive oil
⅔ cup (160 mL) diced cooking onion, about
  ½ a large onion
2 cups (475 mL) sliced leeks, white part only, about
  2 to 3 leeks
1½ celery stalks, cleaned and diced
1 red pepper, seeded and diced
3 medium carrots, peeled and diced

1 28-oz (796-mL) can and 1 14-oz (396-mL) can
  whole tomatoes, drained
1 28-oz. (796-mL) can whole tomatoes, with juice
7 cups (1.7 L) water or vegetable or chicken stock
1½ tsp. (7.5 mL) minced fresh thyme

CROUTONS (FOR 4 SERVINGS)
4 slices white or whole wheat bread, thinly sliced,
  crusts removed
8 to 10 thinly sliced pieces of Gruyère
4 slices thinly sliced Black Forest ham or prosciutto
unsalted butter, at room temperature

Preheat the oven to 350°F (175°C).

FOR THE SOUP

Slice off the top of the garlic bulb about ¼ inch (.6 cm) down the bulb. Wrap the bulb in foil and roast in the oven for 1 hour or until soft. Set aside to cool. Squeeze out the garlic.

Heat the oil. Add the onion, leeks, celery, and red pepper and sauté over medium to medium–low heat for about 15 minutes or until softened. Then add the carrots, tomatoes and juice, and the water or stock. Bring to a boil, cover, and reduce to a simmer for 30 minutes.

Remove from heat. Add the roasted garlic and the thyme.

Purée in a food processor and season with salt and pepper. If you want a smoother purée, force the soup through a fine sieve.

FOR THE CROUTONS

Cover two slices of bread with a layer of cheese, a layer of ham, and another layer of cheese. Top with the other slices of bread. Butter the outsides of both sandwiches, top and bottom. Grill or toast in a toaster oven until the cheese is melted and the bread is golden.

Let sit for 5 minutes and then cut into squares approximately ½ inch (1.2 cm). Pour the soup into bowls and garnish with the croutons.

COOK'S TIP

If using water instead of stock, let the puréed soup sit for at least 2 hours to allow the flavors to blend, then just reheat.

Poitou-Style Fresh Pea Soup

MAKES 9 CUPS (2.1 L) HOT, 11 CUPS (2.6 L) COLD

The French province of Poitou-Charentes was a seat of protest during the French Revolution and sent many of its citizens across the Atlantic. Today it sends some of France's most prized exports, such as brandy from Cognac, chocolates from Angoulême, and pottery from Poitiers. And now this fresh-as-spring soup. Serve it hot as an elegant starter or cold as a pleasant alternative to gazpacho.

3 Tbsp. (45 mL) unsalted butter
1½ thinly sliced cooking onions, approximately
    1½ cups (360 mL)
5 cups (1.2 L) fresh shelled peas or baby frozen peas
1½ tsp. (7.5 mL) chopped fresh thyme
1½ tsp. (7.5 mL) chopped fresh savory
3 Tbsp. (45 mL) chopped fresh parsley
1½ tsp. (7.5 mL) sugar

3 cups (720 mL) lightly packed, roughly chopped
    Boston lettuce
6 cups (1.5 L) chicken or vegetable stock (1 to 2 cups
    [240 to 475 mL] more if serving cold)
¾ tsp. (4 mL) kosher salt
¼ generous tsp. (1.2 mL) freshly ground white pepper
¼ cup (60 mL) fresh ricotta
6 slices white baguette
2 Tbsp. (30 mL) finely chopped walnuts

Heat the butter in a saucepan large enough to hold all the ingredients. Add the onions and sweat until softened but not browned, approximately 5 to 8 minutes. Add the fresh peas, herbs, sugar, and lettuce and toss until coated. Pour in the stock and add the salt and pepper. Cover and simmer until the peas are just cooked, about 20 minutes. Frozen peas should be added in the last 5 minutes.

Purée in batches in a food processor. If you want a perfectly smooth soup, pour it through a sieve, pressing on the solids.

Spread 2 tsp. (10 mL) of ricotta on each slice of baguette and top with some chopped walnuts. Toast in a toaster oven or in the oven until the bread is crisped.

Pour the soup into 6 bowls and float 1 crostini (baguette slice) on top of each. If serving cold, refrigerate the purée for at least 2 hours. The starches in the peas will thicken the chilled soup almost solid. Add extra stock to get the desired consistency. Top with a freshly made crostini if you wish.

"In the vegetable world there is nothing so innocent, so confiding in its expression, as the small green face of the freshly shelled spring pea."
— William Wallace Irwin

Pumpkin – Lemongrass Soup

I got the recipe for this wonderful soup from the chef of the main dining room at the Grand Hotel d'Angor in Siem Reap, Cambodia. The cinnamon, lemongrass, and cumin add wonderful flavor notes, and the splash of coconut milk adds just the right touch of richness. Sugar pumpkins are in the shops from August through December.

2 sugar pumpkins, the kind for cooking, not carving, approximately 3½ lb. (1.6 kg) each *or*
   4 cups (950 mL) pumpkin purée (not pumpkin pie filling)
4 Tbsp. (60 mL) unsalted butter
1 cup (240 mL) chopped cooking onion
1 oz. (28 g) cinnamon sticks, about 4 2½-inch (6.2-cm) sticks

¾ tsp. (4 mL) ground cumin
1 stalk lemongrass
9 cups (2.1 L) light vegetable stock or water
1½ tsp. (7.5 mL) sugar
salt and freshly ground white pepper to taste
½ cup (120 mL) or more unsweetened coconut milk

If using fresh pumpkins, cut them in half and remove the seeds. Reserve the seeds to toast for another time. Peel the pumpkins and cut into 1- to 2-inch (2.5- to 5-cm) pieces. Peel the bottom 5 inches (12.5 cm) of the bulb part of the lemongrass and cut into ½-inch (1.2-cm) pieces.

Melt the butter in a saucepan large enough to hold all the ingredients. Add the onion, cinnamon sticks, cumin, and lemongrass. Sauté on medium low for about 5 minutes or until the onions are translucent but not browned.

Add the pumpkin and toss to cover in butter. Add the stock or water. Cover and bring to a simmer. Cook for about 20 to 25 minutes or until the fresh pumpkin is soft. If using pumpkin purée, simmer for 15 minutes. Remove the cinnamon sticks and purée the soup in batches in a food processor. Stir in the sugar. Add salt and pepper to taste.

Strain through a sieve if you want a finer, thinner soup. Add more water or vegetable stock if the purée is too thick.

Heat, pour into bowls or cups, and drizzle each serving with about 1 Tbsp. (15 mL) coconut milk.

COOK'S TIP

Preheat the oven to 375°F (190°C). To toast pumpkin seeds, thoroughly wash the reserved pumpkin seeds to remove all the connecting pulp, and drain. When dry, toss the seeds in a little canola or vegetable oil and some salt. Spread the seeds on a roasting pan. Bake, stirring occasionally, until the seeds are dark golden and cooked through, about 5 to 8 minutes.

Serve with drinks, toss in a green salad, or make a pumpkin seed brittle.

Although lemongrass — also called citronella — grows well in Australia and North America, the only area of the world where it is commonly used is in Southeast Asia, particularly Thailand.

Avocado and Cucumber Soup

MAKES 7 TO 8 CUPS (1.7 TO 2 L)

This cool, refreshing soup is best on a steamy day. It's light, and the flavors are very delicate. Follow it with Roasted Salmon Salad in Cumin-Scented Yogurt Dressing (see page 114) or Grilled Tuna and Cannellini Bean Salad (see page 113) and then a chocolate dessert. A warm, crusty baguette is a must as an accompaniment.

4 cups (950 mL) strong-flavored vegetable stock, plus 1 extra cup, if needed
1 generous tsp. (5 mL) minced garlic
4 cups (950 mL) English cucumber, cleaned and diced (approximately 1 cucumber)
3 avocados, peeled and roughly chopped
2½ tsp. (12.5 mL) minced fresh chervil
2½ tsp. (12.5 mL) minced fresh parsley
1 tsp. (5 mL) minced fresh tarragon

1½ Tbsp. (22.5 mL) chopped fresh chives
⅛ tsp. (.5 mL) ground hot chilies or cayenne
1 tsp. (5 mL) lemon juice
1 tsp. (5 mL) kosher salt
⅛ tsp. (.5 mL) freshly ground white pepper

GARNISH
5 to 6 Tbsp. (75 to 90 mL) plain yogurt
½ tsp. (2.5 mL) sweet paprika
2 to 3 radishes, thinly sliced

Bring the stock to a simmer. Add the garlic and simmer for about 5 minutes or until soft. Remove from heat and bring to room temperature. Strain the stock through a sieve and reserve the garlic. Mix all the soup ingredients and ¾ tsp. (4 mL) of the cooked garlic in a large bowl.

Purée in batches in a food processor or blender until completely smooth. Taste for seasoning and add more herbs and garlic if you wish. Pulse again and place in the refrigerator until cold. If the soup is too thick, whisk in some of the extra stock.

Serve in individual bowls garnished with 1 Tbsp. (15 mL) of yogurt, a dusting of paprika, and some sliced radishes.

Mariner's Medley

This light and healthy fish soup has all the delights of a substantial stew without the heaviness of added cream. The idea came from a family favorite, Moules Marinière. The addition of various fish adds variety and flavor. Any white fish of your choice, such as halibut or sea bream, can be substituted for the snapper and grouper. Have plenty of warm baguette on hand, as well as the toasts, to soak up the flavorful broth.

2 Tbsp (30 mL) olive oil
2 large shallots, minced
2 large cloves garlic, minced, plus 1 clove for the toast
½ large celery stalk, cut in ¼-inch (.6-cm) dice
2 medium-sized white potatoes, peeled and cut in ½-inch (1.2-cm) cubes
6 cups (1.5 L) Fish Stock (see facing page or use a good store-bought stock)
½ cup (120 mL) dry white wine
2 sprigs fresh thyme
salt and freshly ground white pepper
10 oz. (285 g) snapper, skinned and cut into 6 pieces about 2 inches (5 cm) each

10 oz. (285 g) grouper, skinned and cut into 6 pieces about 2 inches (5 cm) each
10 oz. (285 g) salmon, skinned and cut into 6 pieces about 2 inches (5 cm) each
18 to 24 scallops, depending on appetite
18 to 24 mussels, scrubbed and debearded
1 green onion, green part only, cut in fine rings
⅓ cup (80 mL) roughly chopped fresh parsley
18 cherry tomatoes, sliced
18 ½-inch (.6-cm) slices of baguette, toasted or grilled, and then rubbed with the cut side of a garlic clove
Romesco Sauce (see page 168), for the toasts
extra virgin olive oil

Heat the olive oil over medium heat in a heavy-bottomed pot large enough to hold all the ingredients. Sauté the shallots for 2 to 3 minutes without browning, then add the garlic and continue to cook for an additional 2 minutes or until the garlic is softened but not browned. Add the celery and potatoes and sauté for another 2 to 3 minutes.

Pour the fish stock and wine into the pot. Add the thyme sprigs and simmer for 5 to 6 minutes. The potatoes should be almost cooked through. Add salt and pepper to your taste.

Lower the snapper, grouper, and salmon into the broth. Cover and cook for 1 minute. Then add the scallops and mussels. Cover again and cook 2 to 3 minutes—just until the mussels open.

Ladle the broth and fish into 6 large, heated bowls. Remove the thyme sprigs. Sprinkle the green onion, parsley, and sliced tomatoes among the bowls. Top each bowl with 3 baguette toasts spread with Romesco Sauce and a healthy drizzle of olive oil.

FISH STOCK (OR USE GOOD STORE-BOUGHT STOCK)
3 lbs. (1.35 kg) non-oily fish bones and fish heads
1 Tbsp. (15 mL) vegetable oil
1 small onion, chopped
1 celery stalk, chopped

1 bay leaf
1 carrot, peeled and chopped
10 cups (2.4 L) cold water
½ cup (120 mL) dry white wine
10 white peppercorns
1 bouquet garni of 6 stalks of parsley, 2 stalks of thyme

Rinse the fish bones and heads, making sure there is no blood left on them. Heat the oil in a large stockpot. Add the onion, celery, bay leaf, and carrot. Sauté for 3 to 4 minutes. Do not let the vegetables brown. Add the fish bones and toss with the vegetables. Cook for another 2 to 3 minutes.

Pour in the cold water and wine and drop in the peppercorns and bouquet garni. Cover and bring to a simmer. Skim off any froth. Simmer for 40 minutes. Taste. If you want a more concentrated stock, remove the lid and simmer for 10 more minutes. Drain the stock through a sieve, pressing on the vegetables and fish bones. Freeze any leftover stock.

When buying fresh scallops, make sure they are slightly pinkish in color. Pure white indicates that they have been soaked in water to make them heavier — and more expensive.

White Gazpacho

The original version of gazpacho used almonds, bread, salt, garlic, vinegar, and olive oil. New World foods such as peppers and tomatoes were added later. Culinary scholars may differ in their interpretation of the word *gazpacho*, but they all agree that the base of the soup is Arabic. You can control its thickness with the fineness of your sieve.

1¼ cups (300 mL) skinned whole or halved almonds

9 oz. (255 g) stale white or country bread, crusts removed, 7 to 8 slices

½ to ¾ cup (120 to 180 mL) homogenized milk; just enough milk, at room temperature, to cover the bread

2 medium cloves garlic, roughly chopped

½ to ¾ cup (120 to 180 mL) olive oil

2¼ Tbsp. (34 mL) sherry vinegar

up to 5 cups (1.2 L) cold water

¾ English cucumber, peeled and seeded (reserve the rest for garnish)

¾ cup (180 mL) green seedless grapes plus ½ to ¾ cup (120 to 180 mL) for garnish

salt and freshly ground white pepper to taste

fresh mint, for garnish

Coarsely chop the almonds and set aside. Chop or tear the bread into large pieces. Put in a bowl and cover with the milk. Allow to soak until it has softened, about 5 minutes.

Blend the almonds, garlic, ½ cup (120 mL) of olive oil, vinegar, 4 cups (950 mL) of water, ¾ of the cucumber, and ¾ cup (180 mL) grapes in a food processor or blender in batches until smooth. Add the bread and milk in 3 parts, blending each time until the bread is emulsified. Taste and add salt and pepper.

Press through a sieve and discard the solids. Blend in the extra ¼ cup (60 mL) olive oil and up to 1 cup (240 mL) of water if necessary for flavor or consistency. Taste again and season with more salt and pepper if needed.

Refrigerate until completely chilled. Chop the remaining peeled and seeded cucumber into ¼-inch (.6-cm) dice and cut the remaining grapes in half. Chill those too.

Spoon 2 to 3 Tbsp. (30 to 45 mL) of the diced cucumber and the grapes into each bowl or thin, tall glass. Pour the soup over and garnish with a tiny sprig of mint. Serve immediately.

"Of soup and love, the first is best." — Spanish proverb

4:30 pm :
Madhras divides
multigrain dough
for ovals and
Pullmans.

Salads — Centerpieces and Sides

"Let the salad maker be a spendthrift for oil, a miser for vinegar, a statesman for salt, and a madman for mixing." — Spanish proverb

Tuna and Scallop Ceviche with Tropical Fruits

Grilled Tuna and Cannellini Bean Salad

Roasted Salmon Salad in Cumin-Scented Yogurt Dressing

Persian Chicken Salad with Apricots and Almonds

Belgian Endive Salad with Blue Cheese and Toasted Pine Nuts

Baby Lettuces with Taleggio Croquettes

Field Tomato, Corn, and Grilled Onion Salad with Giant Croutons

Asparagus, Beet, and Chèvre Salad

Croatian Red and Yellow Pepper Salad

Summer Vegetable Bread Salad with Grilled Lemon-Pepper Shrimp

Potato Salad with Green Beans, Corn, and Tomato in a Caper Mayonnaise

Moroccan Roasted Beet Salad with Pomegranates and Almonds

Tuna and Scallop Ceviche with Tropical Fruits

MAKES 6 GENEROUS APPETIZERS

You will love the color and texture of this ceviche as well as the combination of fresh seafood and tropical tastes. That it can be ready in 15 minutes is an added bonus. When making ceviche, it is important to use very fresh fish as it is never cooked by heat, only by the acids contained in the citrus juice. Tamari, a wheat-free soy sauce, is generally available at good supermarkets, gourmet shops, and health food stores. Serve this dish immediately. If left standing, the flavors meld together and become indistinguishable. Accompany the ceviche with warm baguette or ciabatta.

12 oz. (340 g) fresh or fresh-frozen scallops, thinly sliced
12 oz. (340 g) sashimi-grade tuna, thinly sliced
2 to 4 limes, juice only
1 small pink grapefruit
1 mango

2 Tbsp. (30 mL) light soy sauce or tamari (wheat-free soy sauce)
3 Tbsp. (45 mL) finely chopped coriander
¼ tsp. (1.2 mL) sesame oil
¼ to ½ tsp. (1.2 to 2.5 mL) finely minced jalapeño pepper

In two separate bowls, toss the scallops and tuna with the lime juice and let sit for 10 minutes. Meanwhile, peel and section the grapefruit, cutting around the membrane. (See Cook's Tip.) Chop into ¼- to ½-inch (.6- to 1.2-cm) pieces. Peel and slice the mango into ¼-inch (.6-cm) slices.

Drain the scallops and the tuna, reserving the lime juice. In a bowl, gently toss together and then toss with the soy sauce, coriander, sesame oil, and jalapeño pepper. When the fish is thoroughly coated, fold in the grapefruit and mango. Taste, and add some of the reserved lime juice, if necessary.

Using your hands, mound on six plates and serve immediately.

COOK'S TIP

To get citrus slices without the membrane, cut a small piece off the top and bottom of the grapefruit. Set the fruit on a cutting board and, using a sharp knife, follow the contour of the grapefruit, cutting away the skin and the thin membrane. Cut into the grapefruit close to the membrane on both sides of each section of fruit.

Being warm-blooded fish, the only way tuna can get enough oxygen to survive is by constantly swimming, so that there is always water running through their gills. This results in very strong muscles and very dark meat that even the pickiest fish-eaters usually like.

Grilled Tuna and Cannellini Bean Salad

SERVES 4 GENEROUSLY

I love serving this salad warm or at room temperature with a loaf of ciabatta, focaccia, or sourdough bread and a glass of full-bodied red wine. Don't be put off by the bit of chopping involved; everything can be prepared up to a day ahead of time and left to marinate for up to 1 hour. Don't add the tuna until the last moment, though, as the lemon in the vinaigrette will change its color. Finish off the meal with a bowl of seasonal fruit and some shortbread cookies.

MARINADE FOR TUNA

3 Tbsp. (45 mL) olive oil
1 tsp. (5 mL) soy sauce
½ tsp. (2.5 mL) grated fresh ginger
1 medium clove garlic, minced

SALAD

12 to 16 oz. (340 to 455 g) fresh tuna fillets 1- to 1¼-inch (2.5- to 3-cm) thick (at room temperature)
3 19-oz (532-mL) cans cannellini, white kidney or great northern beans, drained and rinsed or 1½ cups (360 mL) dried beans (see page 80 for cooking instructions)
½ medium mild onion, very thinly sliced

1 stalk of celery, cut into ¼-inch (.6-cm) dice
½ to ¾ cup (120 to 180 mL) carrots, cut into ¼-inch (.6-cm) dice
1 to 2 green onions, white and green part, coarsely minced
¼ cup (60 mL) finely chopped Italian parsley
20 to 25 black niçoise or kalamata olives, pitted
salt and freshly ground black pepper to taste

VINAIGRETTE

2 Tbsp. (30 mL) fresh lemon juice
2 tsp. (10 mL) white wine vinegar
4 to 5 Tbsp. (60 to 75 mL) extra virgin olive oil
salt and freshly ground black pepper to taste

FOR THE TUNA

In a shallow dish, mix the olive oil, soy sauce, ginger, and garlic. Marinate the tuna in this mixture for 5 to 10 minutes on each side. The longer it marinates the more pronounced the flavor will be. Heat a grill pan or cast iron skillet over high heat. Sear the tuna for 1 minute on each side. If you prefer tuna medium rare, sear it for an additional 30 seconds on both sides. Remove the pan from the heat and transfer the tuna to a cutting board. Allow the tuna to rest for 10 minutes before cutting into ½-inch (1.2-cm) slices across the grain. Cut each sliced piece into 1-inch (2.5-cm) pieces. Reserve.

FOR THE VINAIGRETTE

Mix the lemon juice and vinegar in a small bowl. Whisk in the olive oil. Season with salt and pepper. The vinaigrette should be quite lemony, to bring out the mild flavor of the beans.

ASSEMBLY

Put the beans, sliced onion, celery, carrots, green onion, parsley, and olives in a serving bowl. Spoon ¾ of the vinaigrette over top. Toss. Gently fold in the tuna. Add more vinaigrette, and salt and pepper, if needed. For extra kick, add the second green onion.

COOK'S TIP

The beans, tuna, and vinaigrette can all be made up to a day ahead and refrigerated. Bring to room temperature before assembling. The salad, except for the tuna, can be tossed together up to an hour before serving.

Roasted Salmon Salad in Cumin-Scented Yogurt Dressing

SERVES 4

The lemongrass and garlic give this salmon salad a delicate Asian flavor, which works well with the cumin and coriander in the yogurt dressing. For a casual spring dinner, consider starting with Poitou-Style Fresh Pea Soup (see page 103). After, since this is a low-fat salad, you can treat yourself to a decadent dessert.

THE SALAD

1 bulb of lemongrass, gently crushed and cut in ¼-inch (.6-cm) rings

2 medium cloves garlic, smashed

approximately ⅛ tsp. (.5 mL) freshly ground black pepper (6 mill turns)

¼ cup (60 mL) vegetable oil

3 8-oz. (225 g) pieces of center-cut salmon fillet, skinned and approximately 1½ inches (3.8 cm) thick

35 yellow beans

35 green beans

half an English cucumber, seeded and cut in 1-inch (2.5-cm) chunks

15 cherry tomatoes

1 tsp. (5 mL) minced fresh coriander (mince just before serving) plus sprigs for garnish

salt and freshly ground black pepper to taste

1 squeeze of lemon juice (optional)

pinch of dried ground chilies (optional)

THE DRESSING

2½ tsp. (12.5 mL) ground cumin, or more, to taste

½ tsp. (2.5 mL) ground coriander, or more, to taste

¾ cup (180 mL) yogurt

FOR THE SALAD

Mix together the lemongrass, garlic, pepper, and oil in a shallow casserole dish large enough to hold the salmon. Place the salmon pieces in the dish, making sure that all of it is covered with marinade. Place 2 or 3 slices of lemongrass on top of each piece of salmon. Marinate, at room temperature, 30 to 45 minutes, occasionally turning the fish over or spooning marinade over top.

Preheat the oven to 400°F (200°C).

Clean and cook the beans in salted water until just barely crisp. Shock under cold water. Drain and place in a serving bowl large enough to hold the salmon and other ingredients. Add the cucumber chunks. Set aside.

Heat a cast iron skillet for 2 minutes. Remove the fish from the marinade and salt 1 side. Place the salmon pieces in the skillet, salted-side down, and cook for 1 minute. Salt the top sides, flip the salmon pieces over and cook for another minute. Move the skillet to the oven for 7 to 9 minutes, depending on how you like your fish cooked. Remove the fish from the skillet and let it rest for 10 minutes. Break into chunks and reserve. If you are using wild salmon, decrease the oven time by at least 2 to 3 minutes.

Slice the tomatoes in half. Add the salmon, tomatoes, and minced coriander to the beans and cucumber mixture.

Gently mix in half the dressing so as not to break up the salmon. Taste, add salt and pepper, more dressing, and more minced coriander as needed. Add the lemon juice and chilies, if desired. Decorate with sprigs of coriander. Serve with warm baguette or pita bread. Use any leftover dressing as a simple sauce for grilled fish.

In a small, dry frying pan, stir together the cumin and coriander over medium heat for 30 seconds to 1 minute or until the spices give off a fragrance and have darkened slightly. Don't let them burn. Mix into the yogurt.

COOK'S TIP

Buy whole cumin and coriander seeds, roast as above, and grind in a clean coffee grinder or with a mortar and pestle. The flavor will be more vibrant than pre-ground spices.

"When one is tired of all seasonings, cumin remains welcome."

— Pliny

Persian Chicken Salad with Apricots and Almonds

This chicken dish is wonderful served slightly warmer than room temperature with a simple green salad and a baguette, or cold the next day as a filling for a sandwich. Save any extra dressing to liven up those next-day leftovers.

¼ cup (60 mL) julienned fresh ginger

2 large cloves garlic, julienned

1 small leek, white part only, cleaned and julienned

1 stalk celery, chopped

1 tsp. (5 mL) kosher salt

10 peppercorns, white or black

1 lb. (455 g) deboned and skinned chicken breasts (about 2 to 3 large breasts)

1½ tsp. (7.5 mL) curry powder, or more, to taste

½ cup (120 mL) Basic Mayonnaise (see page 86) or good store-bought mayonnaise

10 dried apricots, soaked in warm water for 15 minutes, drained, and sliced into 3 pieces each

2 to 3 Tbsp. (30 to 45 mL) slivered almonds (not slices)

3 green onions, green part only, thinly sliced

1 small green apple, peeled and julienned

½ tsp. (2.5 mL) grated ginger

Put the ginger, garlic, leek, celery, salt, and peppercorns into a large, straight-sided frying pan. Fill with enough water to almost cover the chicken breasts. Bring to a simmer and add the chicken breasts. Poach them at the bare simmer, turning after a few minutes, until they are still pink inside, but not raw. The time will depend on the size of the breasts (approximately 5 to 10 minutes). Don't let them cook too long or at too high a heat, as they will become tough.

Turn the heat off and let the meat sit in the liquid for about 15 minutes. Check that the chicken is cooked through. Take the chicken out of the pan and reserve the poaching liquid, which you will need again.

While the chicken is still warm, tear it into pieces with your fingers and place the pieces in a bowl with enough reserved liquid to moisten. Taste and sprinkle with more salt if necessary.

Dry-roast the curry powder in a small frying pan for about 30 seconds and, in a separate bowl, stir it into the mayonnaise. Add the reserved cooking liquid, 1 Tbsp. (15 mL) at a time, until the mayonnaise has the consistency of lightly whipped cream.

Toss the apricots, almonds, green onions, apple, ¾ of the mayonnaise, and the grated ginger with the chicken. Add more salt and pepper, mayonnaise, and grated ginger if you wish.

COOK'S TIPS

1. If you can't be bothered julienning the ingredients, chop them any way you want, as long as the size is consistent. To prepare the apple ahead of time, soak it, after cutting, in a bowl of water with 1 Tbsp. (15 mL) lemon juice. Pat dry before adding to the recipe.

2. Leftover roasted or grilled poultry can be used instead of poached chicken. Simmer 1 Tbsp. (15 mL) julienned fresh ginger and 1 clove crushed garlic in 1½ cups (360 mL) water for 15 minutes. Use the liquid to thin the mayonnaise.

Belgian Endive Salad with Blue Cheese and Toasted Pine Nuts

SERVES 6

A great starter to a grilled fish dinner, this salad can also be doubled and served as a light lunch. Either way, accompany it with thickly cut grilled bread drizzled with good olive oil and sprinkled with coarse salt. Make sure all ingredients are at room temperature before serving.

3½ oz. (100 g) blue cheese (try Papillon Noir or Papillon Rouge, Roquefort, Stilton, or Danish Blue)
¼ cup (60 mL) pine nuts
7 to 8 Belgian endives

1 recipe Basic Mayonnaise made with a whole egg, not just the yolk (see page 86)
salt and freshly ground white pepper
1 Tbsp. (15 mL) minced fresh Italian parsley (optional)

Preheat the oven to 350°F (175°C).

Crumble the cheese.

Toast the pine nuts in the oven for 5 to 7 minutes, stirring once or twice to prevent burning. Remove the nuts from the oven when they are golden, and let them cool.

Wash the endive and pat dry. Slice lengthwise into ¼- to ½-inch (.6- to1.2-cm) spears. Toss the endive with enough mayonnaise to coat. Add salt and pepper if needed, but remember that the cheese is salty.

Divide the endive onto 6 plates and sprinkle with the cheese and pine nuts. Garnish with minced parsley if desired.

COOK'S TIP

The cheese will be easier to crumble when it is cold. After crumbling, bring it to room temperature before using (about half an hour). The endive leaves can be separated and served whole, or the whole endive can be cut into rings for a different presentation. If you serve the leaves whole, you will need only one endive per person. Any excess mayonnaise will keep in the refrigerator for 3 to 4 days.

"First he ate some lettuces and some French beans, and then he ate some radishes; and then, feeling rather sick, he went to look for some parsley." — Beatrix Potter, The Tale of Peter Rabbit

Baby Lettuces with Taleggio Croquettes

There's something spectacularly yummy about a mouthful of crunchy-coated warm cheese together with cool lettuce leaves. Cooking the croquettes is a last-minute job, but they can be assembled hours before. You can hold them in a warm oven for at least 10 minutes if necessary.

CROQUETTES
⅓ cup (80 mL) all-purpose flour
1 egg, white only
1 cup (240 mL) coarse fresh white breadcrumbs
  (see page 43)
10 oz. (285 g) Taleggio cheese, rind removed, and cut
  into ½-inch (1.2-cm) cubes. If you can't find Taleggio,
  substitute fontina.
canola or vegetable oil for cooking
VINAIGRETTE
1 tsp. (5 mL) Dijon mustard

1 Tbsp. (15 mL) sherry vinegar
1 to 2 tsp. (5 to 10 mL) walnut oil
5 to 6 Tbsp. (75 to 90 mL) delicate olive oil
1 sprig of fresh tarragon, crushed
1 small clove garlic, crushed
salt and freshly ground white pepper
SALAD
3 handfuls baby frisée lettuce, cleaned and dried
2 handfuls baby red oak leaf lettuce, cleaned and dried
2 handfuls baby Boston lettuce, cleaned and dried
½ cup (120 mL) pea sprouts

FOR THE CROQUETTES

Place the flour, egg white, and breadcrumbs in three separate bowls and line the bowls up in that order. Roll a cube of cheese in the flour, making sure it is completely coated. Then cover it in egg white, and then completely coat it with the breadcrumbs. Pat the crumbs on if necessary. Place it on a plate. Continue with all the pieces of cheese. Your hands will be a mess. When you've cleaned them up, cover the cheese croquettes with plastic wrap and place in the refrigerator. Remove the croquettes from the fridge half an hour before cooking, to bring to room temperature.

Heat 2 inches (5 cm) of oil in a high-rimmed sauté pan. The oil should be shimmering but not smoking—about 350°F (175°C). Test the temperature by throwing in a piece of bread the same size as a cheese croquette. The oil should bubble up and the bread should be golden in 15 to 20 seconds.

Remove the test piece of bread and lower the croquettes into the oil, a few at a time. You need to be able to turn them and to get them out before they burn. That's impossible if all the croquettes are cooking at the same time. When they've turned golden brown, remove from the oil and drain on a paper towel.

FOR THE VINAIGRETTE

In a bowl, whisk together the mustard and sherry vinegar. Continue whisking, and slowly dribble in the walnut oil, then the olive oil, 1 Tbsp. (15 mL) at a time.

Add the crushed tarragon sprig and the crushed garlic and let stand for 30 minutes, and then take them out and discard. Taste. The garlic taste should be very subtle. You don't want it to overwhelm the delicate lettuces. Add salt and pepper to taste.

In a serving bowl, toss the salad with as much vinaigrette as you like and sprinkle the croquettes on top. Eat while the cheese is still hot.

COOK'S TIP

It is very important that the croquettes be at room temperature before you cook them. If they are put in the oil while they are cold, the coating may separate from the cheese.

Like Parmigiano Reggiano, Taleggio is a name-controlled Italian cheese and is, in fact, the name of a valley in Lombardy, Italy. To be sure that the Taleggio you are purchasing is genuine (produced in Lombardy) look for a mark made up of four circles, each with a different design in the center, embossed on the rind.

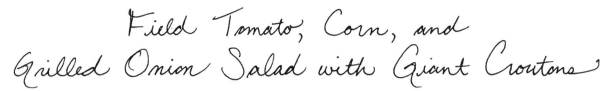

Field Tomato, Corn, and Grilled Onion Salad with Giant Croutons

SERVES 6

Here's one of those versatile recipes you'll find yourself making all summer. I've served it as an appetizer, as a vegetarian lunch, and as an accompaniment to barbecued steaks. For a change of pace, substitute blanched green beans, cooked cannellini beans or raw zucchini for the corn.

½ a large Vidalia onion cut in 4 or 5 crescent-shaped pieces through the root
½ a large red onion cut in 4 or 5 crescent-shaped pieces through the root
2 or more tsp. (10 mL) olive oil for brushing onions
6 large ripe tomatoes, cut in large chunks
2 large ears of sweet corn, husked
3 Tbsp. (45 mL) minced fresh chives or garlic chives

VINAIGRETTE
1 tsp. (5 mL) Dijon mustard
1 tsp. (5 mL) balsamic vinegar
1 Tbsp. (15 mL) red wine vinegar
¼ cup (60 mL) extra virgin olive oil
salt and freshly ground black pepper

CROUTONS
3 large pieces Calabrese, white, or country bread
1 clove garlic, halved
1 Tbsp. (15 mL) olive oil

Preheat the oven to 400°F (200°C) if roasting the onions.

FOR THE VEGETABLES

Brush the onion sections with a little oil and grill or roast them until slightly charred and cooked through. Grilling takes about 15 minutes; roasting will take about half an hour. Cool.

Put the chopped tomatoes in a serving bowl.

Cook the corn in boiling water for 3 minutes. Shock with cold water and drain. Using a very sharp knife, slice the kernels off the cob and add to the tomatoes. Then add the cooled onions to the bowl.

FOR THE VINAIGRETTE

In a small bowl, whisk together the mustard and the 2 vinegars. Slowly add the oil, still whisking. Season generously with salt and pepper. Add the chives just before tossing the salad.

FOR THE CROUTONS

Grill or toast the bread. Rub with the cut garlic clove and brush each piece with olive oil. Cut into 1- x 2 ½-inch (2.5- x 6.2-cm) croutons.

ASSEMBLY

Toss the vegetables with the vinaigrette, adding more salt and pepper if necessary. Decorate with the croutons. For softer croutons, toss them into the salad and let them marinate for 15 to 20 minutes before serving.

Asparagus, Beet, and Chèvre Salad

SERVES 4 AS AN APPETIZER

This simple and easy-to-make salad looks absolutely gorgeous. The colors are so vibrant, and the tastes of the three ingredients really complement one another. Along with some thick slices of baguette or Focaccia (see page 22), it's substantial enough for a light lunch, or it can be served as an elegant appetizer before grilled fish or roasted chicken.

¾ lb. (340 g) beets, boiled or roasted, and peeled (see page 125 for beet preparation)
1 lb. (455 g) asparagus, washed, cooked, and plunged into cold water to maintain color
7 oz. (200 g) creamy chèvre that will keep its shape
1 to 2 Tbsp. (15 to 30 mL) chopped fresh chives

VINAIGRETTE
1 tsp. (5 mL) Dijon mustard
1¼ Tbsp. (20 mL) raspberry vinegar (see below)
4 Tbsp. (60 mL) extra virgin olive oil
½ tsp. (2.5 mL) kosher salt
freshly ground white pepper to taste

Cut the room temperature beets into 1-inch (2.5-cm) chunks. Cut each room temperature asparagus spear into 2 or 3 pieces. Cut the chèvre into 1-inch (2.5-cm) chunks.

For the vinaigrette, whisk together the mustard and vinegar in a small bowl. Drizzle in the oil, whisking continuously. The vinaigrette will become fairly thick. Mix in the salt and pepper.

Toss the beets in half of the vinaigrette and separately toss the asparagus in the other half.

Mound the beets and asparagus beside each other on 1 large plate or 4 smaller ones. Or, if you prefer, toss the 2 vegetables together. Top with the chèvre and garnish with chives.

COOK'S TIP

How to make your own raspberry vinegar:
  2 cups (475 mL) white wine vinegar
  ½ cup (120 mL) raspberries, slightly crushed

Heat the vinegar to just below a simmer. Pour into a canning bottle. Add the raspberries and screw on the top. Leave on your counter for 48 hours or until the vinegar is a rosy color. Strain out the raspberries. Sterilize the jar and pour the vinegar back into it.

Although the ancient Greeks and Romans used the same name for asparagus as we do now, the vegetable has had many different names between their time and ours; the most charming being _sparrow grass._

Croatian Red and Yellow Pepper Salad

SERVES 6 TO 8

My friend Sandy Stermac made this salad for me many years ago. The colors were stunning, and the simple fresh taste exploded in my mouth. Sandy served it as part of an antipasto; I like it with Hungarian Minced Veal (see page 162), with grilled pork tenderloin, or piled into a sandwich made on a baguette and slathered with a tangy chèvre. Accompany the salad with thickly sliced grilled Focaccia (see page 22) or olive bread. Thanks, Sandy.

4 large red peppers
3 large yellow peppers
2 to 3 Tbsp. (30 to 45 mL) or more extra virgin olive oil

salt and freshly ground black pepper
1½ Tbsp. (22.5 mL) finely minced garlic
3 Tbsp. (45 mL) finely minced fresh parsley

Grill or broil the whole peppers, turning often to ensure that the sides are evenly charred. Place in a brown paper bag and let cool; steaming them like this makes the peppers much easier to peel. (But also see the Cook's Tip.) Use your fingers to peel off the skin, and discard the stem and seeds. Slice the peppers lengthwise in halves or quarters, depending on size.

Overlap the peppers on a serving plate, alternating colors, and pour olive oil over them. Sprinkle with salt and pepper, garlic, and parsley.

Let marinate for at least half an hour and up to 5 hours.

COOK'S TIP

Peeling peppers: Place the charred whole peppers on a baking sheet to cool. Put them into freezer bags and use a straw to suck out as much air as possible. Freeze. Remove from the freezer bags when ready to use, and defrost. After defrosting, the charred skin peels off easily. Slice the peppers and pull out the seeds, which also come out more easily than when raw. This is a great way to stock up when peppers are in season.

Summer Vegetable Bread Salad with Grilled Lemon-Pepper Shrimp

SERVES 4 GENEROUSLY

Without the shrimp, this twist on the traditional panzanella salad works well with grilled steak, fish, or chicken. Include the shrimp and it becomes a perfect summer or early fall meal. Vary the proportions of peppers, green onions, croutons, and tomatoes to suit your taste.

10 large shrimp, marinated (see below)
¾ of a yellow pepper, cut lengthwise in 1-inch (2.5-cm) strips, brushed with oil and grilled or roasted
½ of a red pepper, cut lengthwise in 1-inch (2.5-cm) strips, brushed with oil and grilled or roasted
15 green onions, white and pale green part only, brushed with oil and grilled or roasted

20 Spa Croutons (see page 44)
25 cherry tomatoes, cut in half, or the equivalent in chunks of larger tomatoes
3 Tbsp. (45 mL) red wine vinegar
½ tsp. (2.5 mL) finely minced garlic
5 Tbsp. (75 mL) olive oil
salt and freshly ground black pepper
8 to 10 large basil leaves, roughly torn

FOR THE SHRIMP

Ask your fishmonger to cut off the heads of the shrimps and devein them but leave them in the shells. Marinate them in 3 parts olive oil to 1 part lemon juice, black pepper, and some minced garlic, to taste, for 20 minutes to an hour before grilling. Grill the shrimp and let them cool for 10 minutes. Shell and slice them lengthwise. If possible, add them to the salad while they are still slightly warm.

FOR THE SALAD

Put the peppers, onions, croutons, tomatoes and shrimp in a large serving bowl. Pour the vinegar into a small bowl, add the minced garlic and slowly whisk in the oil. Add salt and pepper. Adjust the vinegar and oil mixture to taste. It should be slightly on the tart side. Don't worry if the vinaigrette separates.

Pour ¾ of the vinaigrette over the salad, add more if needed, and let marinate at room temperature for 15 to 20 minutes. Add the torn basil just before serving and toss again. The croutons should be slightly soft but still have crunch.

You can serve the leftovers the next day for a homey lunch. The croutons will be soft but will have soaked up all the flavors.

Panzanella, the traditional Italian bread salad, is very simple, made only with tomatoes, onions, basil, olive oil, vinegar, and, of course, bread.

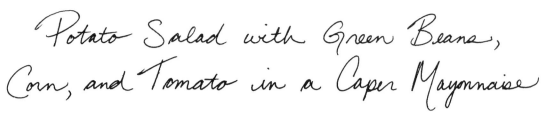

Potato Salad with Green Beans, Corn, and Tomato in a Caper Mayonnaise

SERVES 4 TO 6

I first made this salad in late August when all the vegetables needed for it were harvested from our garden. You could substitute any other late-summer vegetables for the beans and corn—zucchini, diced red pepper, cooked and diced carrot.

2½ lbs. (1.1 kg) white potatoes, peeled and halved (cut them into 1- to 1½-inch [2.5- to 3.8-cm] cubes if you're in a hurry)
2 ears of corn, shucked
1 large handful of green beans, cleaned and washed
4 Roma tomatoes

¾ cup (180 mL) Basic Mayonnaise (see page 86) or good store-bought mayonnaise
1 Tbsp. (15 mL) finely chopped fresh dill
1 Tbsp. (15 mL) chopped capers
2 to 3 Tbsp. (30 to 45 mL) finely chopped fresh chives
juice of ½ lemon
salt and freshly ground white pepper, to taste

Boil the potatoes in salted water until cooked through. Drain, and cool. Cut in cubes, and place in a serving bowl.

Cut the corn off the cob and blanch in boiling salted water for 2 to 3 minutes. Drain, and shock in cold water. Drain again and add to the potatoes.

Boil the beans in salted water until cooked through. Drain, shock in cold water, and drain again. Add to the serving bowl.

Cut the tomatoes; remove the seeds and all the insides. Cut the outside flesh into ¼-inch (.6-cm) slices and add to the serving bowl.

In a small bowl, mix the mayonnaise with the dill, capers, and chives. Add the lemon juice until the mayonnaise has a bright citrus flavor and has thinned considerably. Store-bought mayonnaise will need more lemon. Taste and add salt and pepper if necessary. Spoon over the vegetables. Toss and serve.

"Pray for peace and grace and spiritual food, for wisdom and guidance, for all these are good, but don't forget the potatoes."
—John Tyler Petee

Moroccan Roasted Beet Salad with Pomegranates and Almonds

SERVES 4 TO 6

Moroccans often season beets with cumin, paprika, and cinnamon and serve them before dinner with two or three other salads. They are always accompanied by bread. On its own, this makes a delicious appetizer, but would also be great served with a roasted pork loin rubbed with fresh ginger, garlic, thyme, and black pepper. The pomegranate seeds and almonds give the beets a festive look and a welcome crunch.

6 medium to large beets, leaves attached
1 tsp. (5 mL) Dijon mustard
2½ Tbsp. (37.5 mL) orange juice
1 tsp. (5 mL) raspberry vinegar
1 tsp. or more (5 mL) lemon juice
¼ tsp. (1.2 mL) ground cumin, toasted in a dry pan for about 30 seconds or until the cumin starts to smell aromatic

¾ tsp. or more (4 mL) paprika
¾ tsp. or more (4 mL) ground cinnamon
5 Tbsp. (75 mL) olive oil
salt and freshly ground white pepper to taste (be generous)
5 Tbsp. (75 mL) pomegranate seeds, about 1 large pomegranate, for garnish
1 to 2 Tbsp. (15 to 30 mL) almond slivers, not flakes, for garnish

Cut the leaves off the beets, wash, rip off the red stalks and reserve the leaves. Either boil the unpeeled beets in water and 1 Tbsp. (15 mL) of white wine vinegar or wrap them in foil and cook in a 375°F (190°C) oven for about an hour or until soft. Cool, peel, and cut into ¼- to ½-inch (.6- to 1.2-cm) cubes. You should have about 6 cups (1.5 L) of beets.

Cook the leaves in boiling water until wilted, about 3 to 5 minutes. Drain on paper towels and reserve.

To make the vinaigrette, spoon the mustard into a large bowl and whisk in the orange juice, raspberry vinegar, and lemon juice. Sprinkle in the cumin, paprika, and cinnamon. Slowly dribble in the oil, whisking continuously. Season with salt and pepper. You will have about ⅓ cup (80 mL).

Toss the beets in the vinaigrette and taste. Add more paprika, cinnamon, lemon juice, or salt and pepper, as you like. Toss again.

Arrange the beet greens around the edge of a serving plate. Pile the beets in the middle and garnish with pomegranate seeds and almond slivers.

COOK'S TIP

Pomegranates can be difficult to seed. Cut the fruit in half. Submerge one half in a large bowl of cool water and pick out the seeds with your fingers. The white webbing surrounding the seeds should rise to the top of the water. Remove any webbing that doesn't detach. Drain the seeds and proceed with the recipe.

"For the Lord, thy God, bringeth thee into a good land... a land of wheat, and barley, and vines, and fig trees, and pomegranates; a land of olive oil and honey." — Deuteronomy viii, 8

Sandwiches and Picnics

"If I had some bread I'd make a sandwich if I had a wich."
— Popeye, *Popeye the Sailor Man Meets Ali Baba's Forty Thieves*

ACE Grilled Cheese Sandwich

Wrapped Bocconcini Spiedini

Asiago Cheese with Oven-Roasted Tomatoes and Caramelized Onions on Focaccia

Picnic Cream Cheese with Chives on Ficelle

Open-Face Chèvre and Fresh Figs on Fruit Bread

Curried Egg with Green Apple and Cucumber on Whole Wheat

Two-Minute Cheddar and Apple on Raisin Walnut

Le Pique-Nique Français

Chèvre with Grilled Vegetables on a Calabrese Ring

Low-Fat Japanese-Style Tuna on Ciabatta

Ham and Brie with Crispy Apple

Homemade Almond Butter with Bananas and Apricot Jam

Greek Salad Sandwich

Mediterranean Chicken on Baguette

Ricotta Salata or Fresh Ricotta on Olive Bread

Roast Beef Sandwich with Roasted Garlic and Horseradish Mayonnaise

Vaughan's Thai Chicken Sandwich

Picnic Lemonade

Iced Green Tea with Lime and Mint

ACE Grilled Cheese Sandwich

MAKES 2 SANDWICHES

This adaptation of the classic grilled cheese sandwich is especially good when summer tomatoes are at their peak. Try it with Oven-Roasted Tomatoes (see page 85) in the winter. Just take care not to use too many, as they can overpower the chèvre.

4 slices olive bread *or* 4 slices country bread with 10 pitted and sliced kalamata olives
1½ Tbsp. (22.5 mL) Basil-Garlic Dip (see page 76) or store-bought pesto

4 to 5 Tbsp. (60 to 75 mL) creamy chèvre, depending on size of bread slices
1 to 2 ripe tomatoes, thickly sliced
freshly ground black pepper, to taste
1 Tbsp. (15 mL) extra virgin olive oil

Spread two pieces of olive or country bread with ¾ Tbsp. (12 mL) of Basil-Garlic Dip or pesto. Next spread a generous amount of chèvre over the dip. If using country bread, sprinkle the sliced olives over the cheese.

Layer on the thickly sliced tomatoes and some black pepper. Top with the other two pieces of bread. Brush with olive oil and grill in a grill pan or fry in a cast iron skillet.

Cut each sandwich in half and serve.

Asparagus, Beet, and
Chèvre Salad p. 121

Baby Lettuces with
Taleggio Croquettes p. 118

Whole Wheat Bran Rolls p. 28

Tuna and Scallop Ceviche
with Tropical Fruits p. 112

Field Tomato, Corn, and Grilled Onion
Salad with Giant Croutons p. 120

Picnic Lemonade p. 148

Picnic Cream Cheese with Chives on Ficelle p. 131

Roast Beef Sandwich with Roasted Garlic and Horseradish Mayonnaise p. 145

Chèvre with Grilled Vegetables on a Calabrese Ring *p. 138*

Wrapped Bocconcini Spiedini *p. 129*

Wrapped Bocconcini Spiedini

MAKES 6 SPIEDINI (KEBABS)

These kebabs make a great appetizer before Red Snapper en Papillote (see page 172). I've also served it for an informal lunch with a salad of arugula and baby tomatoes. If you can't find bocconcini—balls of young, soft mozzarella cheese—use 1-inch (2.5-cm) cubes of older mozzarella, but they will take longer to melt. If you want to serve the kebabs as snacks with drinks, just make miniature versions.

12 bocconcini, cut in half
12 to 18 slices prosciutto
30 1½-inch (3.8-cm) cubes of Calabrese, focaccia, country, or white bread

olive oil for brushing kebabs
½ cup (120 mL) olive oil
5 anchovy fillets (tinned), minced
generous squeeze of lemon juice

You will need 2 whole bocconcini, 2 to 3 slices of prosciutto, depending on their size, and 5 cubes of bread for each kebab. You'll also need 6 bamboo skewers soaked in water, or metal skewers.

Wrap each bocconcino half tightly in prosciutto. Starting and finishing with a cube of bread, thread the bread and the wrapped cheese alternately on the skewers. Lightly brush olive oil on all sides of the kebab. You may need 4 to 5 Tbsp. (60 to 75 mL) of oil.

For the sauce, heat the olive oil and minced anchovy until the oil is very warm and the fillets have almost disintegrated. Just before serving, squeeze the lemon juice into the warm sauce. Pour the sauce into a small bowl.

Heat a barbecue, grill pan, or frying pan until very hot. Place the kebabs in the hot pan. Using tongs, turn the kebabs about every 45 seconds so that the prosciutto crisps up, the cheese starts to melt, and the bread toasts. Serve one kebab per person and let them dribble the sauce over it.

Spiedo is the Italian word for a kitchen spit or skewer. Foods cooked on a spiedo, traditionally over a fire, become spiedini.

Asiago Cheese with Oven-Roasted Tomatoes and Caramelized Onions on Focaccia

MAKES 4 LARGE OR 6 SMALL SANDWICHES

This sandwich is our most popular one at the café and is mouthwatering when grilled. It's equally delicious as is, accompanied by a cold glass of beer. As part of a casual buffet, present it whole and let your guests cut off as much as they like.

2½ Tbsp. (37.5 mL) vegetable oil
3 medium yellow onions, cut into thin slices
¼ tsp. (1.2 mL) kosher salt
¼ tsp. (1.2 mL) freshly ground black pepper
½ tsp. (2.5 mL) sugar

1 focaccia, 6 x 8 inches (15 x 20 cm)
4 to 8 lettuce leaves
thinly sliced Asiago cheese, to cover bread, approximately 5 oz. (140 g)
1 recipe Oven-Roasted Tomatoes (see page 85)

Heat the oil in a frying pan, then add the onions and cook for 3 minutes, stirring constantly. Season the onions with the salt, pepper, and sugar. Lower the heat and continue cooking for about 20 minutes to half an hour, until the onions are a deep golden brown. Stir occasionally.

Cut the focaccia in half horizontally so that you have a top and bottom. Cover the lower half with lettuce, then layer with the cheese, onions, and Oven-Roasted Tomatoes. Top with the other half of the focaccia, and cut into 4 large or 6 smaller portions. Grill, if desired, on both sides until the bread is golden and the cheese is slightly melted.

The tomatoes and onions can be stored, separately, for about a week in the refrigerator.

Picnic Cream Cheese with Chives on Ficelle

MAKES 2 SANDWICHES

This simple summer sandwich is a natural for picnics or a lazy light lunch on the deck. The overlapping cucumber and tomato slices make it look wonderfully festive.

3 to 4 Tbsp. (45 to 60 mL) cream cheese
8 to 10 stalks chives, finely chopped
1 ficelle (see below)

3 slices tomato, halved
6 to 8 slices of English cucumber
salt and freshly ground black pepper

Mix the cream cheese and the chives together.

Cut the ficelle ¾ of the way through, from the top. Spread the cream cheese mixture on both halves.

Place an overlapping layer of the tomato slices and the cucumber slices, round side up, on one half of the ficelle, sticking up over the top of the bread. You may have to cut the cucumber pieces in half. Sprinkle with salt and pepper.

Close the sandwich, cut in half, and serve.

Ficelle means twine or string, in French — an apt description for this long and very thin bread that is only 1½ to 2 inches (3.8 to 5 cm) in diameter.

Open-Face Chèvre and Fresh Figs on Fruit Bread

MAKES 4 OPEN-FACED SANDWICHES

We served this sandwich, made with ricotta cheese, at a fundraiser for Willow Breast Cancer Support and Resource Services. The balsamic vinegar really brings out the earthy flavor of the figs.

4 slices fig and almond bread or any fruit or grain bread
½ cup (120 mL) very mild, creamy chèvre or fresh ricotta
2 small green figs

2 small purple figs
coarsely ground black pepper
½ tsp. (2.5 mL) balsamic vinegar

Spread each slice of bread with 2 Tbsp. (30 mL) of creamy chèvre or ricotta. Slice the figs and cover the cheese with contrasting colors of fig. Sprinkle with black pepper. Dribble a few drops of balsamic vinegar on each open-faced sandwich.

The word _sycophant_ is ancient Greek for _one who shows the f_
Figs were particularly valuable to the Greeks as a sweetener, and the first sycophant may well have been someone who exposed fig smugglers in order to curry favor with the authorities.

Curried Eggs with Green Apple and Cucumber on Whole Wheat

MAKES 2 SANDWICHES

My favorite egg recipe. I've found that even people who normally don't like egg salad devour this one. The curry gives the traditional egg mixture warmth, and the apple and cucumber add a pleasant change of texture. If you like a lot of filling, add an extra hard boiled egg. Adjust the other ingredients by an extra half except the apple and cucumber.

½ tsp. (2.5 mL) Curry Powder, or more, to taste (see below)

2 Tbsp. (30 mL) Basic Mayonnaise (see page 86) or good store-bought mayonnaise, or more, to taste

2 hard-boiled eggs, peeled and chopped

⅓ cup (80 mL) diced green apple, cut in ¼-inch (.6-cm) cubes. Peel the apple if the skin is thick.

salt and freshly ground white pepper to taste

4 slices whole wheat bread, or 1 large or 2 medium whole wheat pitas, cut in half

8 slices cucumber

alfalfa sprouts

Place the curry powder in a small skillet. Dry-roast at medium heat for 45 seconds, or until it starts to smell aromatic.

In a bowl, mix the Curry Powder and mayonnaise. Add the eggs and the apple, and mix well. Taste and season with salt and pepper. Add more mayonnaise if desired.

Spread the mixture on 2 slices of bread, or divide between the pita halves. Top with cucumber, sprouts, and the top slices of bread.

The egg salad will keep in the fridge for 3 days.

CURRY POWDER

MAKES ½ CUP (120 ML)

This is my friend Ronica Sanjani's recipe. Ronnie, an actress, host of a vegetarian cooking show, and a caterer, whips up spectacular meals at the drop of a hat. I learned how to cook Indian food in her kitchen.

2½ Tbsp. (37.5 mL) coriander seeds

2½ Tbsp. (37.5 mL) cumin seeds

1 2-inch (5-cm) cinnamon stick

1 tsp. (5 mL) ground cloves

3 bay leaves (optional—add if your garam masala doesn't contain it)

½ tsp. (2.5 mL) paprika (adds color)

2 tsp. (10 mL) ground turmeric

1 tsp. (5 mL) chili powder

1 Tbsp. (15 mL) garam masala

1 tsp. (5 mL) freshly ground black pepper

Dry-roast the ingredients in a frying pan until they begin to smell aromatic. Cool, then grind in a clean coffee grinder or with a mortar and pestle. Store in a cool, dark place for up to 6 months.

To add more heat to the curry, increase the chili powder and garam masala.

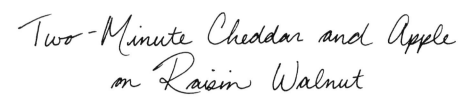

Two-Minute Cheddar and Apple on Raisin Walnut

MAKES 1 SANDWICH

This might not even take two minutes to make. Dinah Koo, a great caterer in Toronto, passed this recipe on to us when we first opened ACE. My husband could eat it every day for lunch. The trick is to use artisan-style bread, not the doughy supermarket stuff. Slice the cheddar and apple thinly and stack them. I don't know why, but they taste so much better than if they're cut into chunks.

2 slices artisan-style Raisin Walnut bread
2 oz. (57 g) old cheddar, thinly sliced
¼ to ½ of a Granny Smith apple, thinly sliced

Cover one slice of bread with the cheddar. Add the apple slices, and cover with the other slice of bread. Cut in half and eat.

COOK'S TIP

If making the sandwich ahead of time, keep the apple soaking in 1 cup (240 mL) of water and 2 tsp. (10 mL) of lemon juice to prevent browning. Drain, pat dry, and put in the sandwich at the last moment.

Le Pique-Nique Français

Pâté and Gruyère with unsalted butter on baguette always conjure up memories of France for me. Perfect picnic food. Just remember to bring along *la bière* and some ripe cherries or nectarines.

1 baguette, about 24 inches (60 cm) long
2 tsp. (10 mL) unsalted butter (optional)
6 oz. (170 g) smooth, good-quality chicken liver pâté
6 oz. (170 g) Swiss Gruyère cheese, thinly sliced

6 to 8 cornichons (small, sour French pickles) or baby dill pickles, thinly sliced, lengthwise
4 to 6 lettuce leaves
1 Tbsp. (15 mL) Dijon mustard, or to taste

Cut the baguette horizontally so that you have a top and bottom and spread butter (if using), then the pâté on the bottom half. Top with a layer of cheese, then the cornichons, and finally the lettuce. Spread the Dijon on the top half of the baguette, and close the sandwich. Wrap in wax paper or foil to transport to your picnic. Don't use plastic wrap, or the crust of the baguette will become soft and chewy.

"Without bread, without wine, love is nothing."
— French proverb

4:45 pm:
Nanthan shapes olive boules.

Chèvre with Grilled Vegetables on a Calabrese Ring

MAKES 5 LARGE SANDWICHES

This sandwich looks great as part of a buffet. You can leave it whole and let guests cut off as much as they want. It's also perfect for a picnic. Grill the vegetables a day ahead and assembly will take just a few minutes. If you can't find a Calabrese ring, a boule or oval will do. You may have to adjust the amounts of the various fillings.

1 small eggplant sliced in ¼-inch (.6-cm) rings *or*
  2 Japanese eggplant cut lengthwise in ¼-inch
  (.6-cm) slices
2 medium peppers, one red and one yellow, sliced in
  ½-inch (1.2-cm) strips lengthwise
2 medium zucchini, cut lengthwise in ¼-inch (.6-cm) slices

1 to 3 Tbsp. (15 to 45 mL) olive oil for grilling vegetables
1 Tbsp. (15 mL) chopped fresh chives (optional)
1 tsp. (5 mL) chopped fresh tarragon (optional)
½ lb. (225 g) chèvre
1 Calabrese ring
salt and freshly ground black pepper

Brush the sliced vegetables with olive oil. Grill until slightly charred, or bake at 375°F (190°C) until cooked through, about 25 minutes.

In a small bowl, mix the chives and tarragon into the chèvre.

Cut the Calabrese ring in half horizontally so you have a top and bottom. Spread both halves with the cheese. Top the bottom half with the grilled vegetables and sprinkle with salt and pepper. Place the other half of the bread on top. Take to your picnic, wrapped in foil or wax paper. Plastic wrap will leave the crust soft and chewy. Let everyone cut the sandwich into pieces when you are ready to eat.

Low-Fat Japanese-Style Tuna on Ciabatta

MAKES 4 GENEROUS SANDWICHES

Andrea Stewart, a superb chef and a former ACE employee, came up with this inventive recipe for a no-mayo tuna sandwich while she was working for us. It stayed on our menu for years. This is a slightly reworked version of her great idea.

⅛ cup (30 mL) pickled ginger
¼ cup (60 mL) rice wine vinegar
1½ tsp. (7.5 mL) wasabi powder
1 Tbsp. (15 mL) mirin
⅓ cup + 1 Tbsp. (95 mL) vegetable oil
2 6-oz. (170-g) cans packed tuna, rinsed and drained

2 green onions, chopped
1 Tbsp. (15 mL) black sesame seeds (optional)
salt and freshly ground black pepper to taste
4 ciabatta rolls or any other crusty roll with a light interior
1 avocado, peeled and sliced
½ cup (120 mL) pea or alfalfa sprouts

To make the vinaigrette, place the ginger—reserving 2 tsp. (10 mL)—the vinegar, wasabi powder, and mirin in a blender or food processor. Blend on high, while slowly dribbling in the oil.

Finely chop the reserved pickled ginger.

In a bowl, mix ¼ cup (60 mL) of the vinaigrette with the tuna. Add the green onion, the sesame seeds, and the reserved, chopped pickled ginger, mixing until combined. Add more vinaigrette if the mixture seems too dry. Season with salt and pepper. Place the tuna on half of the roll. Top with avocado and pea sprouts and the top half of the roll.

Extra vinaigrette will keep in the refrigerator for a week or more.

COOK'S TIP

Rice wine vinegar, wasabi powder, and mirin, all used in Japanese cuisine, can be found in specialty food stores. You can substitute dry sherry for rice wine vinegar, although in this recipe, because of the large amount of vinegar, I would substitute ⅛ cup (30 mL) white vinegar, ⅛ cup (30 mL) sherry, and a pinch of sugar. Taste and adjust the amounts.

Ciabatta loaves are long and wide and must have a very soft interior and thin crust in order to be worthy of their name, which means slipper in Italian.

Ham and Brie with Crispy Apple

This is a good sandwich for a picnic basket or a casual lunch with friends, with the apple adding a new dimension to a comfort food favorite. Place it whole on a cutting board and let everyone cut off as much as they want. Have some Picnic Lemonade (see page 148) on hand for the kids; you could always add a little vodka for the adults.

1 baguette, about 24 inches (60 cm) long
1 Granny Smith apple, or 3 to 4 Tbsp. (45 to 60 mL) apple chutney
½ a lemon
1 tsp. (5 mL) Dijon mustard

2½ Tbsp. (37.5 mL) Basic Mayonnaise (see page 86) or good store-bought mayonnaise
6 to 7 slices Black Forest Ham
8 to 10 ¼-inch (.6-cm) slices brie
freshly ground black pepper, to taste

Cut the baguette in half horizontally so that you have a top and bottom. If using apples, cut them in half, top to bottom, and core. Slice thinly and place the slices in a bowl filled with water and lemon juice to prevent browning.

Mix the mustard and mayonnaise and spread on the bottom half of the baguette. If you are using apple chutney instead of fresh apples, spread it on the bottom half of the baguette and the mustard mayonnaise mixture on the top half of the bread.

Place the ham on the bottom half of the baguette. Top with the cheese and arrange the drained and dried apple slices diagonally over the cheese.

Grind a small amount of black pepper over the apples. Top with the other half of the baguette. Wrap in foil or wax paper to transport to your picnic. Don't use plastic wrap, or the crust of the baguette will become soft and chewy.

"Better to eat bread in peace, than cake amid turmoil."
— Slovakian proverb

Homemade Almond Butter with Bananas and Apricot Jam

MAKES 2 SANDWICHES

If you've never tried almond butter, you're in for a wonderful taste treat. Chances are you'll never eat peanut butter again. Roasting the nuts really intensifies the flavor.

1½ cups (360 mL) slivered or whole chopped, skinned almonds (not flakes)
5 to 6 Tbsp. (75 to 90 mL) canola oil

⅛ tsp. (.5 mL) kosher salt
4 slices good white bread
1 banana
2 Tbsp. (30 mL) apricot jam or more to taste

Preheat the oven to 400°F (200°C).

Sprinkle the almonds in one layer on a baking sheet. Roast in the oven for about 5 minutes, stirring occasionally or until the nuts are dark golden brown. Remove from the oven and cool. Then place the almonds and the salt in a food processor and pulse 2 or 3 times. Slowly add the canola oil until the nuts are smooth and bound together. Taste, and add more oil if necessary. For a chunkier consistency, start by adding 4 Tbsp. (60 mL) of oil to the nuts before processing. Pulse carefully, as the nuts break down very quickly. Add more oil if necessary.

You will get about 1 cup (240 mL) of almond butter, much more than these sandwiches require. The remainder will keep, refrigerated, for at least one month.

Spread 1 to 1½ Tbsp. (15 to 22.5 mL) or more of the almond butter on 2 pieces of bread. Slice the banana in coins and cover the almond butter. Spread at least 1 Tbsp. (15 mL) of apricot jam on each of the other 2 pieces of bread. Place those slices, jam-side down, on the bananas. Cut in half and serve.

Greek Salad Sandwich

This is definitely a summer treat. The crunch of the vegetables, the smoothness of the tapenade, and the saltiness of the feta are a winning combination. Plus, it looks gorgeous.

½ a small red onion, thinly sliced

1 6 x 8 inch (15 x 20 cm) focaccia

3 to 4 Tbsp. (45 to 60 mL) Tapenade (see page 166) or good store-bought tapenade or olive paste

3 to 4 large lettuce leaves, your choice of lettuce

9 to 12 slices tomato

3 oz. (90 g) feta cheese

9 to 12 slices of English cucumber

salt and freshly ground black pepper

1 tsp. (5 mL) minced fresh oregano, or ½ tsp. (2.5 mL) dried oregano

1 Tbsp. (15 mL) red wine vinegar or balsamic vinegar

2 Tbsp. (30 mL) extra virgin olive oil

Soak the red onion slices in cold water for half an hour, then drain. This will mellow their flavor.

Slice the focaccia horizontally so that you have a top and bottom. Spread the tapenade over the bottom piece, then cover with the lettuce, tomato, feta, cucumber, and red onion. Sprinkle with salt, pepper, and oregano. If you plan to eat the sandwich right away, drizzle the combined oil and vinegar over the onion, then top with the other piece of focaccia.

If you're not eating it right away, mix the vinegar and olive oil and put into a container. Wrap in foil or wax paper and transport the sandwich to your picnic whole, then take off the top slice of focaccia and drizzle the sandwich with the oil and vinegar.

Replace the top slice of bread, and cut the sandwich into 4 or 6 pieces.

Mediterranean Chicken on Baguette

MAKES 4 LARGE SANDWICHES

Left whole, this sandwich is a great choice to transport to a friend's house for lunch or a casual supper. Wrap it in foil or waxed paper and then cut it in pieces when you arrive. Radishes are a good accompaniment, and brownies with fresh fruit make a great dessert. You could also serve this chicken salad on a bed of greens. In that case, use a little less vinegar.

8 oz. (225 g) diced, skinless, cooked chicken
¼ green pepper, finely diced
¼ red pepper, finely diced
3 green onions (use all of the white and ¾ of the green part of the onion), quartered lengthwise and then finely chopped

¼ cup (60 mL) Basic Mayonnaise (see page 86) or good store-bought mayonnaise
1 tsp. (5 mL) red wine vinegar
1 tsp. (5 mL) dried, or 2 tsp. (10 mL) minced fresh oregano
salt and freshly ground black pepper
1 baguette
4 to 5 leaves of Boston or leaf lettuce

In a bowl, mix the chicken, peppers, and onion. In a separate bowl, mix the mayonnaise with the vinegar and oregano to taste. Toss the mayonnaise mixture into the chicken and season with salt and pepper. The chicken should taste quite tart. Add more mayonnaise and vinegar if the mixture seems too dry.

Cut the baguette horizontally so that you have a top and bottom. You may need to remove some of the middle. Line the bottom with lettuce leaves, and cover with chicken. Close the baguette and cut into 4 pieces, if serving right away.

In October 1920, a new law came into effect in France that prevented bakers from working before 4 a.m. That didn't leave enough hours to prepare big breads, because they took too long to rise properly before baking. Ever inventive, the bakers created the skinny, quickly prepared baguette to satisfy their morning customers.

Ricotta Salata or Fresh Ricotta on Olive Bread

MAKES 2 SANDWICHES

Here are two recipes using ricotta. Fresh ricotta, which is creamy and delicate, is the easiest to find. Ricotta salata is a hard cheese and has a more pronounced flavor. Add more basil and mayo if you like, and eat right away, as the tomatoes will soak through the bread.

FRESH RICOTTA

Fresh ricotta can be made from either cow's or sheep's milk. Sheep's-milk ricotta is harder to find than the cow's-milk kind, and not quite as smooth, but it's richer tasting, with a slight vanilla tinge.

4 to 6 Tbsp. (60 to 90 mL) fresh ricotta (Tuscan sheep's milk, if possible)

4 slices olive bread, or 4 slices country bread or ciabatta and 10 pitted, black kalamata olives, sliced in half

6 to 8 thick slices very ripe tomato

salt and freshly ground black pepper

1 tsp. (5 mL) minced chives

Spread 2 Tbsp. (30 mL) of ricotta—or more, if you like—on 2 slices of bread. If using country bread, spread the olives over the cheese. Top with the tomato slices. Sprinkle with salt and pepper and minced chives. Top with the remaining bread slices. Slice in half and eat.

RICOTTA SALATA

Ricotta salata can be bought young or old. The younger has the texture of mozzarella and is slightly creamy. The older has the hardness of a young Parmigiano Reggiano and can be very salty. You may wish to test the saltiness of the older version.

2 to 3 basil leaves, depending on size

1 Tbsp. (15 mL) Basic Mayonnaise (see page 86) or good store-bought mayonnaise

4 slices olive bread, or 4 slices country bread or ciabatta and 10 pitted kalamata olives, sliced in half

2 to 4 Boston lettuce leaves

8 to 10 very thin slices ricotta salata

6 to 8 thick slices very ripe tomato

freshly ground black pepper

Mince the basil and mix into the mayonnaise. Spread on 2 slices of bread. Lay the lettuce on the bread. Top with the cheese and tomato. Add the olives if using country bread or ciabatta. Sprinkle with black pepper. Top with bread, cut in half and eat.

Roast Beef Sandwich with Roasted Garlic and Horseradish Mayonnaise

MAKES 4 SANDWICHES

This was one of the original sandwiches at our café. Ten years later, we're still making it. The horseradish and roasted garlic, great accompaniments to beef, raise it above the ordinary. If you prefer to roast your own beef, slice the meat ¼ inch (.6 cm) thick and build an open-faced sandwich. Grilling the bread would be good too. Try any leftover mayonnaise with cold roast pork or smoked trout.

¼ cup (60 mL) Basic Mayonnaise (see page 86) or good store-bought mayonnaise
⅛ cup (30 mL) well-drained horseradish
½ tsp. (2.5 mL) Dijon mustard

1 to 2 cloves roasted garlic (see Cook's Tip)
8 slices sourdough bread
8 to 12 thin slices medium-rare roast beef
baby spinach leaves
salt and freshly ground pepper

In a small bowl, mix together the mayonnaise, horseradish, mustard, and peeled, mashed, roasted garlic.

Spread a thin layer of the mayonnaise mixture on 4 slices of bread. Add 2 or 3 slices of roast beef to each. Top with baby spinach and season with salt and pepper. Top with another slice of bread. The garlic–horseradish mayonnaise will keep, refrigerated, for up to 5 days.

COOK'S TIP

To roast garlic: preheat the oven to 375°F (190°C). Slice ¼ inch (.6 cm) off the top of a garlic bulb, just cutting off the tops of the cloves. Sprinkle with a little olive oil, if you like. Wrap in foil and roast in the oven for 1 hour or until soft. The roasted garlic can then be squeezed out of its skin. The unused cloves of garlic will keep, refrigerated, for 1 week. Try adding them to mashed potatoes or a vinaigrette.

"Roast beef, medium, is not only a food. It is a philosophy. Seated at life's dining table, with the menu of morals before you, your eye wanders a bit over the _entrées_, the _hors d'oeuvres_, and the things `à la` though you know that roast beef, medium, is safe and sane, and sure." — Edna Ferber

Vaughan's Thai Chicken Sandwich

MAKES 2 SANDWICHES

This sandwich takes a bit of planning, but it's worth it. You could also serve it open-faced with an Asian-based coleslaw as a casual supper. In that case, you may want to grill the bread. New Zealand born chef Vaughan Chittock invented this while he was on staff at ACE.

2 Tbsp. (30 mL) light sesame seeds
2 Tbsp. (30 mL) sesame oil
1 Tbsp. (15 mL) light-colored soy sauce
1 Tbsp. (15 mL) balsamic vinegar
1 clove garlic, chopped
1 Tbsp. (15 mL) grated fresh ginger
2 Tbsp. (30 mL) chopped fresh coriander

1 large chicken breast, deboned and skinned, about 8 oz (225 g)
2 baby bok choy
1 to 2 Tbsp. (15 to 30 mL) mango chutney
4 slices country loaf
pea sprouts
chives, for garnish

Toast the sesame seeds in a dry skillet over medium heat until they are dark golden, about 1½ minutes.

In a bowl, combine the oil, soy sauce, vinegar, garlic, ginger, sesame seeds, and 1 Tbsp. (15 mL) of the coriander. Add the chicken and toss gently. Let marinate in the refrigerator for at least 3 hours.

Sear the chicken in a frying pan on high heat for 1 minute on each side. Turn the temperature down to medium low and cook for about 10 more minutes, until the center of the chicken is no longer pink. Be careful not to overcook.

Fill a pot with enough water to cover the bok choy and bring to a boil. Put the bok choy in the boiling water for about 1 minute to blanch; drain and set aside. If the bok choy are large, slice in half lengthwise before cooking.

Remove the chicken from the pan and let rest for 10 minutes. Slice the chicken on an angle to create wide slices. Slice in half, lengthwise, any bok choy that are still whole. Spread the mango chutney on two slices of bread. Add layers of the chicken, bok choy, and pea sprouts. Sprinkle with the remaining coriander and some chives. Top with the other slices of bread.

COOK'S TIP

When toasting any seeds or spices, always start with a cold skillet. You'll have much better control of the toasting process and won't end up burning them.

"...poultry is for the cook what canvas is for the painter."
— Jean-Anthelme Brillat-Savarin

6:10 pm: John
rounds country boules.

Picnic Lemonade

The inspiration for this lemonade comes from Fentons Restaurant, of Toronto. Fentons has been closed for years now, but during its run, every meal there was magical. (Note to travelers: Fentons' proprietors continue to make similar magic at Acton's Bar and Café in Wolfville, Nova Scotia.)

1 cup (240 mL) water
½ cup (120 mL) sugar
juice of 5 lemons or more, to make about 2 cups (475 mL)

1 25-oz. (750-mL) bottle carbonated water
3 cups ice
lemon slices, raspberries, and fresh mint, for garnish

In a saucepan, bring the water and the sugar to a boil. Cool.

In a large pitcher, mix together ¾ cup (180 mL) of the cooled sugar syrup, and all the lemon juice, carbonated water, and ice. Taste and add more syrup if needed.

Garnish each glass with a slice of lemon, three raspberries, and a sprig of mint.

Iced Green Tea with Lime and Mint

MAKES 4 CUPS (950 ML)

I first had this drink in Vietnam and found it even more refreshing than regular iced tea. Do not be tempted to steep the green tea leaves longer than you would normally and add ice. The drink will take on a bitter taste. Instead, add more green tea and steep it for the normal length of time. The extra sugar syrup will keep for weeks refrigerated.

1 cup (240 mL) water
½ cup (120 mL) sugar
4 cups (950 mL) strong green tea
1 lime
fresh mint to garnish

In a saucepan, bring the water and the sugar to a boil. Cool.

Make 4 cups of strong green tea. Cool in the refrigerator.

Slice the lime in half around the middle. Slice one of the halves in slices. Juice the other half.

Pour the tea into 2 or 3 glasses. Then pour 2 teaspoons (10 mL) of sugar syrup into each glass. Add ¼ tsp. (1.2 mL) of lime juice. Taste. Stir and add more of the sugar syrup and lime if you wish. Add one or two ice cubes to each glass—just enough to keep the tea chilled, but not enough to dilute the flavor.

Garnish each glass with a lime slice and a sprig of mint.

Although it comes from the same plant as black tea, green tea is steamed instead of fermented, which is why it tastes so different. In addition to the taste difference, steaming also preserves the vitamin K naturally found in tea leaves, which is used by the body to aid in blood clotting, but which gets lost in fermentation.

Not Just Meat and Potatoes

Burger Quartet

Rack of Lamb with Garlic-Herb Crust

Garlic and Black Pepper–Marinated Fillet of Beef on a Bed of Arugula

Pork Tenderloin in a Prune-Marsala Sauce

Hungarian Minced Veal with Mustard-Yogurt Sauce

Marinated Chicken, Pearl Onion, and Bread Kebabs

Chicken Tagine

Seared Tuna Minute-Steaks with Tapenade and Tomato Confit

Cod and Smoked Salmon Cakes with Romesco Sauce and Lemon Mayonnaise

Spaghetti with Lobster, Cherry Tomatoes, and Toasted Breadcrumbs

Red Snapper en Papillote

Roasted Salmon with Asparagus, Zucchini, Corn, Grilled Onions, and Tomatoes

Apple Onion Bread Pudding

Green Beans with a Soffrito and Toasted Breadcrumbs

Pennette Gratin with Wild Mushrooms

Whole Cauliflower with Dijon-Bechamel Sauce and Buttered Breadcrumbs

Potato Croquettes

Savory Carrot and Minted Pea Pudding

"Strange to see how a good dinner and feasting reconciles everybody." — Samuel Pepys

Burger Quartet
The Cosmopolitan Burger

MAKES 4 LARGE BURGERS

This twist on the basic cheeseburger substitutes Gruyère or chèvre for cheddar (or processed slices), and spicy sweet tomato chutney for ketchup. It can also be served open-faced on a thick slice of grilled bread. The small center of herbed butter keeps the burger moist. Fries tossed with salt and parsley complete the picture.

4 tsp. (20 mL) unsalted butter, at room temperature
1 tsp. (5 mL) finely chopped chives
1½ lbs. (700 g) minced beef
1 egg, lightly beaten
½ tsp. (2.5 mL) kosher salt
¼ tsp. (1.2 mL) freshly ground white pepper
1½ tsp. (7.5 mL) finely minced onion
½ tsp. (2.5 mL) Worcestershire sauce

¼ to ½ cup (60 to 120 mL) coarse fresh breadcrumbs, made from white or Calabrese bread (see page 43)
4 burger rolls, sliced, *or* 4 thick slices white, Calabrese, or sourdough bread

TOPPINGS
Gruyère or chèvre
Dijon mustard
lettuce
Tomato Chutney (see below)

Mix the softened unsalted butter and the chives together. Form into 4 equal-sized disks. Wrap in foil and chill until very cold, at least an hour.

Put the minced meat in a bowl. Add the egg, salt, pepper, onion, and Worcestershire sauce. Mix together lightly (hands are best). Add ¼ cup (60 mL) of the breadcrumbs. Mix. Add more crumbs if needed. The mixture should just hold together.

Divide the beef into 4 portions. Make patties, hiding one pat of the chilled butter and chive mixture in the center of each burger. Make a small ½-inch (1.2-cm) dent in the top of each patty to ensure a flat top when cooking, to hold the condiments better. Chill the patties until half an hour before cooking.

Barbecue, grill, or pan-fry the patties to your desired doneness. If using chèvre, top the burger with it 45 seconds before removing from the heat. The Gruyère cheese will take a little longer to melt. Lay the burger buns on the grill, cut-side down, just before you put the cheese on the burgers.

As soon as the cheese melts, remove the burgers and buns from the grill. Spread mustard on the bun, top with a lettuce leaf, and then add the burger and tomato chutney to taste. Top with the other half of the bun and enjoy. If serving open-faced, lightly grill or toast the bread and build the sandwich the same way.

TOMATO CHUTNEY
5 cups (1.2 L) tomatoes, peeled and cut into chunks *or*
3 28-oz. (796 mL) cans tomatoes, drained and peeled
¾ to 1 cup (180 to 240 mL) sugar

1½ inch (3.8-cm) piece of ginger, about 1 inch (2.5 cm) in diameter, peeled and grated
3 Tbsp. (45 mL) minced garlic
½ tsp. (2.5 mL) crushed red pepper flakes
1½ to 1¾ cups (360 to 420 mL) cider vinegar
1½ tsp. (7.5 mL) kosher salt

Combine all the ingredients in a heavy-bottomed stainless steel pot, starting with ¾ cup (120 mL) sugar and 1½ cups (360 mL) cider vinegar. Simmer over low heat until thick, stirring occasionally. There should still be some texture to the tomatoes. This should take about 1 to 1 ½ hours, depending on the water content of the tomatoes. Canned tomatoes will cook in less time. If there is still a lot of liquid left, increase the heat and bring the chutney to a simmer, but watch that it doesn't burn and that the tomatoes don't reduce to a paste.

Tomatoes vary in acidity, depending on the type and the season. Taste and add more sugar and vinegar, if needed. If you add more sugar, heat until the sugar has dissolved. Cool. Taste again, and if the cooled chutney needs more sugar or vinegar, add those now, reheat the chutney, and let it cool again before using. Tomato chutney will keep in the refrigerator for 1 month or can be canned using traditional methods.

COOK'S TIP

If using canned tomatoes, the drained juice can be used in your favorite soup or risotto recipe. Or, freeze the juice in ice trays and use the cubes for Bloody Marys.

Indian-Style Chicken Burger with Chutney and Raita

MAKES 3 REGULAR-SIZED BURGERS OR 6 MINI-BURGERS

This light, delicious burger is a favorite at our house. Try serving it with steamed corn covered in butter and sprinkled with a little chili powder and lime juice, a simple green salad, and Indian beer. Finish with sliced melon drizzled with honey and lemon. As with all the burgers in this book, you can also serve it open-faced on a thick slice of grilled bread. Raita, an Indian condiment made with yogurt, is perfect used as a topping.

1 lb. (455 g) minced chicken
1 large clove garlic, very finely minced
1 egg, lightly beaten
½ tsp. (2.5 mL) curry powder
up to 1 cup (240 mL) fine, dry breadcrumbs made
   from white or Calabrese bread
¾ tsp. (4 mL) kosher salt
½ tsp. (2.5 mL) freshly ground white or black pepper

TOPPINGS
¼ cup (60 mL) mango chutney
I large handful of mixed greens (avoid stronger flavored greens
   such as arugula as they will overpower the chicken)
3 burger rolls, *or* 6 small dinner rolls, *or* 3 thick slices white,
   country white, Calabrese, or ciabatta bread
Raita (see page 154)

Place the minced chicken in a bowl. Add the garlic, egg, curry powder, ½ cup (120 mL) of breadcrumbs, and salt and pepper. Mix together. The chicken should be quite moist and just loosely bound. Add more breadcrumbs if necessary.

Shape into 3 patties or 6 mini-patties. They will feel sticky and be more delicate than minced beef. Make a small indentation about the size of a quarter in the middle of each burger to ensure a flat cooked burger, not one that all your condiments will slide off.

Brush the patties with vegetable oil and grill the large ones for approximately 5 to 6 minutes per side or until cooked through. The mini-patties will take approximately 3½ to 4 minutes per side.

ASSEMBLY

Toast or heat the burger buns. Spread the chutney on the bottom part of the bun. Place the greens on the chutney. Put the hot burger on the lettuces. Spoon the raita over the chicken and top with the other half of the bun.

If using bread, lightly grill or toast the bread and build the open-face sandwich on a single slice, in the same way.

RAITA
1 cup (240 mL) 2% or 4% yogurt
1 tsp. (5 mL) ground cumin
1 5-inch (12.5-cm) piece English cucumber, seeded
   and coarsely grated

1 small tomato, seeded and finely chopped
1 to 2 tsp. (5 to 10 mL) minced fresh mint (optional)
2 grinds of white pepper

If you have time, drain the yogurt for up to 1 hour, to thicken. Lightly toast the cumin in a dry frying pan at medium high for about 30 seconds. Pat the grated cucumber dry with a paper towel. Add the cucumber, tomato, mint (if using), and white pepper to the yogurt and mix. Keep cool until serving time.

COOK'S TIP

The raita can be made the day before and held in the refrigerator, but you may have to drain off some liquid. The burgers can also be made beforehand, but bring them to room temperature before cooking.

The word _chutney_ has been adopted into the English language from the Indian _chatni_, which, in Sanskrit, means "licking good."

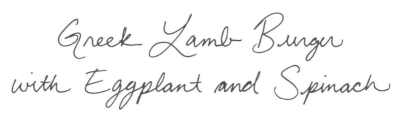

Greek Lamb Burger with Eggplant and Spinach

MAKES 4 BURGERS

Lamb, roasted garlic, and spices combine to make a great burger. The grilled eggplant adds a low-fat creaminess and tastes delicious served with oven-roasted sweet potatoes. The burger can also be served as an open-faced sandwich.

1¼ lb. (565 g) minced lamb
4 to 5 cloves roasted garlic, mashed (see page 145)
½ heaping tsp. (2.5 mL) ground cinnamon
½ tsp. (2.5 mL) ground allspice
1 heaping Tbsp. (15 mL) minced fresh oregano
1 egg, lightly beaten
salt and freshly ground black pepper
2 to 3 Tbsp. (30 to 45 mL) coarse fresh breadcrumbs made from white or Calabrese bread (see page 43)

4 burger buns, *or* 4 thick slices white, country white, or olive bread
Basic Mayonnaise, to taste (see page 86) or good store-bought mayonnaise
1 Japanese eggplant, sliced in coins, brushed with olive oil and grilled
8 to 12 leaves baby spinach, cleaned and drained
1 large ripe tomato

Mix the lamb, garlic, cinnamon, allspice, and oregano in a bowl. Add the egg to the meat mixture, using either a fork or your hands. Add salt and pepper to taste and enough breadcrumbs to bind the mixture.

Form 4 patties. Make a small indentation about the size of a quarter in the center of each patty, to ensure a flat cooked surface for condiments.

Grill the burgers and cut the buns. (The buns can also be toasted.)

ASSEMBLY

Spread as much mayonnaise as you like on the bottom half of each bun, top with the grilled eggplant, then the burger. Finish with the spinach, a slice of tomato, and the top half of the bun. If serving open-face, lightly grill or toast the bread and build the sandwich on a single slice as described above.

The uncooked burgers and the cooked eggplant can be prepared up to a day ahead. Warm the eggplant before serving.

Serve with oven-roasted chunks of peeled sweet potato sliced into giant half moons. Spray them with canola oil or olive oil, sprinkle with salt, and roast at 375°F (190°C) for about 45 minutes, turning if needed.

6:20 pm: Sabeysan and Roy
sheet dough for cheese twists.

12 am: Sergio
scores the baguettes
moments before they head
for the oven room.

6:30 pm: John loads country boules into the proofer.

Swedish Pork Burger with Onion and Apple Sauté

By the middle of summer I'm ready for a burger that's a little different, and sometimes it's nice to be able to offer your guests a choice off the grill. Accompany this one with Croatian Red and Yellow Pepper Salad (see page 122) and some potato chips. Lemon or raspberry sorbet and some cookies would be great for dessert. Serving the burger open-face on a thick slice of grilled bread works too.

1½ lbs. (700 g) minced pork
1 egg, lightly beaten
½ tsp. (2.5 mL) kosher salt
¼ tsp. (1.2 mL) freshly ground white pepper
2 tsp. (10 mL) grated fresh ginger
½ tsp. (2.5 mL) finely minced garlic
¼ heaping tsp. (1.2 mL) fresh thyme or a large pinch of dried thyme

¼ to ½ cup (60 to 120 mL) coarse fresh breadcrumbs made from white or Calabrese bread (see page 43)
4 burger buns, sliced, *or* 4 thick slices Calabrese, country white bread, or focaccia

TOPPINGS
honey mustard
baby frisée
Onion and Apple Sauté (see below)

Put the minced meat in a bowl. Add all the ingredients except the breadcrumbs. Mix together lightly with your hands. Then sprinkle the breadcrumbs on the mixture and mix in. The mixture should just hold together.

Divide the mixture into 4 patties, with a ½-inch (.6-cm) indentation in the top of each burger to ensure a flat top for condiments. Chill the patties until half an hour before cooking.

ASSEMBLY

Barbecue, grill, or pan-fry the burgers. Pork is safe served slightly pink. Grill or toast the buns. Remove the burgers and buns from the grill. Spread the honey mustard on the bottom half of each bun, top with the frisée or lettuce of your choice, and then add the burger and some of the Onion and Apple Sauté. Top with the other side of the bun. If serving open-face, lightly grill or toast the bread and build the sandwich on a single slice, as described above.

ONION AND APPLE SAUTÉ
1 large Granny Smith apple, peeled and cut in ¼-inch (.6 cm) slices.
2 Tbsp. (30 mL) unsalted butter
3 medium cooking onions, thinly sliced

Put the apple slices in a bowl of cold water with 2 tsp. (10 mL) of lemon juice to prevent browning.

Melt the butter over medium heat and add the onions. Sauté, stirring, for about 10 minutes or until the onions are soft and start to go dark golden. Drain and pat the apples dry. Add to the frying pan and sauté until golden but not falling apart. Reserve.

COOK'S TIP

If you don't have time to make the onion and apple garnish, you may want to add more ginger, garlic, and thyme to the pork mixture.

Rack of Lamb with Garlic-Herb Crust

SERVES 4 GENEROUSLY

I cannot claim credit for this simple and delicious recipe. It was given to me by Amos Bomze of Toronto's wonderful butcher shop, Olliffe. If you like perfectly pink rack of lamb, follow the cooking times to the minute. I promise, you won't be disappointed. You could serve this with Savory Carrot and Minted Pea Pudding (see page 182). A simple carrot purée would also be good.

3 cloves garlic, minced
2 tsp. (10 mL) chopped fresh or 1 tsp. (5 mL) dried rosemary
1 tsp. (5 mL) chopped fresh or ½ tsp. (2.5 mL) dried oregano
2 tsp. (10 mL) extra virgin olive oil
1 cup (240 mL) coarse white or country fresh breadcrumbs (see page 43)

salt and freshly ground white pepper to taste
2 medium-sized racks of lamb at room temperature
2 cloves garlic
salt and pepper (be generous)
1 Tbsp. (15 mL) unsalted butter
1 Tbsp. (15 mL) canola or vegetable oil
½ cup (120 mL) Dijon mustard

Preheat the oven to 350°F (175°C).

Mix the minced garlic, herbs, and olive oil together. Gently toss into the breadcrumbs. Add the salt and pepper. Set aside.

Bring the lamb racks to room temperature; otherwise it will affect the cooking time. Score the fat on the racks into large diamond shapes. Cut the 2 remaining garlic cloves in half and rub over all sides of the fat and meat. Sprinkle all sides of the meat liberally with salt and pepper. Heat the oil and butter in a frying pan and sear the meat on all sides for about 1 minute per side. Wrap the bones in tin foil so they do not darken. Transfer to a baking pan and roast for 15 to 16 minutes.

Remove from the oven and spread ¼ cup (60 mL) of mustard on each rack. It seems like a lot, but don't worry—it needs it. Pat ½ cup (120 mL) of the breadcrumbs firmly on top of the mustard on each rack. Return to the oven for 10 minutes. This will give you rosy lamb. Cook for another 4 minutes for medium. Let the lamb rest for at least 10 minutes before cutting. Cut between every second bone.

"Next to eating good dinners, a healthy man with a benevolent turn of mind must like, I think, to read about them."
— William Makepeace Thackeray

Garlic and Black Pepper–Marinated Fillet of Beef on a Bed of Arugula

SERVES 8 VERY GENEROUSLY

Serving steak on a bed of arugula drizzled with oil is an old Tuscan recipe. This updated version substitutes fillet for beef steak and includes a dry marinade as well as a good squeeze of lemon juice. A grilled vegetable salad and boiled baby potatoes tossed in butter and chopped chives make a perfect summer dinner. In colder weather, if arugula is not available, serve the sliced fillet on sourdough or Calabrese bread rubbed with garlic. The beef juices will permeate the bread, making for a truly decadent dinner.

Two rules you should follow to ensure a perfectly cooked fillet:

1. Bring the meat to room temperature before cooking so that it is not cold in the middle when it goes into the oven.

2. Let the meat rest for at least 10 to 15 minutes to allow it to finish cooking and the juices to redistribute throughout the fillet.

6 to 8 cloves garlic, peeled and mashed
up to 3 Tbsp. (45 mL) coarsely ground black pepper
3½ to 4 pounds (1.6 to 1.8 kg) fillet of beef
1 to 2 Tbsp. (15 to 30 mL) extra virgin olive oil

1 Tbsp. (15 mL) kosher salt
6 to 8 heaping handfuls of baby arugula
1 Tbsp. (15 mL) lemon juice
1 to 2 Tbsp. (15 to 30 mL) assertive-tasting extra virgin olive oil (Tuscan, if possible)

Rub the garlic and black pepper onto all sides of the fillet. Wrap in plastic wrap and marinate in the refrigerator for up to 12 hours.

One hour before serving, remove the fillet from the fridge and allow it to come to room temperature. If one end is thicker than the other, roll the thinner side under itself.

Preheat the oven to 450°F (230°C).

Brush the garlic off the fillet, leaving on as much pepper as possible. With your hands, rub 1 to 2 Tbsp. (15 to 30 mL) of oil over all sides of the beef. Season very generously with salt and more black pepper.

Roast in an uncovered pan for 22 to 24 minutes for rare, 27 to 29 minutes for medium rare. Let the meat rest for at least 10 to 15 minutes before cutting into ¼- to ½-inch (.6- to 1.2-cm) slices.

Cover the serving plate with a good layer of arugula, overlap the fillet slices onto the greens, and drizzle the meat with the lemon juice and then the olive oil. Make sure that everyone gets a generous helping of arugula with their meat.

COOK'S TIP

The thickest part of the meat registers 105° to 108°F (40° to 42°C) on a meat thermometer for very rare, 115° to 118°F (46° to 48°C) for medium rare, 125° to 128°F (52° to 53°C) for medium. The meat will continue to cook after it is removed from the oven. If you don't let it rest 15 minutes, your meat will be undercooked and will lose a lot of its juices.

Spaghetti with Lobster, Cherry Tomatoes, and Toasted Breadcrumbs p. 170

Iced Green Tea with Lime and Mint p. 149

Indian-Style Chicken Burger
with Chutney and Raita p. 153

Savory Carrot and Minted Pea Pudding p.182

Seared Tuna Minute-Steaks with
Tapenade and Tomato Confit p. 166

Pork Tenderloin in a Prune-Marsala Sauce

This is a simple supper that can easily be prepared ahead. Make the sauce and sauté the pork, keeping them separate until just before serving. Combine and heat for a few minutes. Serve, heaped onto pieces of grilled Calabrese (see page 26), or with rustic Jalapeño Cornbread (see page 36) or garlic mashed potatoes and steamed carrots or roasted squash.

PRUNE-MARSALA SAUCE

1 Tbsp. (15 mL) unsalted butter or vegetable oil
1 cup (240 mL) finely chopped shallots (approximately 4 to 6 shallots)
½ cup (120 mL) chicken stock
20 prunes, sliced in half
generous ½ tsp. (2.5 mL) fresh thyme leaves
5 Tbsp. (75 mL) Marsala

PORK TENDERLOIN

2 pork tenderloins, approximately 1 lb. (455 g) each, cut into ½-inch (1.2-cm) thick medallions
salt and freshly ground white pepper, to taste
2 Tbsp. (30 mL) vegetable oil or butter
1 cup (240 mL) chicken stock
1 Tbsp. (15 mL) unsalted butter

FOR THE PRUNE-MARSALA SAUCE

Melt the butter or oil in a medium-sized frying pan. Add the shallots and sauté over medium-low heat for 3 to 4 minutes. Add the ½ cup (120 mL) of stock and simmer until the liquid has almost disappeared, about another 3 to 4 minutes. Add the prunes, thyme, and Marsala and simmer until the Marsala is syrupy, about 2 to 3 minutes. Set aside.

FOR THE PORK TENDERLOIN

Season the pork medallions with salt and pepper. Heat the oil or butter in a frying pan until shimmering. Add the pork and sauté on each side for about 2 minutes. Lower the heat if the meat starts to burn. Remove the pork and place in a bowl. Deglaze the pan with 1 cup (240 mL) of chicken stock and simmer until it is reduced by half.

Pour the reduced stock and pork juices into the Prune-Marsala Sauce and heat. Then mix in the 1 Tbsp. (15 mL) of butter. Finally, add the pork medallions and heat through.

Overlap the medallions on the bread or on a serving dish and spoon the prune sauce overtop.

Prunes were first brought to France by pilgrims and crusaders returning from thirteenth-century Damascus. They planted the trees in Toulouse, where the monks who gathered the fallen fruit noticed that, when dried, it would last into the cold winter months.

Hungarian Minced Veal with Mustard-Yogurt Sauce

SERVES 6 GENEROUSLY

I think that this is the most versatile recipe in this book. It makes a delicate and delicious meatloaf and can also be formed into hamburgers. But my favorite way to serve it is to wrap the meat around kebab skewers, brush them with oil and grill them on an open fire. Serve the meat with the Mustard-Yogurt Sauce, a tomato-and-red-onion salad, the Croatian Red and Yellow Pepper Salad (see page 122) and some warm olive or sourdough bread. Mashed potatoes and boiled carrots make good wintertime accompaniments, too.

4 slices white bread, crusts removed
¾ cup (180 mL) homogenized milk
2 lbs. (900 g) minced veal or a combination of minced pork and veal
2 eggs, lightly beaten
1¼ cups (300 mL) finely chopped cooking onion (approximately 2 medium onions)

2 tsp. (10 mL) finely minced garlic (optional)
½ generous cup (120 mL) minced fresh parsley
¾ tsp. (4 mL) kosher salt
¼ tsp. (1.2 mL) freshly ground white pepper
4 hard-boiled eggs (optional)
¼ to ½ cup (60 to 120 mL) dried breadcrumbs (optional) (see page 43)
Mustard-Yogurt Sauce, for topping (see over)

In a shallow bowl, soak the bread in the milk until soggy. Squeeze the milk out of the bread with your hands. It will be very mushy.

Put the meat in a bowl large enough to hold all the ingredients. Add the soaked bread, eggs, onion, garlic, parsley, salt, and pepper. Use your hands to completely mix things together.

1. MEATLOAF

Preheat the oven to 375°F (190°C).

The meatloaf can be made free-form or in a loaf pan. If you want to do a free-form loaf with hard-boiled eggs, cover a baking pan with foil and pat a little more than ⅓ of the meat mixture onto the foil in an oblong shape. Slice the ends off the eggs to ensure that all servings have some egg yolk. Roll them in breadcrumbs and butt them together down the length of the meat. Cover with the rest of the mixture.

Bake for 50 minutes to 1 hour. If you don't use the boiled eggs, the meatloaf will need to bake a little longer.

You can also make individual meatloaves in muffin tins. Mound the meat up over the top of the cups to resemble muffins. Bake for about 30 to 40 minutes, depending on the size of the muffin cups.

2. BURGERS

Form the meat into 6 to 8 patties. Brush with a little vegetable oil before grilling. Serve on grilled Calabrese (see page 26) or focaccia slices. Top with the sauce and a healthy portion of a tomato and onion salad or the Croation Red and Yellow Pepper Salad (see page 122).

3. KEBABS

Make the kebabs using metal or water-soaked bamboo skewers. The number of skewers depends on how large you want your kebabs. Using your hands, form the meat around each skewer. They are very delicate, so treat them gently. Brush them with a little vegetable oil before grilling for about 8 minutes, depending on size, and remember to turn them very carefully. Serve the kebabs with the sauce on the side.

MUSTARD-YOGURT SAUCE
1 cup (240 mL) 4% yogurt or sour cream
1 Tbsp. (15 mL) Dijon mustard

Combine the yogurt or sour cream with the mustard and blend. Serve at room temperature.

"I do not think that anything serious should be done after dinner, as nothing should be before breakfast."
— George Saintsbury

Marinated Chicken, Pearl Onion, and Bread Kebabs

SERVES 4

You could precede the chicken with the Baby Lettuces with Taleggio Croquettes (see page 118) or a large tomato salad. Adding pieces of peppers or zucchini to the kebab would be good too, although I would try it first with just chicken, onion, and bread. For a more substantial dinner, I also like to serve these with a medley of grilled vegetables.

16 to 20 red or white pearl onions
5 Tbsp. (75 mL) combined, chopped fresh sage, oregano, and thyme or rosemary
1 large clove garlic, minced
2 Tbsp. (30 mL) lemon juice
generous ½ cup (120 mL) olive oil

3 to 4 deboned, skinned chicken breasts, cut into 1½-inch (3.8-cm) cubes
16 1- to 1½-inch (2.5- to 3.8-cm) cubes of Calabrese (see page 26) or any other dense, white bread
5 to 6 stalks fresh rosemary, thyme (or a combination of both)
salt and freshly ground white pepper

Put the onions, with the skins on, in boiling water for about 3 minutes, or until just barely cooked. Drain and cool, and then remove the skins.

In a shallow bowl large enough to hold the chicken pieces, mix together the chopped herbs, garlic, lemon juice, and olive oil. Marinate the chicken at room temperature in this mixture for half an hour to an hour, or, alternatively, in the refrigerator for up to 2 hours. Return to room temperature.

Using 4 metal or water-soaked bamboo skewers, make the kebabs, alternating the chicken, pearl onions, and bread cubes. Insert sprigs of the stalks of rosemary or thyme between the other ingredients. Brush each kebab with the marinade, and sprinkle with salt and pepper.

Preheat the oven to 400°F (200°C).

Briefly sear the kebabs on a hot grill, turning very gently, then place them on a pan and bake in the oven for about 10 minutes. Remove from the oven, tent with foil, and let rest for 5 minutes.

According to English folklore, a rosemary plant growing outside a house is a sure sign that inside the house, it's a woman who is in charge. This superstition was once so strongly ingrained that men would kill off any rosemary plants growing near their houses to prove their manhood.

The word <u>tagine</u> is the name for a pot with a unique pointed cover traditionally used to cook this, or any, tagine (Moroccan stew).

Chicken Tagine

SERVES 6 TO 8

This recipe for tagine, or Moroccan stew, is adapted from the wonderful restaurant La Maison Bleu in Fez, Morocco. The tomatoes and onions are not traditional, but maybe should be. The preserved lemons have to be made at least three weeks ahead, but you can make enough to last you for months. If you can't be bothered, just use lemon zest and a squeeze of lemon juice. The flavor won't be as authentic, but it will still be delicious. In Morocco, Chicken Tagine would be preceded by small dishes of various salads that are scooped up with pieces of warm bread. I serve this tagine with couscous, buttered broad beans, and lots of warm baguette.

4 chicken breasts and 4 chicken legs
1½ tsp. (7.5 mL) kosher salt
1 tsp. (5 mL) freshly ground white pepper
1 tsp. (5 mL) ground ginger
1 tsp. (5 mL) sweet paprika
½ tsp. (2.5 mL) saffron, finely ground
1 medium red onion, puréed
2 Roma tomatoes, puréed

¼ cup (60 mL) olive oil
¼ cup (60 mL) melted unsalted butter
2 cups (475 mL) water
2 cups (475 mL) mixed green and black olives, pitted
1 preserved lemon, skin only, cut into ¼-inch (.6-cm) slices (see below) *or*, use zest of ½ a lemon and 1 tsp. (5 mL) lemon juice
1 tsp. (5 mL) chopped fresh coriander, or more, to taste

Place the chicken pieces in a large skillet with high sides and a lid that will hold all the ingredients. Mix the salt and pepper together and rub it all over the chicken pieces. Let them rest for 15 minutes. Mix the ginger, paprika, and saffron and sprinkle evenly over the meat. Then mix the onion purée and the tomato purée and gently pour over the spices. Make sure the spices and purée are spread evenly over the chicken. Drizzle the combined oil and butter over the mixture and let it sit for 15 minutes.

Bring the water to a boil and carefully pour it down the side of the pot rather than directly on top of the mixture. Place the pot on the stove and bring to a simmer. Cover and cook, turning the pieces several times, for about 30 minutes or until the chicken is cooked. Add more boiling water if the sauce starts to stick to the pan.

Remove the chicken from the pot, place on a warm plate, and tent it with foil. Add the olives and the preserved lemon rind to the liquid in the pot. It should be the consistency of thick cream. Simmer for a few minutes if it is too thin.

Place the chicken on a serving dish, pour the sauce overtop, and sprinkle with the coriander.

PRESERVED LEMONS
6 lemons
approximately ½ to ¾ cup (120 to 180 mL) kosher salt

At least 3 weeks before they are needed, cut the lemons in quarters almost all the way through, but making sure they are still joined at the bottom. Rub lots of salt onto the cut sides and close them up again. Place the lemons in a clear jar, place a heavy weight, such as a washed stone, on top of them, close the jar, and refrigerate. The lemons will start to extrude juice. Leave them for at least 3 weeks.

Seared Tuna Minute-Steaks with Tapenade and Tomato Confit

SERVES 4

Please don't be put off by the long list of ingredients. Each component of this dish can be prepared ahead of time. Grill the tuna at the last minute, and you'll be eating dinner in no time. If it's a casual kitchen dinner, put a plate of antipasto and a bottle of wine on the counter and give your guests a choice of making the Tapenade, the Tomato Confit, or the Lemon Garlic Mayonnaise. Then all you'll need is a quick assembly. Serve with a good portion of grilled or roasted asparagus or surrounded by a baby frisée and arugula salad.

TAPENADE

1 cup (240 mL) pitted niçoise olives (pitted, rinsed, and drained kalamatas can be substituted, but the taste will be different)

6 anchovy fillets, drained, patted dry, and minced
1 tsp. (5 mL) minced garlic
4 Tbsp. (60 mL) capers
up to 1 Tbsp. (15 mL) extra virgin olive oil

Place all the ingredients except the oil in a food processor and pulse until the mixture is puréed but still has some texture. If you prefer a moister tapenade, mix in olive oil 1 tsp. (5 mL) at a time until the tapenade holds together. The amount of oil you need will depend on the moisture in the olives.

TOMATO CONFIT

6 plum tomatoes, blanched and peeled
¼ cup (60 mL) balsamic vinegar
⅓ cup (80 mL) olive oil

1 Tbsp. (15 mL) fresh thyme leaves
2 tsp. (10 mL) chopped fresh basil
2 cloves garlic, thinly sliced
2 shallots, roughly chopped

Preheat the oven to 325°F (165°C).

Cut the tomatoes in half lengthwise and place face down in a baking dish. Mix together the vinegar, olive oil, thyme, basil, garlic, and shallots and pour over the tomatoes.

Bake for 25 to 30 minutes or until the tomatoes are slightly soft but not collapsed.

Drain and reserve.

LEMON GARLIC MAYONNAISE

Follow the recipe for Lemon Mayonnaise (see page 87) adding 2 to 4 cloves of roasted garlic, or add roasted garlic to store-bought mayonnaise and thin the mayonnaise with a little lemon juice.

3 Tbsp. (45 mL) olive oil
2 tsp. (10 mL) grated lemon rind

4 ½-inch (1.2-cm) thick slices of fresh tuna,
    approximately 5 to 6 oz. (140 to 170 g) each,
    cut the long way, resembling minute steaks
salt and freshly ground black pepper to taste
4 large slices Calabrese, country, or focaccia bread

Mix the olive oil and lemon rind. Brush the tuna on both sides with this oil. Sprinkle with salt and pepper. Heat a grill or frying pan over high heat. When it is very hot, sear the tuna on both sides for 25 to 30 seconds. Remove from heat.

ASSEMBLY

Grill or toast the bread. Brush the toasted bread on one side with any leftover oil and lemon mixture. Spread a thin layer of tapenade over the bread. Top with the tuna and 2 or 3 pieces of the tomato. Drizzle with the lemon garlic mayonnaise.

COOK'S TIP

The tapenade can be made up to 5 days ahead; the tomato confit 3 days ahead, and the mayonnaise 1 day ahead. You will have more tapenade and mayonnaise than you need for this recipe. The extra tapenade can be used in a chèvre, tomato, and grilled eggplant sandwich, while the mayo can be fancied up with chopped mixed herbs to accompany fish and chips.

Traditionally a confit is either poultry or meat, cooked and covered with its own fat before being preserved in a covered pot. The word comes from the French _confire_, to preserve. It no longer denotes only meat, but can describe a vegetable or even a fruit cooked in its own juices.

Cod and Smoked Salmon Cakes with Romesco Sauce and Lemon Mayonnaise

MAKES 12 2-INCH (5-CM) OR 8 3-INCH (7.5-CM) CAKES

You will be able to serve 6 appetizers or 3 main-course portions with this recipe. In either case, a small green salad beside the cod cakes adds color and texture to the plate. If using as an appetizer, you may want to try the Garlic and Black Pepper–Marinated Fillet of Beef (see page 160) as a main course followed by Summer Pudding with Ginger Crème Anglaise (see page 206) or Baked Apples Stuffed with Dates, Walnuts, and Ginger (see page 188), depending on the season.

20 oz. (570 g) skinned fresh cod fillets, cut in ¼-inch dice
6 oz. (170 g) smoked salmon, thinly sliced and minced
4 Tbsp. (60 mL) finely minced red onion
2 tsp. (10 mL) finely minced garlic
2 tsp. (10 mL) capers, minced
1 Tbsp. (15 mL) minced fresh jalapeño pepper
2 Tbsp. (30 mL) minced chives
1 to 2 eggs
2 to 3 Tbsp. (30 to 45 mL) lemon juice

kosher salt to taste
¼ tsp. (1.2 mL) freshly ground white pepper
2 to 3 cups (475 mL to 720 mL) coarse fresh sourdough, Calabrese (see page 26), or white breadcrumbs (see page 43)
3 to 4 Tbsp. (45 to 60 mL) olive oil
3 to 4 Tbsp. (45 to 60 mL) unsalted butter
1 recipe Romesco Sauce (see below)
Lemon Mayonnaise, for topping (see page 87)

Preheat the oven to 400°F (200°C).

If time is of the essence, mince the onion, garlic, capers, jalapeño pepper, and chives in a mini food processor. Always cut the fish by hand.

Put the cod, smoked salmon, onion, garlic, capers, jalapeño pepper, and chives in a bowl and toss gently. Lightly whisk 1 egg. Add the egg, lemon juice, salt and pepper and toss again. The mixture should be fairly loose. Add more lemon juice and another egg if it seems too dry.

Put the breadcrumbs in a shallow bowl. Shape one-sixth of the fish mixture into a disk. Cover all sides with breadcrumbs. Continue until all the fish is used. The cakes will be very delicate and moist.

Melt 1 Tbsp. (15 mL) oil and 1 Tbsp. (15 mL) butter in a non-stick frying pan. When just sizzling, add the cod cakes. Brown on both sides, turning gently to prevent the cakes from breaking. Add more oil and butter as needed.

Remove to a baking tray. Bake in the oven for 10 minutes. Serve immediately with a spoonful of Romesco Sauce on the side and a drizzle of Lemon Mayonnaise overtop.

ROMESCO SAUCE

It seems there are as many versions of Romesco Sauce as there are Spanish flamenco dancers. Almonds, garlic, olive oil, tomatoes, and bread turn up in most traditional recipes for this sauce. Some modern versions have dispensed with the almonds and substituted roasted red peppers for the tomatoes. Here are two versions—authentic and contemporary. Take your pick. Don't restrict the use of these sauces to this dish. They go equally well with any grilled white fish, shrimp, or chicken and are an integral part of Mariner's Medley (see page 106). Some Spaniards enrich their cardiologists by mixing them with aïoli or mayonnaise.

1 cup (240 mL) whole blanched almonds
2 slices white or Calabrese bread, crusts removed,
   sliced ¾ inch (1.9 cm) thick and then into 1-inch
   (2.5-cm) cubes
1 clove garlic

⅛ tsp. (.5 mL) kosher salt
2 good-sized Roma tomatoes, peeled, seeded, and
   coarsely chopped
2 Tbsp. (30 mL) sherry vinegar
up to ¾ cup (180 mL) olive oil
salt and freshly ground white pepper

Preheat the oven to 375°F (190°C).

Toast the almonds on a cookie sheet in the oven for about 10 minutes or until light golden. Then toast the bread cubes until slightly dry and just golden.

Grind the almonds into a fine powder using a spice grinder or with a mortar and pestle. Mince the garlic clove and mash with ⅛ tsp. (.5 mL) salt into a paste. (See Cook's Tip.) In a food processor, combine the almonds, bread, garlic, tomatoes, and sherry vinegar. Pulse for 2 or 3 10-second bursts, scraping down the bowl in between, until the ingredients are combined. With the machine on, slowly pour ½ cup (120 mL) oil through the spout. The sauce should be thick enough to just hold its shape in a spoon. Add more olive oil if needed. Taste and season with salt and pepper.

3 red peppers, roasted, peeled, and seeded (see page 122
   for how to roast)
2 large cloves garlic, coarsely chopped
2 slices white or Calabrese bread, crusts removed, lightly
   toasted, sliced ¾ inch (1.9 cm) thick and cut into
   1-inch (2.5-cm) cubes

⅛ tsp. (.5 mL) cayenne pepper
¼ tsp. (1.2 mL) kosher salt
⅛ tsp. (.5 mL) freshly ground white pepper
up to ¾ cup (180 mL) olive oil

Put the red peppers, garlic, bread, cayenne, salt, and pepper in the bowl of a food processor. Process for 2 10-second bursts, scraping down the bowl in between bursts. Turn on the machine and slowly drizzle in ½ cup (120 mL) oil. Check for seasoning and consistency. The sauce should be thick enough to just hold its shape in a spoon. Add the extra oil if necessary.

To turn garlic and salt into a paste, start by finely mincing the garlic. Sprinkle the salt over the garlic, and using the flat side of a large chef's knife, press down and draw the garlic and salt across the cutting board. Scrape the mixture together and continue the motion until the garlic is a paste.

Archeologists in Ireland have found remains of what appears to be a fish-smoking house on the river Bann that dates back about four thousand years.

Spaghetti with Lobster, Cherry Tomatoes, and Toasted Breadcrumbs

Toasted breadcrumbs sprinkled over pasta originated in Southern Italy as an economical substitute for cheese. This particular recipe came about due to an overabundance of lobsters and tomatoes left over after a dinner party.

For this dish to turn out at its best, it is imperative to undercook the pasta. It will continue cooking in the sauce. If your lobster is precooked and you're serving this as a main course, you'll have the dinner on the table in 25 minutes. Should you decide to serve it as a first course, following it with a simple roasted chicken accompanied by room-temperature grilled vegetables tossed in a garlic-infused vinaigrette would be nice.

¾ lb. (340 g) spaghetti
1 cup (240 mL) reserved pasta water
2 Tbsp. (30 mL) olive oil
20 red cherry tomatoes, sliced in half
10 yellow cherry tomatoes, sliced in half
3 cloves garlic, finely minced
salt and freshly ground white pepper

2 2-lb (900-g) lobsters, cooked, shelled, and cut into
   1-inch (2.5-cm) pieces
1 Tbsp. (15 mL) finely chopped chives
1 Tbsp. (15 mL) unsalted butter
GARNISH
⅔ cup (160 mL) fresh, coarse white or Calabrese
   breadcrumbs, sautéed in 1 Tbsp. (15 mL) of olive oil
   until golden brown

Bring enough water to a boil to cook the pasta. Add a large pinch of salt and then the pasta. Cook for about 7 to 8 minutes. It should still have a small white core down the middle. Drain the pasta while it still has this core and reserve 1 cup (240 mL) of cooking water.

Meanwhile, in a sauté pan large enough to hold all of the ingredients including the pasta, heat the olive oil until it shimmers, then add the tomatoes. Lower the heat to medium and sauté the tomatoes for 1 minute. Add the garlic and a pinch of salt and pepper, and cook for about 2 to 3 minutes. The garlic and the tomatoes will have softened, but the tomatoes should still hold their shape. Remove from the heat and add the lobster.

Put the sauté pan over medium heat, add the spaghetti and ⅓ cup (80 mL) of the reserved water. Toss gently so as not to break up the tomatoes. Add another ⅓ to ⅔ cup (80 to 160 mL) of reserved water and the chives. Toss again. Add the butter, and salt and pepper if needed. There will not be a real sauce, but rather a glaze made up of the water and butter coating the pasta.

Place in a heated serving bowl and sprinkle generously with toasted breadcrumbs.

COOK'S TIP

Simmer the lobster shells in about 9 cups (2.1 L) of water with 1 bay leaf, 1 roughly chopped carrot, and 1 chopped celery stalk for about half an hour. Let sit for 1 hour and then strain, cool, and freeze. Use as a delicate alternative to fish stock.

Several schools of thought exist on how to best (and most humanely) cook a lobster. Starting the lobster in a pot of cold water, for example, is said to gently lull it into an unconscious state. For brave souls who want extremely flavorful lobster, try cutting the live lobster in half lengthwise. As horrible as this sounds, quickly stabbing the lobster in the back of the head kills it instantly and this method allows for the removal of the stomach sac, located just behind the head, and the long intestinal vein, before cooking. A third method calls for placing the lobster in the freezer for half an hour before plunging in boiling water.

Red Snapper en Papillote

Fish roasted in parchment paper always stays moist and full of flavor. This recipe should be treated as a guideline. Change or delete any of the vegetables if you want, or season the fish with any kind of herbs and spices that you like. You can make the parcels hours before and refrigerate. Bring to room temperature before cooking.

2 fresh artichoke hearts
2 Tbsp. (30 mL) lemon juice
½ yellow pepper, cleaned and cut into 6 pieces
½ red pepper, cleaned and cut into 6 pieces
1 red onion, cut into 6 wedges through the root
3 Japanese eggplant, cut into thin slices
vegetable oil, for grilling
1 Tbsp. (15 mL) balsamic vinegar
9 baby white potatoes

12 asparagus spears, washed and drained
12 cherry tomatoes
parchment paper or foil
6 6-oz. (170-g) pieces of skinned red snapper fillets
sea salt
freshly ground white pepper
4 Tbsp. (60 mL) pesto or Basil-Garlic Dip (see page 76)
2 Tbsp. (30 mL) olive oil
2 Tbsp. (30 mL) finely minced fresh Italian parsley

Clean the artichokes and cut the hearts into thin slices. Quickly immerse them in a bowl of water with 1 Tbsp. (15 mL) of the lemon juice to prevent browning.

Brush the peppers, onion, and eggplant with the oil and grill over medium-high heat until softened and charred, or roast in a 400°F (200°C) oven until three-quarters cooked. They will be cooking again in the parchment, so do not need to be cooked through. Toss the onion in the vinegar.

Boil the potatoes in salted water until almost cooked. Shock in cold water and drain. Boil or steam the asparagus until barely cooked. Shock in cold water and drain. Cut the potatoes and the cherry tomatoes in halves. If the asparagus are very long, cut them into smaller pieces, too.

Cut 6 pieces of parchment paper or foil about 20 inches (51 cm) long. Place 3 slices of eggplant on one side of each piece of paper. Cut the pieces of fish in half and place 2 halves on top of the eggplant. Surround all the fish with equal amounts of the peppers, onion, potatoes, artichoke hearts, asparagus, and cherry tomatoes. Sprinkle the fish very generously with salt and pepper. Drizzle each piece of snapper with ½ tsp. (2.5 mL) lemon juice. Pat 1 tsp. to 2 tsp. (5 to 10 mL) of pesto on top of each fillet and drizzle all the contents with 1 tsp. (5 mL) olive oil and 1 tsp. (5 mL) parsley. Fold the other side of the parchment or foil over the fish and crimp along the edges.

Preheat the oven to 425°F (220°C).

If the packages have been refrigerated, bring them to room temperature. Bake the packages in the oven for 12 minutes. Cooking time will vary depending on the thickness of the fish. You may want to take one out to test that it is done to your liking.

Open each package and slide the contents into a large-rimmed soup bowl. There should be 2 to 3 Tbsp. (30 to 45 mL) of liquid in each bowl. Serve with warm baguette to sop up the juices.

Picking out fresh artichokes can be tricky, but here are some good indications: tight leaf formation, and leaves that squeak when the artichoke is squeezed.

Roasted Salmon with Asparagus, Zucchini, Corn, Grilled Onions, and Tomatoes

Consider putting a bowl of Red Pepper and White Bean Hummus (see page 80) with Baked Tortilla Shards (see page 42) on the kitchen counter and have everyone join you in the kitchen, wine in hand, while you make a mushroom risotto to start the meal. I have prepped this dish in the morning, stuck it in the fridge, brought it to room temperature, and popped it in the oven while we were eating our appetizer. Make sure to have a warm baguette on hand to sop up the flavorful broth. Ginger, Almond, and Lemon Cake (see page 195) would be a good dessert.

1½ lbs. (680 g) green asparagus (to generously serve 6), peeled if thick
1 large red onion, cut in eighths through the root
6 6- to 7-oz. (170- to 200-g) fillets skinned salmon, 1½ to 2 inches (3.8 to 5 cm) thick
4 large Roma tomatoes, seeded

2 small zucchini, seeded and sliced ⅛ inch (.3 cm) thick
kernels from 2 ears of corn
1 to 1½ cups (240 to 360 mL) chicken or vegetable stock, at room temperature
salt and freshly ground white pepper
3 tsp. (15 mL) olive oil
6 small sprigs chervil

Preheat the oven to 400°F (200°C).

Steam or boil the asparagus for about 2 minutes, until it is half cooked. Plunge into ice water to stop the cooking, drain, and pat dry.

Brush the onion pieces with a little olive oil and grill or roast in the oven until almost cooked through. Ten minutes on the grill or half an hour in the oven should do it.

Place the asparagus in a single layer in a roasting dish that can be taken to the table. Lay the salmon fillets diagonally across the asparagus. Tuck the tomatoes and zucchini around the fish. Sprinkle the corn kernels in between the fillets and pour in enough stock to just cover the asparagus. Salt and pepper to taste. Cover with foil and cook for 12 to 15 minutes. If you like your salmon rare or are using wild salmon, decrease the cooking time by about 4 minutes.

Take off the foil, check the fish and cook until done, approximately 5 minutes. Remove the dish from the oven and drizzle each piece of salmon with ½ tsp. (2.5 mL) oil and a sprig of chervil. Bring the roasting dish to the table and let guests help themselves, or, using large-rimmed soup bowls, place some asparagus in the bottom of each bowl, put a piece of salmon on top, and divide the vegetables among the six bowls. Pour the liquid down the side of each bowl and serve with thick slices of baguette to dunk in the flavored broth.

10 pm: Oven mitts, ready for use,
hang on the oven door.

10:10 pm: Sourdough Pullmans
wait their turn for the oven.

1:30 am: Maduras pulls a loader of baguettes out of the hearth oven.

Apple Onion Bread Pudding

SERVES 6

Grilled pork tenderloin, sautéed duck breasts, or roasted chicken are all great matches for this bread pudding. It can be assembled hours before—very important to me—and finished when you need it.

1 Tbsp. (15 mL) canola oil
2 Tbsp. (30 mL) unsalted butter
2 cups (475 mL) onion, in ¼-inch (.6-cm) slices
  (about 2 medium cooking onions)
1 tsp. (5 mL) minced garlic (about 1 medium clove)
2 Granny Smith apples, peeled, cored, and sliced into
  ¼-inch (.6-cm) thick by 1-inch (2.5-cm) long slices
1 tsp. (5 mL) chopped fresh thyme leaves

1 heaping tsp. (5 mL) chopped fresh marjoram leaves
1½ cups (360 mL) chicken stock
3 eggs
1 egg yolk
1¾ cups (420 mL) 10% cream
salt and freshly ground white pepper to taste
1 to 1½ loaves sourdough, white, or Calabrese bread,
  crusts removed and cut ½ inch (1.2 cm) thick
¼ to ⅔ cup (120 to 160 mL) grated Gruyère

Heat the canola oil and 1 Tbsp. (15 mL) butter in a sauté pan. Add the onion and sauté, stirring occasionally, over medium-low heat for approximately 10 minutes. Add the second tablespoon of butter, and the garlic. Sauté for 1 minute, add the apples, and cook for about 5 minutes until the apples are softened on their surface but still crisp inside. Add the thyme and marjoram and sauté for 1 or 2 minutes. Sprinkle with a large pinch of salt. Remove from the pan and reserve in a bowl.

Deglaze the pan with ½ cup (120 mL) of the stock until it is reduced to about ¼ cup (60 mL). In a bowl, whisk the eggs, egg yolk, and cream together. Slowly whisk in the warm deglazed stock, the other ½ cup (120 mL) of stock, ½ tsp. (2.5 mL) of salt, and a pinch of white pepper.

In an approximately 7- x 11-inch (18- x 28-cm) casserole dish that is 2 inches (5 cm) high, place a layer of bread, followed by half the apple and onion compote. Top with another layer of bread and the rest of the compote. Finish with a slightly overlapping layer of bread. Pour the cream and stock mixture over the bread. Press down on the bread and then drizzle the remaining ½ cup (120 mL) stock overtop. Press down again and leave for at least half an hour.

Preheat the oven to 375°F (190°C).

Bake for 30 minutes. Remove from the oven and sprinkle the top with the Gruyère and bake for an additional 5 minutes or until the cheese is melted. Then put under the broiler until the top is crisp and golden.

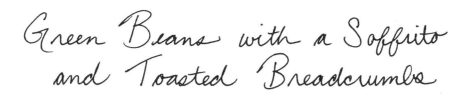

Green Beans with a Soffrito and Toasted Breadcrumbs

SERVES 4 TO 6

Soffrito, usually made of olive oil, garlic, onion, parsley, and tomato, is the base of many Italian dishes. This easy way to dress up green beans could be served as a cold salad if you tossed the beans in a light vinaigrette before heaping the soffrito and crumbs on top. I like it warm served with roasted cod that has a grating of lemon zest on top, or cold served with fried chicken.

2 Tbsp. (30 mL) olive oil
⅓ cup (80 mL) finely chopped cooking onion
1 clove garlic, minced

2 Roma tomatoes, seeded and finely chopped
½ cup (120 mL) fresh white, country or Calabrese breadcrumbs (see page 43)
½ lb. (225 g) French haricot vert or green string beans

To make the soffrito, heat 1 Tbsp. (15 mL) of the oil in a small frying pan over medium heat. Sauté the onion until pale gold and translucent. Add the garlic and cook for 30 seconds before adding the tomatoes to the pan. Cook, stirring, until the tomatoes have disintegrated and the onion is soft. Reserve.

Sauté the breadcrumbs in the remaining 1 Tbsp. (15 mL) of oil and reserve.

Boil or steam the beans until slightly crispy. Drain. Toss the beans into the warm soffrito. Turn into a bowl and sprinkle with as much of the breadcrumbs as you like.

The soffrito can also be heated on its own and spooned over the beans after they have been tossed in a little olive oil. Then sprinkle the breadcrumbs over the soffrito.

Pennette Gratin with Wild Mushrooms

This is grown-up macaroni and cheese. You can prepare the mushrooms, sauce, and even the pennette ahead of time, refrigerate them until needed, then bring them to room temperature, assemble, and pop the dish in the oven. Served with a green salad, this makes a great casual lunch or dinner. For a hearty but simple supper, I sometimes serve it as a side dish with oven-roasted sea bass or grilled lamb. You could also add some buttered broccoli tossed with a little sautéed garlic.

MUSHROOMS

- 1 generous lb. (455 g) mixed mushrooms, cleaned and sliced (I like a combination of chanterelle, portobello, and porcini, or shiitake and button)
- 3 Tbsp. (45 mL) olive oil
- ½ tsp. (2.5 mL) kosher salt
- ⅛ tsp. (.5 mL) freshly ground white pepper
- 1 Tbsp. (15 mL) finely minced garlic
- ½ tsp. (2.5 mL) chopped fresh thyme

SAUCE

- 4¼ generous cups (1 L) homogenized milk
- 5 Tbsp. (75 mL) unsalted butter
- 5 Tbsp. (75 mL) all-purpose flour
- 5 oz. (140 g) fontina cheese, finely chopped or grated
- 5 oz. (140 g) Asiago cheese, grated
- ⅛ tsp. (.5 mL) ground nutmeg
- ½ to 1 tsp. (2.5 to 5 mL) kosher salt, or to taste
- ⅛ tsp (.5 mL) freshly ground white pepper, or to taste
- 1⅛ lb. (500 g) package pennette rigate or any short pasta
- 5 oz. (140 g) mozzarella cut into ½-inch (1.2-cm) cubes
- 5 oz. (140 g) Parmigiano Reggiano, grated
- 1 to 1½ cups (240 to 360 mL) coarse fresh white breadcrumbs, (see page 43)

FOR THE MUSHROOMS

Preheat the oven to 400°F (200°C).

Brush a baking dish with a little olive oil. Put the mushrooms in the dish and toss with the 3 Tbsp. (45 mL) of olive oil. Add the salt and pepper. Bake for 10 minutes, stirring once. The salt will release moisture from the mushrooms. Add the minced garlic and thyme, and mix. Bake for another 10 minutes, stirring once or twice. Remove from the oven and reserve.

FOR THE SAUCE

Heat the milk.

Melt the butter over medium heat in a saucepan large enough to hold all the sauce ingredients. Slowly whisk in the flour and cook, stirring for 2 minutes. Still on the heat, gently pour in the warm milk, whisking continuously to prevent lumps from forming. Cook, stirring occasionally, for about 7 minutes until the sauce has thickened slightly. You do not want a thick sauce, as adding the cheese will further thicken it. Remove from the heat and stir in the fontina and Asiago. When completely melted, add the nutmeg, salt, and pepper. Taste. Season more if needed.

Lower the oven to 375°F (190°C).

Cook the pasta in salted water. Drain when the pasta is still very undercooked. There should be a tiny white core in the center of the pennette. Return the pasta to the pot it was cooked in and add the sauce. Stir to coat, and add the mozzarella and half of the Parmigiano. Then, gently stir in the roasted mushrooms. Taste, and add more salt and pepper, if needed. Toss the other half of the Parmigiano and the breadcrumbs together in a bowl.

Butter a 9- x 12-inch (23- x 30-cm) ovenproof dish and fill with the mixture. Sprinkle with all of the breadcrumb mixture.

Bake for about 30 minutes or until hot and the pennette is cooked through. If you want a darker top, put the dish under the broiler for a minute or so. For a different presentation, use individual gratin dishes and cook for 20 minutes.

COOK'S TIP

If your milk is cold or is added too quickly to the flour, small lumps may form in the sauce. Pour the sauce through a fine sieve, pressing the lumps through the sieve with a spoon. Proceed with the recipe.

Whole Cauliflower with Dijon-Bechamel Sauce and Buttered Breadcrumbs

SERVES 6 TO 8

This is an easy but grand-looking dish. The unusual presentation of a whole cauliflower draped in a pale sauce and topped with dark, golden breadcrumbs is guaranteed to impress even the most blasé diner. The sauce can be made ahead of time. When reheating, do not bring it to a boil, as the cheese in the sauce will cause it to become stringy. The cauliflower can also be partially cooked and finished by dropping it in boiling water for 2 minutes. If you prefer a more casual-looking presentation, break the cauliflower into florets before cooking it.

1 medium-sized cauliflower
1½ Tbsp. (22.5 mL) unsalted butter
½ tsp. (2.5 mL) grated garlic
1 heaping Tbsp. (15 mL) all-purpose flour
1 tsp. (5 mL) Dijon mustard
1½ cups (360 mL) homogenized milk, warmed

½ cup (120 mL) grated Gruyère
⅛ tsp. (.5 mL) ground nutmeg
salt and freshly ground white pepper to taste
1 Tbsp. (15 mL) unsalted butter
½ cup (120 mL) fresh Calabrese (see page 26) or white breadcrumbs (see page 43)
1 Tbsp. (15 mL) minced fresh Italian parsley

Clean and wash the cauliflower, discarding the leaves, and remove about 1 inch (2.5 cm) of the hard core, making sure the florets don't fall off. Submerge the whole cauliflower in a large pot of salted boiling water. Cover and cook about 10 to 12 minutes until cooked but not mushy. Remove from the water and wrap in foil.

Melt the 1½ Tbsp. (22.5 mL) of butter over low heat in a medium-sized saucepan. Add the grated garlic, stirring constantly, and sprinkle in the flour. Cook for about 1 minute. Mix in the mustard and add the warm milk. Stirring, bring to a simmer and cook until slightly thickened. Remove from heat and add the cheese. This will thicken the sauce. Add the nutmeg and salt and pepper to taste. If necessary, add more warm milk to bring it to the consistency of melted chocolate.

Melt the 1 Tbsp. (15 mL) of butter in a frying pan. Add the breadcrumbs and sauté until golden brown.

Put the whole cauliflower on a serving dish that has a lip. Spoon the sauce overtop and sprinkle with the breadcrumbs and then the parsley.

Potato Croquettes

These elegant-looking, delectable-tasting croquettes are the real thing—no nouveau touches of cheese, bacon, or herbs—even though there is a classic recipe for cheese croquettes—no potatoes in those, though. My mom likes to serve these with grilled steak or roasted chicken. I think they're delicious with anything.

3 lbs. (1.35 kg) Yukon Gold or white potatoes,
  peeled and cubed
1 tsp. (5 mL) kosher salt
3 eggs, separated

2 Tbsp. (28 g) unsalted butter, cubed
2 to 3 cups (475 to 720 mL) dry white breadcrumbs
  (see page 43)
8 cups (2 L) vegetable oil for deep frying

Cook the potatoes in salted water until soft. Force through a ricer or a medium sieve. Lightly whisk the egg yolks and add immediately, with the butter, while the potatoes are still warm. Taste and add more salt and butter if necessary. Cool to just above room temperature.

Shape the mashed potato into logs about 1 inch (2.5 cm) in diameter and 3 inches (7.5 cm) long. Roll them in the egg white, covering all sides, and then in the breadcrumbs.

Cover and refrigerate until half an hour before frying.

Preheat the oven to 375°F (190°C). Heat the oil in a deep saucepan to 350° to 375°F (175° to 190°C).

Using a slotted spoon or Chinese sieve, gently lower 4 to 5 croquettes into the oil. The oil will bubble up. Deep-fry until the croquettes are a golden brown. This will happen quite quickly. Remove from the oil and place on a baking sheet lined with paper towel. Put them in the oven to keep warm. Repeat with the remaining croquettes. The croquettes can be kept in a warm oven for 20 minutes. Any more than that and you run the risk of the potatoes drying out.

COOK'S TIP

The uncooked croquettes must be removed from the refrigerator half an hour before cooking. If you fail to do so, the hot oil may lift the breadcrumb coating away from the potatoes.

Developed at the University of Guelph, Ontario, the Yukon Gold is the first Canadian potato marketed by name. In 1980, it was licensed and began to be exported.

Savory Carrot and Minted Pea Pudding

SERVES 8

This delicate-tasting but satisfying side dish tastes good with the Pork Tenderloin (see page 161) or any grilled or roasted meat. Decorated with pea shoots and drizzled with a touch of warm lemon butter, it can be served as an appetizer. For variety, try using any combination of vegetables that are in season.

3 cups (720 mL) homogenized milk
1 large clove garlic, crushed
8 Tbsp. (120 mL) unsalted butter—reserve 1 Tbsp.
  (15 mL) for later use
7 Tbsp. (105 mL) flour
½ tsp. (2.5 mL) kosher salt
½ tsp. (2.5 mL) freshly ground white pepper
large pinch of nutmeg

1 cup (240 mL) ¼-inch (.6-cm) diced carrots
1 cup (240 mL) fresh peas (if using frozen, don't cook
  before adding to white sauce)
2 large fresh mint leaves, plus more for garnish
2 Tbsp. (30 mL) minced shallots
2 eggs
1 cup (240 mL) Parmigiano Reggiano
1½ cups (360 mL) dry or fresh white breadcrumbs,
  toasted dark golden brown (see page 43)

Preheat the oven to 400°F (200°C).

Pour the milk into a saucepan and add the crushed garlic. Bring to a simmer and remove from heat to allow garlic to steep.

Melt 6 Tbsp. (90 mL) of the butter in a saucepan large enough to accommodate the flour and milk. When the butter is melted, slowly whisk in the flour. Cook over medium-low heat, stirring continuously, until the mixture is a light golden. Quickly whisk the warm milk into the butter mixture and continue stirring until all the lumps have disappeared. Raise the temperature to medium and continue to stir until the sauce has become thicker and pulls away from the pan. Add the salt, pepper, and nutmeg. Remove from heat and reserve.

Blanch the carrots in boiling salted water for about 3 to 4 minutes. They should still be crisp. Drain and shock under cold water. Drain again. Place in a small bowl.

Blanch the peas and mint in boiling salted water for 3 minutes. Drain and shock under cold water. Drain again and remove the mint leaves. Add the peas to the carrots.

Sauté the shallots in 1 Tbsp. (15 mL) of butter for about 4 or 5 minutes or until golden but not browned. Toss into the vegetables.

Whisk the eggs, add the Parmigiano, and mix together. Remove the garlic from the cooled white sauce and add the egg mixture to it. Fold the vegetables into the sauce. The dish can be assembled to this point up to a day ahead and refrigerated.

If you have assembled the pudding and refrigerated it, bring it to room temperature before proceeding.

Generously butter 8 half-cup (120-mL) glass ramekins with the remaining 1 Tbsp. (15 mL) of butter, using more if needed. Coat each ramekin bottom and sides thickly with breadcrumbs, patting them in, if necessary. Spoon the pudding into the ramekins. Place them on a baking pan that has a rim. Put the pan in the oven and pour hot water in the pan until it reaches halfway up the outside of the ramekins.

Bake for 45 minutes or until a tester comes out almost clean.

Place on a cooling rack and let sit for 20 minutes. Resist the urge to try to turn them out sooner as they will stick in the molds. Invert the ramekins onto individual plates or a large serving platter and serve with a garnish of fresh mint. For a more casual presentation, leave the puddings in the ramekins and serve immediately.

Before sugar and other sweeteners became common in Europe, cooks there often used carrots in desserts and other sweet dishes. This tradition was revived during World War II, when the British Ministry of Food distributed recipes for Carrot Christmas Pudding and Carrot Cake.

Sweet Things

Apple, Pear, and Cranberry Charlotte with Crème Anglaise

Chocolate Pain Grillé with Raspberry Coulis and Honey-Almond Ice Cream

Baked Apples Stuffed with Dates, Walnuts, and Ginger with Marsala Custard

Steamed Fig, Date, and Prune Pudding with Sticky Toffee Sauce

Blueberry-Lemon Crisp

Baked Banana Spring Rolls with Rum Sauce

Vanilla Ice Cream Topped with Warm Strawberry Compote and Cinnamon
Melba Toast Crunch

Ginger, Almond, and Lemon Cake

Maple-Orange Bread and Butter Pudding

Warm Chocolate Brownie Pudding

Honey-Pecan Brown Bread Ice Cream

Summer Ice Cream Sandwich with Dolce de Leche

Pumpkin Bread Pudding with Caramel Sauce

Pan-Fried Pineapple on Caramelized Toast with Almond Crème Fraîche

Summer Pudding with Ginger Crème Anglaise

"I remember that at one time I saw two of my young mistresses and some lady visitors eating ginger cakes, in the yard. At that time those cakes seemed to me to be the most tempting and desirable things that I had ever seen; and then and there I resolved that, if I ever got free, the height of my ambition would be reached if I could get to the point where I could secure and eat ginger cakes in the way I saw those ladies doing." —Booker T. Washington

Apple, Pear, and Cranberry Charlotte with Crème Anglaise

SERVES 6 GENEROUSLY

The most common, and likely the original, charlotte is apple charlotte, presumably named for Queen Charlotte (wife of George III) who enthusiastically patronized local apple growers. If there is such a thing as gorgeous-looking comfort food, this is it—a crisp, golden dome encasing a mélange of autumn fruits. Be sure to bring the charlotte to the table whole so your guests can appreciate your handiwork. The dessert will not keep its shape after the first piece is cut, but nonetheless will taste delicious. You could make the fruit compote the day before, bring it to room temperature before spooning it into the tin and bake it while you're getting dinner ready. The crème anglaise will keep in the refrigerator for 3 to 4 days.

2 Tbsp. (30 mL) unsalted butter
6 cups (1.5 L) peeled and cored Bosc pears, cut in 1-inch (2.5-cm) pieces (about 6 pears)
6 cups (1.5 L) peeled and cored Spy, Northern Spy, Gala, or Granny Smith apples cut in ½-inch (1.2-cm) pieces (about 4 large apples)
1 star anise (or dried star-shaped spice)
1 vanilla bean, split lengthwise
1 tsp. (5 mL) lemon juice
2 Tbsp. (30 mL) sugar

4 Tbsp. (60 mL) maple syrup
⅔ cup (160 mL) dried cranberries
2 tsp. (10 mL) sweet sherry
1 scant tsp. (5 mL) orange zest
⅔ cup (160 mL) unsalted butter, melted
16 to 20 ½-inch (1.2-cm) slices white bread, sandwich-loaf shaped, crusts removed
1 recipe Ginger Crème Anglaise made without the ginger (see page 207) (heat over warm water before serving) or vanilla ice cream
1 to 2 Tbsp. (15 to 30 mL) icing sugar to garnish

Melt the butter in a frying pan large enough to hold all the fruit.

Add the pears, apples, star anise, vanilla bean, and lemon juice. Stir and cook over medium heat for 3 to 4 minutes. Add the sugar and maple syrup and cook, stirring occasionally, for another 5 minutes, approximately, or until the juice from the fruit is almost all evaporated and the fruit is slightly softened but still holds its shape. Remove from the heat. Add the cranberries, sherry, and orange zest. When the mixture is cool, scrape the seeds from the vanilla bean into the mixture and remove the star anise. You will have about 6 cups (1.5 L) of fruit.

Preheat the oven to 375°F (190°C).

Brush 1 side of each slice of bread with melted butter. Cut enough slices of bread into triangles to line the bottom of an 8-cup (2-L) charlotte tin. The triangles should be overlapping and butter-side down. (Metal charlotte tins look like small angel food tins without the center cone. It is hard to find a substitute.) Brush lightly with more melted butter. Cut the rest of the bread slices into wide strips and line the side of the pan, buttered side against the pan. Again, overlap the pieces of bread. Fill the middle of the tin with the fruit, pressing against the bread with a spoon. Cover the fruit filling with overlapping slices of bread and brush with more melted butter. Place in the oven and cook for 40 minutes. Check after 20 minutes to make sure the top is not over-browning. Cover with foil if it is.

Remove from the oven and let rest for 20 to 30 minutes. Turn out onto a plate, dust with icing sugar, and pour the crème anglaise around the edge of the plate. Serve warm.

Chocolate Pain Grillé with Raspberry Coulis and Honey-Almond Ice Cream

SERVES 2 VERY GENEROUSLY

A favorite Paris restaurant of mine, in the 8th Arrondissement, inspired this dessert. Basically a grilled sandwich, oozing with warm, melted chocolate, it can be prepared ahead of time and finished at the last moment. Take five minutes between courses to grill it, and you'll satisfy even the least likely chocolate lover. A good quality chocolate bar is integral to the recipe. Don't use cooking chocolate; in all probability the fat content will be too high.

2 3½ -oz. (100-g) dark semi-sweet European chocolate bar

4 slices either Pain au Lait (see page 19), brioche, challah (not braided), or white sandwich loaf at least ½ inch (1.2 cm) thick

1 Tbsp. (15 mL) salted butter, at room temperature

1 recipe Raspberry Coulis (see below)

1 recipe Honey-Pecan Brown Bread Ice Cream (see page 198, made without the breadcrumbs and substituting toasted almonds for the pecans) or a good quality store-bought vanilla ice cream

Place the chocolate onto 2 slices of bread, and cover with the remaining bread slices. The chocolate should fit neatly inside the bread and not stick out at the edges. Butter the outsides of each sandwich and place on wax paper.

Heat a grill pan or frying pan and cook the buttered sandwiches on one side until dark golden; flip and cook for the same amount of time on the other side. Press the sandwich gently with a spatula while it cooks to join the chocolate and bread together. The chocolate should be soft but not liquid.

Transfer to a cutting board and cut each sandwich into two triangles. Place, overlapping, on a dessert plate. Put a scoop of ice cream on the plate and either drizzle the raspberry coulis over the ice cream or pour a pool of it on one side of the plate.

RASPBERRY COULIS

10½ oz. (300 g) frozen unsweetened raspberries, defrosted

1 to 2 Tbsp. (15 to 30 mL) sugar

1 tsp. (5 mL) lemon juice

Drain the defrosted raspberries through a fine sieve into a bowl. Press on the raspberries to release as much juice as possible. Pour the juice into a small saucepan and add 1 Tbsp. (15 mL) sugar and all of the lemon juice. Bring to a simmer and cook for 3 or 4 minutes or until the mixture has thickened slightly. Taste and add more sugar if needed. Chill in the refrigerator.

"You can take some chocolate... and you take two pieces of bread... and you put the candy in the middle of it and you make a sandwich of it. And that would be cake." — Andy Warhol

Baked Apples Stuffed with Dates, Walnuts, and Ginger with Marsala Custard

SERVES 6

Baked apples always signify the beginning of cold-weather cooking for me. Marsala, a fortified wine from Italy, gives the custard a scrumptious lift. I specify medium-sized apples because my many attempts to treat friends to a larger dessert too often resulted in the fruit splitting open and making an awful mess. Sometimes smaller is better. If you prefer a dessert with no alcohol, substitute unfiltered apple cider for the Marsala and red wine.

4 to 6 large dates, pitted
16 walnut halves
1 tsp. (5 mL) roughly grated orange peel
⅛ tsp. (.5 mL) freshly grated ginger
large pinch of freshly grated nutmeg
5 Tbsp. (75 mL) fine fresh breadcrumbs (white, challah, or Pain au Lait or brioche) (see page 43)
2 tsp. (10 mL) Marsala
6 russets, Golden Delicious, Cortland, Macintosh, or other medium-sized baking apple

1 cup (240 mL) red wine
2 Tbsp. (30 mL) liquid wildflower honey
1 Tbsp. (15 mL) unsalted butter
unsalted butter to grease baking dish

MARSALA CUSTARD
2 cups (475 mL) homogenized milk
½ vanilla bean (cut in half lengthwise) or 1 tsp. (5 mL) vanilla extract
5 egg yolks
3 Tbsp (45 mL) sugar
1½ Tbsp. (22.5 mL) Marsala

FOR THE APPLES

Chop the dates and walnuts into ¼-inch (.6-cm) pieces. Place in a medium-sized bowl and add the orange zest, ginger, nutmeg, and breadcrumbs. Toss. Sprinkle in the Marsala. Gently mix together. Taste and adjust the ingredients to your liking.

Preheat the oven to 350°F (175°C).

Cut a small slice off the bottom of each apple so it can stand upright. Using a melon baller or a sharp small spoon, starting at the bottom, core out the middle of the apple almost to the top, making sure to get out all the seeds. Peel the skin off the top third of the apple. Stuff each apple firmly from the bottom with the date and walnut mixture. Put the apples, peeled-side up, in a buttered baking dish small enough so that they almost touch.

In a small saucepan, warm the red wine, honey, and butter just long enough to melt the honey, then pour the mixture over the apples. Bake in the oven for about half an hour or until soft, basting the apples every 10 minutes or so. Let rest 10 to 20 minutes before serving. Serve each apple with a generous puddle of room temperature Marsala Custard.

FOR THE MARSALA CUSTARD

Bring the milk and vanilla bean to a simmer. Remove from stove.

In a bowl large enough to accommodate the milk, gently whisk the egg yolks and sugar for about a minute. While whisking the egg mixture, slowly pour in ¼ cup (60 mL) of the warm milk. Continue until all the milk is used.

Place ice in a large bowl until half full and rest a bowl in it large enough to accommodate all the custard. Set aside. Pour the egg and milk mixture back into the saucepan and cook over medium-low heat. Stir continuously with a wooden spoon for about 6 to 9 minutes or until the mixture has thickened to the consistency of very loose whipped cream. To tell if the custard is ready, lift the spoon out of the liquid and draw your finger down the back of it. It's ready when the line doesn't fill in. Stir in the Marsala.

Pour the custard into the bowl resting in the ice to stop the crème anglaise from continuing to cook. Remove the vanilla bean. Scrape out the seeds and whisk them into the custard. For a smoother, velvety texture, put the custard through a sieve after cooking. Bear in mind you may lose some of the vanilla seeds.

COOK'S TIP

Making custard for the first time can be intimidating. There is less chance of the mixture "scrambling" if you use a double boiler. Make sure the water in the lower pot doesn't come in contact with the top pot of the double boiler. Follow the same procedure as cooking directly on the heat. The custard may take a bit longer to thicken.

Steamed Fig, Date, and Prune Pudding with Sticky Toffee Sauce

SERVES 8

Best suited to cool evenings, this is the "feel good" recipe of this book. A friend told me it brought back all the good memories of childhood, but with an adult twist. I assume she means the splash of whisky in the ingredients. The whipped egg whites lighten the pudding, and the sticky toffee sauce makes it very luxurious. Please don't be put off by the length of the recipe; it includes a lengthy description of how to steam the pudding.

PUDDING

⅓ packed cup (80 mL) of ¼-inch (.6-cm) diced, dried figs (approximately 4)

¾ packed cup (180 mL) of ¼-inch (.6-cm) diced prunes (approximately 20)

¾ packed cup (180 mL) of ¼-inch (.6-cm) diced dates (10 to 20 depending on size)

3 Tbsp. (45 mL) Scotch

⅔ cup (160 mL) boiling water

4 large eggs, separated, plus 2 egg yolks

6 Tbsp. (90 mL) unsalted butter, at room temperature

⅓ cup (80 mL) plus 1 Tbsp. (15 mL) maple syrup

1½ Tbsp. (22.5 mL) sugar

1 tsp. (5 mL) vanilla

2¼ cups (535 mL) very fine, fresh white, Pain au Lait (see page 19), challah, or brioche breadcrumbs (see page 43)

1 Tbsp. (15 mL) baking powder

1 tsp. (5 mL) ground cinnamon

½ tsp. (2.5 mL) kosher salt

STICKY TOFFEE SAUCE

9 Tbsp. (135 mL) unsalted butter

6 Tbsp. (90 mL) white sugar

7 Tbsp. (105 mL) brown sugar

6 Tbsp. (90 mL) 18% cream

FOR THE PUDDING

Use an 8-cup (2-L) non-stick mold or generously butter a metal, glass, or enamelware 8-cup (2-L) mold. I like a dome-shaped mold but any shape will do.

Mix the dried fruit together in a small bowl. Toss with the Scotch and boiling water and let sit for about 10 minutes or until most of the liquid has been absorbed.

Whisk all 6 egg yolks in a small bowl. Reserve the 4 egg whites.

In a bowl large enough to hold all the ingredients, mix the butter, maple syrup, sugar, and vanilla for 1 minute until well blended. Add the egg yolks and mix for another minute, until well blended. Next mix in the breadcrumbs, baking powder, cinnamon, and salt. Then fold the marinated dried fruit into this mixture.

Whip the egg whites until they mound in soft peaks. Stir a third of the whites into the batter until completely combined. Gently fold in the remaining whites.

Fit a trivet or shallow bowl (upside down) into the bottom of a pot that is at least 4 inches (10 cm) wider and 2 inches (5 cm) higher than your mold. Pour the batter into the mold, leaving the top inch (2.5 cm) free for the pudding to expand. Lay a buttered circle of parchment paper over the batter, buttered-side down, and cover the top of the mold with foil, securing it over the edge to keep out any condensation.

Lower the mold onto the trivet in the pot and carefully pour boiling water ¾ of the way up the mold. Cover with the pot lid and steam for 1 hour and 40 minutes, if your mold has a center hole. If not, extend the steaming time by 10 to 15 minutes. Add more boiling water if necessary to keep the level constant.

FOR THE STICKY TOFFEE SAUCE

Melt the butter and two sugars in a saucepan. When the mixture liquefies and becomes glossy, lower the heat and continue stirring for about 3 to 4 minutes until you can smell the caramel. Be careful to not let it burn. Pour the cream into the center of the caramel. It will bubble up and be swallowed into the sauce. Remove from the heat immediately. If the toffee sauce seizes up when it cools, place it over low heat and stir until the sugar dissolves. You may need to add more cream to thin it out.

ASSEMBLY

Heat the oven to broil.

Remove the pudding from the pot, set on a rack, and allow to cool for 10 minutes. Take off the parchment paper and invert the mold onto a baking sheet. If the pudding sticks, try gently easing the sides away from the baking dish with a knife.

Drizzle a few tablespoons of toffee sauce over the top of the pudding and place under the broiler for 2 minutes. Turn off the broiler and allow the residual heat to warm the pudding. Transfer to a serving plate. Gently warm the rest of the toffee sauce and either pour it from a pitcher over individual pieces or pour the sauce around the base of the entire pudding on the serving plate. Serve with a scoop of butterscotch or vanilla ice cream.

COOK'S TIPS

1. If you fill a tall glass or jar with very hot water and keep dipping your knife blade into it while dicing the dried fruit, the fruit won't stick to the knife.

2. Forgot to bring butter to room temperature? Run the cold block of butter down a grater; the grated butter will be soft.

"A smell like an eating-house and a pastry cook's next door to each other, with a laundress's next door to that. That was the pudding."
— Charles Dickens, A Christmas Carol

Blueberry-Lemon Crisp

My friend Susan Perren makes a simplified version of this crisp at her beautiful, rustic cottage in Northern Ontario. She picks the blueberries that grow near her cottage, uses yesterday's bread, and delights all her friends. Almond ice cream or lemon sorbet is a nice accompaniment.

4 cups (950 mL) blueberries, preferably wild
1 tsp. (5 mL) minute tapioca
4 tsp. (20 mL) white sugar
½ tsp. (2.5 mL) lemon zest
⅛ tsp. (.5 mL) almond extract

2 cups (475 mL) fresh Pain au Lait (see page 19), brioche, challah, or white breadcrumbs (see page 43)
5 Tbsp. (75 mL) cold butter cut into ¼-inch (.6-cm) cubes
generous ½ cup (120 mL) brown sugar
2 to 3 Tbsp. (30 to 45 mL) sliced almonds

Preheat the oven to 350°F (175°C).

Toss the blueberries, tapioca, white sugar, lemon zest, and almond extract in a 12- x 7-inch (30- x 18-cm) casserole dish.

In a separate bowl, mix the breadcrumbs, butter, and brown sugar together with your fingers. Spoon over the blueberry mixture.

Bake for 30 minutes, then sprinkle with the almonds and bake for another 15 minutes, or until the crust is golden.

Note: If you like a thicker crumb topping, increase the breadcrumbs, butter, and brown sugar by 25%.

Buy a large basket of wild blueberries in August and wash and freeze the berries you can't eat or cook right away; you can then bake with blueberries all winter. Don't defrost the berries before adding them to a recipe.

Blueberry-Lemon Crisp p. 192

Summer Pudding with Ginger Crème Anglaise p. 206

*Summer Ice Cream Sandwich
with Dolce de Leche p. 200*

Ginger, Almond,
and Lemon Cake
p. 195

Baked Banana Spring Rolls with Rum Sauce

MAKES 5 3-PIECE SERVINGS (WITH EXTRA FOR THE COOK) OR 8 2-PIECE SERVINGS

Bread as a spring roll wrapping? I know it sounds odd, but I promise you these are delicious and light as well as being easy to make. Put them together hours ahead of time and just pop them in the oven 15 to 20 minutes before serving. If you are feeling decadent, add some rum-raisin or vanilla ice cream. Native to India and Southeast Asia, the banana is related to ginger, cardamom, and turmeric. Botanically, the fruit is a berry, and Europeans originally called it the "Indian fig."

SPRING ROLLS

16 thin, ¼-inch (.6-cm) slices Pain au Lait (see page 19), brioche, challah, or white bread

2 to 3 Tbsp. (30 to 45 mL) unsalted butter, softened

2 ripe bananas, peeled

¼ to ⅓ cup (60 to 80 mL) fine white sugar

icing sugar for decoration

2 oz. (57 g) bittersweet chocolate, melted (optional)

RUM SAUCE

¾ cup (180 mL) white sugar

½ cup (120 mL) lime juice

¼ cup (60 mL) dark rum

2 Tbsp. (30 mL) unsalted butter, chilled

FOR THE SPRING ROLLS

Preheat the oven to 350°F (175°C).

Cut the crusts off the slices of bread and roll them out individually with a rolling pin until each is about ⅛ inch (.3 cm) thick. Butter one side of each rolled piece of bread.

Cut both bananas in half, then cut each half in quarters lengthwise, yielding 16 pieces.

Place a slice of bread, butter-side down, near the bottom edge of a piece of plastic wrap. Put a banana spear on the bottom edge of the bread. Using the plastic wrap to create some tension, roll the bread over and around the banana, continuing to the upper edge of the bread slice, making sure the edges of the bread slightly overlap. Press the seams together. Trim the banana to the length of the roll, if necessary, then roll the spring rolls in the sugar, and place on a plate, seam-side down.

FOR THE RUM SAUCE

Put the sugar and lime juice in a small saucepan and bring to a simmer. Remove from the heat and stir in the rum. Return to the heat. If the mixture flames up, reduce the heat until the flames go out. Let the mixture simmer for 1 or 2 minutes until it thickens slightly. Remove from the heat and reserve. As the sauce cools, it will continue to thicken to a syrupy consistency.

Transfer the spring rolls onto a foil-lined baking tray and bake for 15 to 20 minutes, or until golden brown. After 5 minutes, check to see that the rolls are not burning on the bottom. Turn so that all sides get crisp, if necessary.

Warm up the sauce and stir in the chilled butter to give it a glossy finish. Do not bring to a boil or the butter will separate.

Pour pools of sauce on 5 or 8 dessert plates and arrange 2 or 3 spring rolls on each plate. Drizzle with melted chocolate, if using, and dust with icing sugar. Serve very warm. The spring rolls can be made ahead and covered with plastic wrap. If you have stored them in the refrigerator, return to room temperature before baking.

Vanilla Ice Cream Topped with Warm Strawberry Compote and Cinnamon Melba Toast Crunch

This recipe is a snap. Gently warming the strawberries really intensifies their flavor. Make the compote when strawberries are at their peak. Those woody, pale, winter ones just won't do.

2 cups (475 mL) strawberries
6 to 8 Decadent Melba Toast (see page 41)
⅛ cup (30 mL) fine white sugar

squeeze of lemon juice
Honey-Pecan Brown Bread Ice Cream (see page 198) made without the pecans and bread, or good store-bought vanilla ice cream

Wash and hull the strawberries. Cut into quarters and roughly mash with a fork or an electric wand.

Break the Melba toast into large crumbs.

Put the strawberries in a saucepan. Add the sugar and heat, stirring occasionally.

Remove from the heat, add the lemon juice, and taste. Add more sugar and lemon juice if necessary. You can prepare the recipe to this point up to 8 hours ahead. Reheat before serving.

Scoop ice cream into bowls, ladle some warm strawberries on top, and garnish with Melba toast crumbs. Serve immediately.

Extra ice cream will keep in the freezer for 2 weeks, and extra compote will keep in the refrigerator for 4 to 5 days.

"The only emperor is the emperor of ice cream."
—Wallace Stevens

Ginger, Almond, and Lemon Cake

SERVES 8 TO 10

Cut small slices; this cake is rich, and also best eaten the day it is made. I like to put a couple of large spoonfuls of marinated strawberries and nectarines on the plate beside the cake in the summer, or a compote of pineapples and raisins in the winter. Top with whipped cream, if you like. My friend Mechtild would drop the whipped cream and instead use her Lemon-Wine Sauce, included at the end of this recipe.

7 Tbsp. (105 mL) fine sugar, plus extra for dusting cake tin
1 cup (240 mL) very fine dry white breadcrumbs (see page 43)
1 Tbsp. (15 mL) baking powder
1 cup (240 mL) roughly chopped skinned whole almonds

¼ lb. (113 g) butter, melted and cooled to lukewarm
½ tsp. (2.5 mL) lemon zest
¼ cup (60 mL) finely chopped crystallized ginger
6 egg whites
icing sugar for garnish

Preheat the oven to 350°F (175°C).

Cut a round piece of parchment paper large enough to fit the bottom of a 8 to 9-inch (20 to 23-cm) round cake tin. Grease the inside of the tin, put the parchment in the bottom, butter the parchment, and dust it and the sides of the tin with fine sugar.

Mix the 7 Tbsp. (105 mL) sugar, breadcrumbs, baking powder, and almonds in a bowl large enough to hold all the ingredients including the whipped egg whites. Transfer into a food processor, and add the lukewarm butter. Pulse until the mixture is the consistency of brown sugar. Return to the mixing bowl, sprinkle in the lemon zest, and add the crystallized ginger. Mix well so that they are well distributed throughout the batter.

Whip the egg whites until they hold stiff peaks, but are not glossy. Mix 1 cup (240 mL) of the egg whites into the batter to lighten it up. Gently fold half of the remaining egg whites into the batter, and then fold in the second half. Pour the batter into the cake tin, and bake for 50 to 60 minutes. Cool for 10 minutes before removing from the cake tin.

LEMON-WINE SAUCE

1 egg, extra large
¼ cup (60 mL) sugar

1 Tbsp. (15 mL) lemon juice
1 cup (240 mL) dry white wine
zest of ¼ lemon

In a small bowl, whisk the egg and sugar together until it turns pale yellow, about 2 minutes. Add the lemon juice and wine to the egg mixture and combine. Transfer to a double boiler and whisk continuously until it is warm and slightly thickened. Be careful not to overcook, as the egg could scramble. Remove from the heat and add the lemon zest.

COOK'S TIP

Egg whites freeze well. Defrost slowly; return to room temperature and proceed with your recipe.

Maple-Orange Bread and Butter Pudding

SERVES 10

We served this homey and satisfying pudding in the café for brunch and dessert. It was our most requested recipe. The addition of maple syrup and orange zest make second helpings hard to resist. I suggest you make the whole lot, not divide the recipe, as it freezes well. Defrost overnight in the refrigerator and heat.

4 cups (950 mL) homogenized milk
2 cups (475 mL) whipping cream
2 tsp. (10 mL) vanilla extract
9 large eggs
½ cup (120 mL) sugar
¾ cup (180 mL) maple syrup

15 to 20 slices white bread, crusts removed
2 to 3 Tbsp. (30 to 45 mL) unsalted butter, melted
½ cup (120 mL) sultana raisins
zest of two oranges
½ tsp. (2.5 mL) ground nutmeg
½ tsp. (2.5 mL) ground cinnamon
icing sugar for garnish

In a saucepan, scald the milk, whipping cream, and vanilla. Remove from the heat. In a large bowl, whisk the eggs and sugar together until pale yellow, and then slowly whisk the hot liquid into the egg mixture until combined. Stir in ½ cup (120 mL) of the maple syrup, and set aside. The remaining syrup is for drizzling overtop when ready to serve.

Cut each slice of bread into four triangles and brush with melted butter. Spread overlapping bread slices on the bottom of an approximately 12- x 7-inch (30- x 18-cm) casserole dish and sprinkle with half the raisins and orange zest. Repeat with a second layer of bread, followed by the remaining raisins and orange zest. Top with any extra bread cut in 1½-inch (3.8-cm) cubes or laid in overlapping rows.

Pour the cream mixture over the bread and sprinkle with the nutmeg and cinnamon. Let sit for half an hour to absorb the liquid.

Preheat the oven to 350°F (175°C).

Place the casserole dish in a baking pan and fill the pan halfway up the casserole dish with warm water. Bake for 35 to 40 minutes, until golden brown.

Allow the pudding to cool for 10 minutes before cutting into squares or triangles. Serve drizzled with the remaining maple syrup and dusted with icing sugar.

This recipe will keep, refrigerated, for up to 5 days. Remove from the fridge, wrap individual pieces loosely in foil, and bake in a 375°F (190°C) oven for 10 minutes or until warm, or microwave each piece individually for 45 seconds on high.

Warm Chocolate Brownie Pudding

SERVES 12

What's great about this chocolate dessert is that you can serve it two ways—hot and slightly puffy, right out of the oven, or cool and dense a few hours later. Ginger Crème Anglaise (see page 207) goes with either version. The chocolate breadcrumb mixture can be prepared up to 6 hours ahead of baking.

1½ cups (360 mL) homogenized milk
1¼ cups (300 mL) 35% whipping cream
1 vanilla bean, sliced half through, lengthwise
6 large eggs, separated
4 Tbsp. (60 mL) sugar

10 oz. (285 g) semi-sweet chocolate, melted
3 Tbsp. (45 mL) crème de cacao
2½ cups (600 mL) fresh Pain au Lait (see page 19), brioche, or white breadcrumbs (see page 43)
1 tsp. (5 mL) sugar, for egg whites
1 recipe Ginger Crème Anglaise (see page 207)

Preheat the oven to 350°F (175°C).

Scald the milk and whipping cream with the vanilla bean. In a bowl, whisk the egg yolks and the 4 Tbsp. (60 mL) sugar together. Add a little of the hot liquid to the yolks as you continue stirring. Slowly add the rest of the liquid to the yolks, whisking constantly. Scrape the seeds from the vanilla bean into the mixture.

Whisk the melted chocolate and crème de cacao into the liquid. Mix in the breadcrumbs. Cool to room temperature, about ½ hour.

Note: You can prepare this much of the recipe up to 6 hours before serving. Bring to room temperature before continuing with the next step.

Whip the egg whites and add the 1 tsp. (5 mL) sugar when peaks start to form. Do not over-whip. Stir a third of the whites into the chocolate mixture and then gently fold in the other two-thirds making sure there are no streaks of egg white to be seen.

Spoon into 12 1-cup (240-mL) ovenproof dishes. Fill almost to the top and bake for 26 to 28 minutes. The middle should be slightly runny when you puncture it with a cake tester.

Serve immediately for a puffed look. Let sit if you prefer a denser cake-like pudding.

COOK'S TIP

If using white breadcrumbs, add one more teaspoon (5 mL) sugar.

If your vanilla bean has dried out, soak it in cream in the refrigerator for a few days. The bean will be reusable again and you will have vanilla-flavored cream.

Honey-Pecan Brown Bread Ice Cream

MAKES 8 CUPS (2 L)

Brown bread ice cream has been around forever. Open any British cookbook published before the 1970s and you'll find a recipe. I've updated an old classic by adding honey and chopped pecans to the mix. Make sure you use dense brown bread, not light whole wheat, for the crumbs. Whole Wheat Bran Bread (see page 28) works beautifully. If you do not have an ice cream maker, this is the time to invest in one. When you're feeling really ambitious, serve it with a warm dried apricot and prune compote laced with Armagnac, a French brandy from the province of Gascony, and simple meringues made from the egg whites left over from making the ice cream.

3 cups (720 mL) homogenized milk
½ cup (120 mL) wildflower honey (or any delicate-
  tasting honey)
1 vanilla bean, cut in half, lengthwise
9 egg yolks

⅓ cup (80 mL) sugar
1½ cups (360 mL) 35% cream
5 oz. (140 g) coarse fresh brown breadcrumbs
  (see page 43)
1 cup (240 mL) very roughly chopped pecans

Preheat the oven to 325°F (165°C).

Pour the milk into a saucepan. Add the honey and the vanilla bean. Bring to a simmer then take it off the stove. Make sure the honey is dissolved.

Place the egg yolks and sugar in a bowl and whisk until the yolks turn a very pale yellow. The mixture will have thickened and should come off the whisk in ribbons.

Whisk a little of the hot liquid into the egg mixture; this will prevent the eggs from curdling. Continue whisking as you slowly pour the rest of the milk into the eggs.

Pour the mixture back into the saucepan and reheat on medium low. Stir with a wooden spoon. Don't let the mix heat up too quickly or you'll end up scrambling the eggs. You will know when the custard is ready—after about 5 to 7 minutes—when you can lift the spoon out of the liquid and draw your finger down the back of the spoon and the line doesn't fill in. If the cream needs to cook any longer, the line will fill in.

Pour the custard mixture into a bowl and quickly whisk in the cream. Scrape the vanilla seeds out of the bean and whisk into the mixture.

Cool the mixture in the refrigerator until completely chilled.

Toast the breadcrumbs in a 325°F (165°C) oven for about 20 minutes, until they are dark golden. Let cool.

Pour the chilled cream into an ice cream maker and start the machine. When the ice cream is three-quarters finished, about the consistency of yogurt, add the breadcrumbs and pecans and continue the process until the ice cream is ready.

COOK'S TIP
Brown bread ice cream is best eaten within 12 hours of making. The breadcrumbs tend to soften as the ice cream ages.

1:50 am: A packer loads sourdough and oval bâtardes into large delivery bags.

Summer Ice Cream Sandwich with Dolce de Leche

I love this marriage of South American and Sicilian tastes. Dolce de leche, much loved in Latin America as a sweet treat, is basically caramelized condensed milk. It may not sound too appetizing, but this is worth taking a flyer on. The practice of sandwiching ice cream in a sweet roll comes from Southern Italy, where bread is eaten with almost everything. Use small, dinner-sized rolls if you can find them and serve 2 per person.

4 large, or 8 dinner-sized Pain au Lait, brioche or challah rolls
1 11-oz. (300-mL) can condensed milk (not evaporated milk) (see below)
1 quart (1 L) good vanilla, chocolate or hazelnut ice cream

To caramelize the milk, place the unopened can of condensed milk upright in a saucepan at least 3 inches (7.5 cm) taller than the can. Pour enough water into the saucepan to cover the can by 1 to 2 inches (2.5 to 5 cm). Cover and bring to a boil. Lower the heat and simmer for 1½ to 2 hours, checking periodically that the can is always covered with water.

Remove the can from the water and let cool for at least 15 minutes. Be careful opening, as the mixture may still be warm. Spoon what is now dolce de leche out of the can and reserve.

Cut the rolls in half and toast under a broiler.

Spread a thick layer of dolce de leche on the bottom half of each roll, spoon on a scoop of ice cream, and top with the other half of the roll.

You'll have some dolce de leche leftover. It will keep in the refrigerator for up to 2 weeks, although in our house it seems to disappear much more quickly.

COOK'S TIPS

1. Although I have never had a can of condensed milk explode while boiling, I recommend knocking a dent in the can as a precaution. This will enable you to see any build-up of pressure. Remove the saucepan from the heat and discard the can.

2. There is some confusion concerning condensed and evaporated milk. What is the difference? Both go through a vacuum process that evaporates about half of the water content. At this point, however, evaporated milk is canned and heat-sterilized for preservation, while condensed milk is canned and preserved with sugar.

3:05 am: Completed customer orders wait to be loaded into the trucks

5:30 am: Raj delivers his first order of the day.

Pumpkin Bread Pudding with Caramel Sauce

SERVES 6 TO 8

Andrea Stewart and Dawn Woodward, two past employees of ACE, came up with the idea for this dessert as an alternative to pumpkin pie. It was so popular that we kept it on the menu from Thanksgiving through Christmas. This is an adaptation of their recipe. Canned pumpkin purée works well here, so don't feel obliged to steam fresh pumpkin.

unsalted butter to grease the pan
7 large eggs
2 egg yolks
heaping ¾ cup (180 mL) sugar
2 cups (475 mL) pumpkin purée, canned or fresh
  (see end of recipe)—do not use pumpkin pie filling
5 cups (1.2 L) whipping cream
1 vanilla bean, cut in half, lengthwise
¼ tsp. (1.2 mL) kosher salt
¼ tsp. (1.2 mL) ground nutmeg
¾ tsp. (4 mL) ground cinnamon

½ tsp. (2.5 mL) ground ginger
1 Tbsp. (15 mL) dark rum
11 ½-inch (1.2-cm) slices white bread, brioche,
  or challah, crusts on (about 1 large loaf)
⅓ cup (80 mL) sultana raisins *or* ⅓ cup (80 mL)
  dried cranberries

CARAMEL SAUCE
1 cup (240 mL) sugar
1¾ cups (420 mL) whipping cream
1 tsp. (5 mL) vanilla extract
2 tsp. (10 mL) cold, unsalted butter

FOR THE PUDDING

Generously butter 8 1-cup (240-mL) ramekins or one 8-cup (2-L) casserole dish.

In a bowl, whisk the eggs, egg yolks, and sugar until the sugar is dissolved. Add the pumpkin purée and stir until combined.

In a saucepan, scald the whipping cream with the vanilla bean, salt, nutmeg, cinnamon, and ginger. Slowly pour the scalded liquid into the pumpkin mixture, whisking continuously. Strain the mixture through a sieve into a clean bowl, pressing the solids through, and scrape out the seeds of the vanilla bean into the mixture. Stir in the rum.

Cut the bread into 1-inch (2.5-cm) cubes and add to the pumpkin mixture. Then add the raisins or cranberries. Toss gently until the bread is covered and thoroughly soaked. Let rest for at least half an hour. Divide the mixture among the ramekins or pour into the casserole.

Preheat the oven to 325°F (165°C).

Bake the ramekins for about 25 minutes or the larger dish for 40 to 45 minutes or until just set. It will continue cooking in the pan. Remove from oven. Let rest for 5 to 8 minutes and remove from ramekins. If using a casserole, serve the pudding from it.

Drizzle each serving with caramel sauce. Extra canned pumpkin purée freezes well.

FOR THE CARAMEL SAUCE

Put the sugar in a small heavy-bottomed saucepan over medium-low heat. Stir the sugar until it starts to melt. The sugar will form clumps. Don't be concerned; they will eventually melt. Just keep stirring. Cook the caramel until it turns a medium-dark amber. It should take about 10 minutes. Don't overcook, or the caramel will take on a bitter taste.

Remove the saucepan from the heat and slowly add the cream. The mixture will bubble up. Return the mixture to medium-low heat and simmer gently until smooth and thickened, about 4 to 5 minutes.

Remove from the heat and stir in the vanilla and butter. Reheat the sauce before serving. It will keep, refrigerated, for up to one month.

FRESH PUMPKIN PURÉE

Small sugar pumpkins are available from late September through December. To make your own pumpkin purée, buy 3 pumpkins. Cut in half horizontally, scoop out the seeds, and set them aside. In a closed pot, with 2 to 3 inches (5 to 7.5 cm) of water in it, simmer the pumpkin halves, cut-side up, until you can pierce them easily with a knife. Check regularly to be sure they don't boil dry and burn. Cool and then scoop out the pulp. If the purée is very watery, drain in a sieve for 1 hour. Any leftover purée can be frozen for future use. For what to do with the seeds, see Pumpkin-Lemongrass Soup (see page 104).

Pan-Fried Pineapple on Caramelized Toast with Almond Crème Fraîche

SERVES 4

This is a great winter dish, when pineapples are at their best. The crème fraîche must be made at least 12 to 24 hours before you plan to serve the dessert. Everything else can be prepared ahead of time, too, except for sautéeing the pineapple while the sugared toast warms. You could also serve this for a decadent special breakfast. If you don't have time to make the crème fraîche, use heavy cream whipped with sugar and almond extract.

ALMOND CRÈME FRAÎCHE

2 cups (475 mL) whipping cream
½ cup (120 mL) buttermilk
3 drops almond extract (or vanilla extract can be substituted)
1 to 2 Tbsp. (15 to 30 mL) fine white sugar

TOAST AND PINEAPPLE

4 1-inch (2.5-cm) slices Pain au Lait (see page 19), brioche, challah, or white bread

3 Tbsp. (45 mL) unsalted butter, at room temperature
⅓ cup (80 mL) fine white sugar
1 Tbsp. (15 mL) unsalted butter
½ cup (120 mL) orange juice
2 tsp. (10 mL) orange zest
2 Tbsp. (30 mL) dark rum
1 Tbsp. (15 mL) brown sugar
6 ½-inch (1.2-cm) thick slices fresh pineapple, cored and cut in half

FOR THE CRÈME FRAÎCHE

Combine the whipping cream and the buttermilk in a wide-mouthed bowl. Cover with a towel and leave at room temperature until thickened, about 12 to 24 hours. Cover with plastic wrap and refrigerate. Put ½ cup (120 mL) of the crème fraîche in a bowl and add the almond extract and sugar to taste. The rest of the crème fraîche will stay fresh in the fridge for at least a week.

FOR THE CARAMELIZED TOAST

Preheat the oven to 375°F (190°C).

Spread one side of the bread slices with the softened butter. Put the sugar in a shallow bowl and press the buttered side of the bread into the sugar. Then butter the other side of the bread, turn it over, and press it into the sugar. Heat a non-stick frying pan, or a lightly buttered ordinary pan. When warm, cook the buttered bread slices on each side until they are a dark gold color. Reserve. The toast can be made up to 5 hours in advance and left at room temperature. When ready to use, bake it in the oven for 5 to 6 minutes, or until very hot.

FOR THE PINEAPPLE

Melt the 1 Tbsp. (15 mL) butter in a frying pan. As soon as it is melted, add the juice, zest, rum, and brown sugar and bring to a boil. Reduce the heat, and let the mixture simmer until it is reduced by just less than half. Add the pineapple slices and cook on each side for 1 minute, basting with the liquid.

Place each slice of the toast on a plate and top with 3 pieces of pineapple. Drizzle a quarter of the sauce on one side of the plate, and put a large spoonful of the crème fraîche beside it.

COOK'S TIPS

Uses for Crème Fraîche

1. Use 1 cup (240 mL) of crème fraîche instead of the whipping cream in the Honey-Pecan Brown Bread Ice Cream (see page 198).

2. Flavor with vanilla and sugar and substitute for whipped cream.

3. Toss 2 Tbsp. (30 mL) crème fraîche, 1 small seeded chopped tomato, and 2 tsp. (10 mL) sautéed minced onions into steamed green beans.

Most European languages call pineapple *ananas*, from the Paraguayan word *nana*, meaning "exquisite fruit." Its form, carved either in wood or stone, has long been a symbol of hospitality.

Summer Pudding with Ginger Crème Anglaise

SERVES 6 GENEROUSLY

It's amazing how a little liqueur and some fresh ginger can jazz up an old standard. You can make this as one large dessert mold or in six individual molds. I prefer bombe-shaped or domed containers, if you're making individual servings, and a loaf pan for the larger dessert. This recipe should be refrigerated overnight. Occasionally the pudding will cling to the mold and perseverance will be needed to get it loose. You may feel more comfortable lining the container with plastic wrap before you start. Some cooks prefer to dip the bread slices into the juice given off by the cooked berries before they assemble the pudding. If this appeals to you, by all means try it. Float the puddings on the Ginger Crème Anglaise and garnish them with fresh mint leaves.

SUMMER PUDDING

24 slices day-old white bread, crusts removed
1 cup (240 mL) red currants *or* ½-inch (1.2-cm) slices
  of rhubarb, rinsed and drained
2½ cups (600 mL) blueberries, rinsed and drained
3 cups (720 mL) raspberries, rinsed and drained
1 Tbsp. (15 mL) lemon juice
1¼ cups (300 mL) water
7 to 8 Tbsp. (105 to 120 mL) sugar
up to 2 Tbsp. (30 mL) raspberry liqueur such as Chambord
3 nectarines or peaches, peeled and cut into ½-inch
  (1.2-cm) pieces

1 cup (240 mL) strawberries, washed, drained,
  hulled, and cut into ½-inch (1.2-cm) pieces
1 tsp. (5 mL) lemon juice
1 tsp. (5 mL) sugar
fresh mint for garnish

GINGER CRÈME ANGLAISE

2 cups (475 mL) homogenized milk
1¼-inch (3-cm) chunk of fresh ginger 1½ inches
  (3.8 cm) in diameter
1 tsp. (5 mL) vanilla extract
4 egg yolks
½ cup (120 mL) sugar

FOR THE PUDDING

Line a 6-cup (1.5-L) mold or individual 1-cup (240-mL) molds with the bread, reserving 6 slices for later. Put the red currants (or rhubarb), blueberries, raspberries, 1 Tbsp. (15 mL) lemon juice, water, and 7 Tbsp. (105 mL) of sugar in a saucepan and place on medium heat. Cook, stirring occasionally, for about 5 minutes, until the berries have broken down. Taste and add more sugar if necessary. Remove from heat, add the Chambord, and let the mixture cool to room temperature.

Mix the nectarines, strawberries, 1 tsp. (5 mL) lemon juice, and 1 tsp. (5 mL) sugar together. Fill the molds with the cooked berry mixture and top with the nectarine mixture. Drizzle some of the juices on top. Cover the top of the molds with the extra pieces of bread and drizzle more juice on top so that the bread turns red. Cover them with plastic wrap. Reserve any extra juice.

The puddings need weight on them so that the juice will permeate the bread casing. With the individual molds you can use pie weights or washed stones. If you are making one large pudding, place a plate a little smaller than the mold over the plastic wrap and weigh down with canned food.

Refrigerate overnight. Check in the morning that the top and sides of the molds have turned a ruby red. If they have not, pour a little more of the reserved juice over each mold and return to the fridge. See Cook's Tip #2 if you need more liquid.

Pour the milk into a saucepan large enough to hold all the ingredients. Slice the ginger into ¼-inch (.6-cm) coins, add to the milk, and bring to a simmer. Remove from stove and stir in the vanilla. Whisk the egg yolks and sugar together in a bowl until they are pale yellow and fall from the whisk in ribbons.

Place a bowl large enough to hold all the ingredients into a larger bowl of ice.

Slowly whisk the warm milk into the egg mixture. Pour the mixture back into the saucepan and return to the stove over medium-low heat. Stir continuously with a wooden spoon for about 5 to 7 minutes or until the mixture has thickened just slightly. The custard is ready when you lift the spoon out, draw your finger down the back of the spoon, and the line doesn't fill in.

Quickly pour the crème anglaise through a fine sieve into the bowl resting in ice. Taste to see if it is gingery enough. Remember that the taste of the ginger will fade as the custard cools. Take the ginger out, if you wish, or leave it in longer for a more pronounced taste. When it reaches room temperature press plastic wrap onto the surface to prevent a skin from forming, and refrigerate until half an hour before serving.

Carefully unmold the summer puddings and place them in the middle of each plate. Drizzle with the remaining juice if any white bread shows through. Pour the room temperature crème anglaise around the puddings and garnish with mint leaves.

COOK'S TIPS

1. If the custard gets overcooked and turns grainy, remove it from the heat, take out the vanilla bean, add 2 Tbsp. (30 mL) of cold 35% cream, and mix in an electric blender until smooth. Then proceed with the recipe.

2. Depending on the time of year, the berries may not yield enough juice. If this is the case, simply simmer 2 cups (475 mL) of raspberries and a handful of blueberries until they give up their liquid. Strain and add 1 Tbsp. (15 mL) of raspberry liqueur.

This concoction of fruit and juice-saturated bread was originally created in the nineteenth century as a dessert for patrons of health resorts where pastry was forbidden.

Back Matter

"In Paris today millions of pounds of bread are sold daily, made the previous night by those strange, half-naked beings one glimpses through cellar windows, whose wild-seeming cries floating out of those depths always make a painful impression. In the morning one sees those pale men, still white with flour, carrying a loaf under one arm, going off to rest and gather new strength to renew their hard and useful labour when night comes again. I have always highly esteemed the brave and humble workers who labour all night to produce those soft but crusty little loaves that look more like cake than bread."
— Alexandre Dumas, 1802–1870

Glossary and Baker's Lingo

active dry yeast or traditional yeast: The yeast most commonly found in the average kitchen. It is very potent and keeps for a relatively long time, up to a year sealed in its package, and a few months once opened, or longer if stored in the refrigerator. It needs to be rehydrated in lukewarm water before being added to a recipe.

all-purpose flour: Flour whose protein content falls between those of soft and hard flour and can be substituted for either, although the results won't be quite as pleasing as with the flour specifically suited for that purpose. When baking bread, hard flour should be used. (See *hard flour*.)

ascorbic acid: Another name for vitamin C. Bakers sometimes add minute amounts to the dough to prevent it from collapsing.

autolyse: A resting period for dough, prior to the addition of salt, yeast, or pre-ferment, during which the flour can hydrate and the gluten can develop, smoothing the dough. The salt tightens the gluten, and the leaveners— the yeast or pre-ferment—acidify the dough, inhibiting hydration.

baguette: A long, relatively thin loaf of bread, developed in France.

bain marie: The French term for a double boiler or water bath.

banneton: A woven basket lined with raw linen cloth. When sprinkled with flour, it is used to rise boule-shaped pieces of dough.

bâtard: A shape similar to the baguette, but shorter and fatter.

benching: See *resting*.

biga: An Italian pre-ferment, made of flour, water, and yeast, which is quite stiff. It can be fermented in a cool environment for up to 18 hours.

boule: A round bread, proofed upside-down in a basket (if it is a wet dough) designed to give it its shape.

butter: Most professional recipes and the ones in this book, base their butter measurements on unsalted (or sweet) stick butter. The use of any other type of butter will result in a different end product unless other adjustments are made.

compressed yeast: The most active of the baking yeasts, preferred by most professional bakers. It should be stored in the refrigerator, tightly wrapped. If using it in a recipe that calls for active dry yeast, multiply the weight of active dry yeast called for by about two and a half, and simply crumble that amount of compressed yeast directly into the dough—no need to rehydrate.

couche: A heavy, raw-linen cloth that shaped breads, especially baguettes, can proof inside without forming a crust. The fabric is quite stiff and naturally non-stick, helping breads keep their shape as they rise.

crumb: The interior of the bread, especially with reference to the texture.

crust: The outside of a loaf of bread. In an artisan bread, color is valued as well as crispness. A dark crust indicates good caramelization, which will have added some of its flavor to the bread.

fermentation: The professional baker's term for the first rising of a dough, and any subsequent rising before it reaches its final shape.

ficelle: Like a baguette, but very thin, almost like a length of thick rope—about 1½ inches (3.8 cm) in diameter.

folding: This process is called for by many recipes when combining a light and a heavy mixture (for example, beaten egg whites into a batter) without destroying the delicacy of the lighter one. There are two methods. One, pour all of the lighter mixture onto the heavier one, use a spatula to drag the heavy mixture across the bottom and over the top of the lighter one, and continue—turning the bowl as you go—until the two mixtures combine. The second method is slightly different. Thoroughly mix a third of the lighter mixture into the heavier one as described above. The rest of the lighter mixture can be gently dragged through the heavier one until completely mixed. Folding a lighter mixture into a heavier one is easier than the other way around.

gluten: The protein formed when flour containing relatively high amounts of *glutenin* and *gliadin* is moistened. Gluten is what allows dough to keep its shape as it rises, preventing the air bubbles formed by the rising agent from collapsing.

hard flour: Flour milled from specific wheats with a relatively high protein content that turns into gluten when moistened. It is well suited to bread making.

hearth: The stone baking surface of a baker's oven.

instant yeast: Compared to active dry yeast, instant yeast has a much higher surface area relative to the size of its grains, so it absorbs moisture much more easily and doesn't need to be rehydrated in advance. It can take up to 20 minutes to activate, so you may want to add it to bread dough sooner than a recipe suggests, maybe before a short autolyse.

intermediate proofing: See *resting*.

iodized salt: Salt with iodine added to combat hypothyroidism, a condition often caused by a dietary lack of iodine. But a diet too high in iodine is not healthy either, so if you get iodine from other sources it is best to use non-iodized salt.

kosher salt: Far less regular in shape than table salt, its crystals often form hollow, four-sided pyramids. It dissolves more quickly than table salt, but because of its irregular shapes it has a higher air content. If you measure by volume, you must use considerably more kosher salt to get the same effect as with table salt. That's why it is always better to measure salt by weight, or be flexible in following recipes.

lame: The tool bakers use to slash the tops of their breads. It is usually a razor blade mounted on a wooden or plastic handle. A very sharp knife or scalpel can also be used.

marinate: To soak meat or seafood in a specially prepared liquid. The flavor acquired from marinating is only one of the results. An acidic marinade will tenderize even the toughest meat. Leaving fish to stand in lemon or lime juice has the same effect as cooking it, and an oily marinade will make lean or dry meat more appetizing by adding some flavor-carrying fat. Today the term is also used for a mixture of dry ingredients that are rubbed into meat, poultry, or fish.

non-wheat flours: Flours made from grains other than wheat, such as rye, semolina, or oats. These don't contain the proteins that allow a dough to rise, and so must be combined with wheat flour unless you want a very dense final product.

oils: Aside from flavor, two factors help determine what kind of oil to use in a recipe: the predominant type of fat in the oil, and the smoke point. Of the common vegetable oils used in cooking, coconut and palm oil are highest in saturated fat, safflower oil is highest in polyunsaturated fat, and olive oil is highest in mono-unsaturated fat. Grapeseed oil has the highest smoke point, allowing it to heat well, while olive oil has the lowest.

oven spring: The rapid expansion of bread dough in the first few minutes of baking, caused by the increased temperature and stopped when the heat reaches the point at which it kills the yeast cells. Up to a third of a bread's final volume can be added during this time.

pâte fermentée: A French pre-ferment, started 6 to 9 hours ahead of use.

peel: The paddle used to transfer bread into and out of the oven. It is usually wooden—essentially a flat, edgeless tray with a long handle.

poolish: A Polish pre-ferment, made of flour, water, and yeast, that is quite liquid. It is fermented at room temperature for up to 14 hours.

pre-ferment: A portion of dough mixed ahead of time and allowed to ferment. It is a leavening agent, and its fermentation time allows it to develop a flavor that impacts the final product.

proofing: The professional's term for the rising that happens after a dough is in its final shape—a loaf in its pan, a boule in its basket—but before baking.

Pullman: Bread baked in a loaf pan—so named because it looks a little bit like a rail car.

resting (or benching, or intermediate proofing): The period after a quantity of dough has been cut into loaf-size portions and rounded, when it is left to relax before being shaped. This is the second-last rising of the dough, the last being proofing, after the dough is shaped.

retarding: Refrigerating yeast or pre-ferment dough to slow down the fermentation or proofing. The bread takes on more of the fermented flavor the longer it is retarded.

rock salt: Salt from underground deposits left by ancient seas, which may contain impurities that have to be removed before it is used for cooking.

rounding: After dough has been cut into loaf-sized portions, the cut sides are folded into the dough in a free-form shape. This keeps the dough from drying out while it is benching, and prevents the gasses released by the yeast from escaping. After the dough has rested, this round edge helps it to spread evenly when it is being shaped.

salt: See *iodized salt, kosher salt, rock salt, sea salt,* and *table salt.*

sautéing: Cooking food over very hot, direct heat in a small amount of fat in a pan. The difference between sautéing and frying is that sautéing is very quick.

searing: Cooking meat briefly over a high heat before turning down the heat for the balance of the cooking time. This will seal in the juices and generally improve the flavor of the end product.

sea salt: Salt formed by evaporation of sea water. Because it has not been in the ground for eons, it is often purer than rock salt, and prized by connoisseurs.

slashes: Cuts made in an unbaked loaf before it goes into the oven. In addition to making the bread look nice, they provide an escape for excess gasses released during the baking; without them, the bread's crust would tear randomly.

soft or cake flour: Flour milled from wheats that have a relatively low protein content, therefore well suited to cakes and other baked goods with a delicate texture.

sour starter: A natural pre-ferment made without commercial yeast. Flour and water are allowed to ferment for several days and develop yeasts of their own, or dried or fresh fruit may be mixed in, for their yeasts to activate the starter. More flour and water are then added until the starter is strong enough to leaven bread. This method of fermentation imparts a sour flavor that can be clearly tasted in the final "sourdough" bread.

sponge: Another type of pre-ferment, in which the yeast, some of the flour, and all the liquid called for in the recipe are mixed together and allowed to ferment for several hours before the rest of the dry ingredients are added to the dough.

table salt: Salt that has been processed to make it resistant to humidity. The cubical shape of the crystals allows them to flow better from salt shakers.

turning: A method used by most professional bakers in place of the home baker's "punching down the dough." The risen dough is turned out of its fermentation bowl, spread gently, and folded into a neat package before being returned, smooth side up, to the fermentation bowl. Turning the dough and letting it rise again will make it stronger.

whipped butter: Butter with air incorporated into it through whipping, making it much more spreadable and increasing its volume by about 25 per cent. If you are using whipped butter in a recipe, increase the volume of butter called for by about one-third.

whipping: Beating wet ingredients vigorously so as to trap air within them, making them light and fluffy.

whisking: A gentler version of whipping, generally using a hand-held whisk and stopping when the ingredients are just beginning to foam.

whole grain flours: Flours that include the grain's germ and bran as well as just its endosperm. The germ of any grain contains unsaturated fat, which can cause whole grain flours to go rancid if stored unrefrigerated or for long periods of time.

yeast: See *active dry yeast, compressed yeast,* and *instant yeast.*

A List of Sources

Agriculture Canada website: *www.agcanada.com*

Bain, Jennifer. "Muskoka's cran-tastic bounty," *The Toronto Star*, October 17, 2001.

Bastianich, Lidia Matticchio. *Lidia's Italian Table*. New York: William Morrow and Company, 1998.

Bayless, Rick. *Rick Bayless's Mexican Kitchen*. New York: Scribner, 1996. p 69.

Better Baking website: *www.betterbaking.com*

Calvel, Raymond. *The Taste of Bread*. Trans. Ronald L. Wirtz. Maryland: Aspen, 2001.

Davidson, Alan. *The Oxford Companion to Food*. New York: Oxford University Press, 1999.

Dupaigne, Bernarde. *The History of Bread*. New York: Abrams, 1999.

Fabricant, Florence. "In France the Prune Holds a Noble Station," *The New York Times*, October 31, 2001.

Feibleman, Peter S. *The Cooking of Spain and Portugal*. New York: Time Life Books, 1969.

Glezer, Maggie. *Artisan Baking Across America*. New York: Workman Publishing, 2000.

Gugino, Sam. "Getting Your Goat," *Wine Spectator*, May 31, 2000.

Herbst, Saron Tyler. *The New Food Lover's Companion*. New York: Barron's, 1990 (2001).

Hillman, Howard. *Kitchen Science*. Boston: Houghton Mifflin, 1989.

Home Cooking website: *www.homecooking.about.com*

Jenkins, Steven. *The Cheese Primer*. New York: Workman Publishing, 1996.

Kleiman, Evan. *Cucina Del Mare: Fish and Seafood Italian Style*. New York: William Morrow, 1993.

Mariani, John. *The Dictionary of Italian Food and Drink*. New York: Broadway Books, 1998.

McGee, Harold. *On Food and Cooking*. New York: Fireside, 1997.

Monette, Solange, ed. *The Visual Food Encyclopedia*. Montreal: Quebec/Amerique, 1989.

Montagné, Prosper. *New Larousse Gastronomique*. Trans. Nina Froud, Patience Gray, Maud Murdoch, and Barbara Macrae Taylor. Middlesex: The Hamlyn Publishing Group, 1960 (1983).

Moosewood Collective. *Moosewood Restaurant Low Fat Favorites*. New York: Clarkson N. Potter Publishers, 1996.

Pham, Mai. *Pleasures of the Vietnamese Table*. New York: Harper Collins, 2001.

Reader's Digest. *Foods That Harm, Foods that Heal*. Montreal: The Reader's Digest Association (Canada) Ltd, 1997.

Swain, Margaret. "A Bluffer's Guide to Balsamics," *The Weekend Post*, April 7, 2001.

Tsuji, Shizuo. *Japanese Cooking, A Simple Art*. Japan: Kodansha International, 1980.

Index

About the Author

Linda Haynes

Linda Haynes is the co-founder and co-owner of ACE Bakery. Established in 1993, ACE Bakery has become Toronto's premier supplier of artisan breads to hotels, restaurants, caterers, gourmet food stores and airlines.

Having grown up with cooking and family meals as essential rituals, Linda was an accomplished home chef by the time her husband Martin Connell decided to bake bread as a weekend hobby in 1985. While traveling in France, they observed village bakers at work and slowly refined their baking skills at home in Canada. Martin even built a wood-burning bakehouse at their country retreat. Linda pinpointed the lack of artisan bakeries as a gap in the local market. After she studied the operations of such bakeries in New York and California, she and her husband Martin opened ACE Bakery in 1993. In 1997, it expanded into a larger facility, and in 2000 opened an on-site bread store and café.

Linda studied journalism and worked as an ad copywriter, interviewer and producer before turning her attention to food. She is a member of the International Association of Culinary Professionals and the Women's Culinary Network. She and Martin founded Calmeadow, an organization that supports the provision of credit and financial services to micro-entrepreneurs in developing countries who are unable to access traditional sources. A portion of ACE Bakery's profits were donated until recently to the charity; now the bakery focuses charitable efforts on food and nutrition programs for low-income families. ACE Bakery contributes to over 100 fundraisers annually, and Linda's recipes appeared in the *Eat to the Beat* and *Great Soup, Empty Bowls* cookbooks.

Linda divides her time between Toronto and Caledon, Ontario. She is currently developing a cooking show. Her active lifestyle includes skiing, yoga, travel, and enjoying the culinary creations of her two grown children, Devin and Luke.